Spiritual Doctrine

OF

FATHER LOUIS LALLEMANT,

OF THE COMPANY OF JESUS.

PRECEDED BY

SOME ACCOUNT OF HIS LIFE.

Translated from the French.

———

EDITED BY

FREDERICK WILLIAM FABER, D.D.
PRIEST OF THE ORATORY OF S. PHILIP NERI.

This Translation is made from the edition published at Paris by Lecoffre and Co. in the year 1846, which contains a dedication of the work, by Father Peter Champion, of the Company of Jesus, to Mgr de Beauveau, Bishop of Nantes.

CONTENTS.

	PAGE
ADVERTISEMENT	1
LIFE OF FATHER LOUIS LALLEMANT	3

FIRST PRINCIPLE.

THE CONSIDERATION OF THE END.

CHAP.
I. God alone can make us happy	37
II. Our happiness depends on our perfect submission to God, who ought to reign alone in our hearts . .	41

SECOND PRINCIPLE.

THE IDEA OF PERFECTION.

SECTION I.

OF PERFECTION IN GENERAL.

I. The first act of a soul seeking perfection . . .	43
Art. I. How we ought to seek God in all things, and to seek but Him alone	43
II. We must give ourselves wholly to God . .	47
III. How subtlety and dissimulation keep us far from God	49
II. The principal means of perfection	50
Art. I. The sacraments are the principal means of acquiring perfection	50
II. The use of penances	51
III. The exercise of the virtues that are most necessary to perfection	52
Art. I. Of faith	52

CONTENTS.

CHAP.		PAGE
III. Art. II.	How much our want of confidence displeases God and injures ourselves	54
III.	Of humility	56
IV.	Of the love of crosses	59

SECTION II.

OF THE PERFECTION PECULIAR TO THE COMPANY OF JESUS.

I. Wherein consists the perfection peculiar to this Company . 61
   Art. I. The end of the institution of the Company of Jesus, and the means of arriving thereat . 61
     II. The Company belongs to Jesus Christ as Saviour 63
     III. St. Ignatius the model of the perfection of the Company . 64
II. Of the different dispositions of religious with regard to perfection . 65
III. The motives that induce us to labour at our perfection . 67
   Art. I. The desire of our own salvation . 67
     II. The order of a well-regulated zeal . 68
     III. The fruit of our labours . 68
     IV. How many persons are interested in our perfection . 69
IV. The means of perfection peculiar to the Company . 70
   Art. I. In what way the exercise of prayer in the Company should be practised . 70
     II. The obedience and exact observance of the rules peculiar to our Company, and the motives thereto . 72
V. Zeal for the salvation and perfection of our neighbour . 74
   Art. I. Motive for zeal . 74
     II. What use we ought to make of knowledge, after the example of St. Ignatius . 74
     III. The means by which the reputation and influence of the Company are to be maintained . 75
VI. Divers counsels . 77
   Art. I. Advice to a teacher of young religious on their coming out of the noviciate . 77
     II. Advice to the Fathers of the third year for the time of their noviciate . 82
     III. Advice to the Fathers of the third year, on com-

CONTENTS.

CHAP.		PAGE
	pleting their noviciate, for their conduct during the rest of their life	86
VI. Art. IV.	Advice to preachers	90
V.	Advice for various employments in the Company	92

THIRD PRINCIPLE.

PURITY OF HEART.

I.	Its nature and properties	96
Art. I.	In what purity of heart consists	96
II.	How necessary purity of heart is to us	96
III.	The order to be observed in purity of heart, and the different degrees of purity	98
II.	The things from which we must cleanse our hearts	100
Art. I.	Venial sins	100
II.	The passions	103
III.	The fund of pride there is in us	105
IV.	We must not neglect our least imperfections	109
V.	Of the denial of our inclinations, in order to put ourselves in a state of holy indifference	110
VI.	How we ought to comport ourselves with respect to divine graces, and with what self-abnegation we must receive them	113
III.	The care we ought to take to preserve purity of heart in action	117
Art. I.	We must perform our actions with a pure intention	117
II.	We ought to act on supernatural principles	118
IV.	Mental causes of the corruption of the heart	118
Art. I.	Error and false maxims	118
II.	Ignorance	119
V.	External causes of the corruption of the heart	122
Art. I.	The harm that results from particular friendships, and the conversations of the imperfect	122
II.	The faults we ought to avoid in conversation	123
III.	Of unprofitable visits and conversation	124

FOURTH PRINCIPLE.

OF THE GUIDANCE OF THE HOLY SPIRIT, AND DOCILITY THERETO.

CHAP.   PAGE

I. The nature of docility to the guidance of the Holy Spirit 126
   Art. I. In what this docility consists 126
      II. The means of attaining this docility . . . 127
      III. Objections against this doctrine of the guidance of the Holy Spirit 128

II. The motives which lead us to the practice of this docility 131
   Art. I. That perfection, and even salvation, depend on docility to grace 131
      II. There are but few perfect souls, because there are but few who follow the guidance of the Holy Spirit 135
      III. The excellence of grace, and the injustice of the opposition we offer to it 137
      IV. The Holy Spirit exercises the office of comforter to faithful souls 139

III. Of the gifts of the Holy Spirit in general . . . 141
   Art. I. Of the nature of the gifts of the Holy Spirit . 141
      II. Of the effects of the gifts of the Holy Spirit . 143
      III. Whence it comes that the gifts of the Holy Spirit produce so little effect in souls . . . 147

IV. Of the gifts of the Holy Spirit in detail . . . 150
   Art. I. Of the gift of wisdom 150
      II. Of the gift of understanding 158
      III. Of the gift of science 162
      IV. Of the gift of counsel 171
      V. Of the gift of piety 178
      VI. Of the gift of fortitude 182
      VII. Of the gift of the fear of God 188

V. Of the fruits of the Holy Spirit 193
   Art. I. Of the nature of the fruits of the Holy Spirit . 193
      II. Of the fruits of charity, joy, and peace . . 195
      III. Of the fruits of patience and meekness . . 198
      IV. Of the fruits of goodness and benignity . . 199
      V. Of the fruits of longanimity 199
      VI. Of the fruits of faith 199
      VII. Of the fruits of modesty, temperance, and chastity 201

CONTENTS.

CHAP.   PAGE

VI. The obstacles which the devil puts in our way in the practice of docility to the guidance of the Holy Spirit 202
    Art. I. How the devil prevents our spiritual advancement 202
        II. Different artifices of the devil to deceive us . 203
        III. Of distinguishing between the operations of God and those of the devil 205
        IV. Secret illusions 206
        V. Marks of a deluded soul 207
        VI. What we ought to observe in the movements leading us to good 208

FIFTH PRINCIPLE.

RECOLLECTION, AND THE INTERIOR LIFE.

I. Of the nature and causes of the interior life . . . 209
    Art. I. In what the interior life consists . . . 209
        II. How we ought to imitate the interior life of God 211
        III. How it is that we make so little progress in the interior life 212
II. Of the motives that lead us to the interior life . . 213
    Art. I. We make no progress in the ways of perfection unless we give ourselves to the interior life . 213
        II. Without prayer we cannot acquit ourselves of the duties of our vocation, nor gather fruit from our ministrations 215
        III. Peace is not found except in the interior life, and our dissatisfactions spring only from our not being interior men 219
III. The occupations of the interior life 220
    Art. I. Of watchfulness over our interior . . . 220
        II. How important it is that we should join the interior life with our exterior occupations . 225
        III. We ought not to engage in exterior occupations of our own accord 227
IV. Advice for the interior life 228
    Art. I. We ought to cultivate the will more than the understanding 228
        II. The path of faith is a safer way to perfection than that of sensible graces 229
        III. The best mode of practising the virtues . . 229

CONTENTS.

SIXTH PRINCIPLE.
UNION WITH OUR LORD.

SECTION I.
OF THE KNOWLEDGE OF OUR LORD.

CHAP.	PAGE
I. Of the mystery of the Man-God	231
Art. I. Of the excellence of the Incarnation	231
II. Of the Person of the Word	233
III. Why the Son of God was to become incarnate, and not the Father or the Holy Spirit	235
IV. Why the Son of God became incarnate by way of generation	236
II. The properties of the Man-God	236
Art. I. The self-annihilations of the Man-God	239
II. The alliances of the Sacred Humanity of Jesus Christ with the Three Persons of the Holy Trinity	238
III. Of the three crowns which Jesus Christ received from His Holy Mother in His Incarnation	239
IV. Of the royalty of Jesus Christ	240
V. Of the three principles of the actions of Jesus Christ	243
III. The different states of the life of Jesus Christ	245
Art. I. Of the infancy of Jesus Christ	246
II. Of the hidden life of Jesus Christ	247
III. Of the glorious life of Jesus Christ	248
IV. Of the state of Jesus Christ at the last judgment	251
IV. Of the Blessed Virgin	255
Art. I. The dignity of the Most Holy Virgin	255
II. The Blessed Virgin stands alone in each of her alliances with the Three Persons of the Holy Trinity	256
III. The glory of the Blessed Virgin in the Incarnation	257

SECTION II.
THE LOVE OF OUR LORD.

I. Motives for loving our Lord in Himself	259

CONTENTS.

CHAP.   PAGE

II. Motives for loving our Lord in the Holy Sacrament of the Altar 263
    Art. I. The wonders of the Holy Eucharist, and especially the sacramental species . . . 263
    II. The excellence of the Body of our Lord . . 264
    III. The eucharistic Presence of our Lord is more profitable to us than His sensible Presence was to the Jews 266
    IV. Of our union with our Lord in the Holy Sacrament 270
    V. Some thoughts on Communion 272

SECTION III.

ON THE IMITATION OF OUR LORD.

I. Motives for imitating our Lord 275
II. Of imitating our Lord in separation from all creatures 277
III. Of imitating our Lord in His poverty . . . 278
IV. Of imitating our Lord in IIis chastity . . . 280
V. Of imitating our Lord in His obedience . . . 284
VI. Of imitating our Lord in His humility . . . 287
VII. Of imitating our Lord in His interior life . . . 289
VIII. How greatly the mystery of the Incarnation serves to advance us in the way of perfection . . . 290
IX. A mode of effectually honouring the Incarnate Word, the Blessed Virgin, and St. Joseph . . . 292

SEVENTH PRINCIPLE.

THE ORDER AND DEGREES OF THE SPIRITUAL LIFE.

I. Of prayer in general 294
    Art. I. The great advantage of being a man of prayer . 294
    II. Advice on mental prayer in general . . . 295
II. Of meditation 297
III. Of affective prayer 298
IV. Of contemplation 298
    Art. I. There are two sorts of contemplation . . 298
    II. Of the gift of the presence of God. The first step in contemplation 300

CONTENTS.

CHAP.	PAGE
IV. Art. III. The advantages of contemplation	301
IV. Contemplation, so far from being opposed thereto, is necessary to the Apostolic life	304
V. What contemplation is	306
VI. Of the properties and effects of contemplation	308
VII. Different divisions of the degrees of contemplation	312
VIII. Another division of the degrees of contemplation	317
IX. Opinion on the above divisions	321

ADDITIONS.

I. Of perfection in general	327
Art. I. Motives that excite us to perfection	327
II. Wherein perfection consists, and what dispositions we ought to bring thereto	327
III. Of the practice of perfection	329
II. Of purity of heart	330
III. In what the faithful service of God consists	332
IV. Important advice for the advancement of souls	332
V. Of humility	333
VI. Of holy simplicity	334
VII. Of the spirit of devotion	335
VIII. Of different kinds of religious, and of the things that are most prejudicial to certain holy communities	337
IX. Of the spirit of the Company of Jesus	338
X. Of the kingdom of God in souls	344
Art. I. In what the kingdom of God consists, and its advantages	344
II. Of the conduct of the kingdom of God	345
III. Of the happiness of the kingdom of God	347
IV. Of the practice of the interior kingdom of God, or the means of establishing it within us	349

ADVERTISEMENT.

FATHER LOUIS LALLEMANT left behind him an odour of sanctity which still survives amongst us. It is to preserve it and transmit it to posterity that I have undertaken to give to the public his *Spiritual Doctrine*, together with a short account of his life. I should have fulfilled my object better, had I had access to the documents which were placed in the hands of one of our Fathers of the province of Champagne, who had engaged to write a complete biography of this holy man.

The following narrative is supported by the public testimony of all who knew him, and particularly his own disciples. His interior graces, which it was not possible to learn from himself, were observed by certain of his confessors and most intimate friends, as F. Peter Meflant, F. John Bagot, F. Antony Vaher, F. James Grandami; four theologians who, by their eminent virtues and great abilities, were worthy of being admitted to his confidence.

His *Spiritual Doctrine* was carefully compiled by F. John Rigoleu, who was born in 1595, and died in 1658; and who, so far from detracting from the force and unction of the work, rather added thereto. The collection which he made was preserved by another holy man, whom we are bound in gratitude to mention, F. Vincent Huby, under whose influence it was that I undertook the little works to which I devote the small portion of time which my occupations leave at my disposal.

I lately discovered among the papers of F. John Joseph Seurin, who was born in 1600, and died on the 21st of April, 1665, a manuscript, in which he had written with his own hand certain pious sentiments of his director, F. Louis Lallemant. As it was no longer possible to insert them each in its appropriate place in the collection of F. Rigoleu, they have been given separately, just as F. Seurin had noted them down.

And now, that I may comply with the decrees of Urban VIII. and other Sovereign Pontiffs, I protest that as regards the Life of F. Lallemant I ask from the reader but a human faith; and that in speaking of this Father as a Saint, I in no wise pretend to invest him with a title which it belongs only to the Apostolic See to give to those whom it judges worthy of it.

THE LIFE

OF

FATHER LOUIS LALLEMANT,

OF THE COMPANY OF JESUS.

FATHER LOUIS LALLEMANT was born in Champagne at Châlons-sur-Marne, in 1588. He was the only son of a *bailly* of the *comté de Vertus*, which was formerly an appanage of the princesses of France. His father sent him from his tenderest years to Bourges, to commence his studies at the College of the Fathers of the Company of Jesus.

God had bestowed upon him all the dispositions, both of nature and of grace, which were necessary for the accomplishment of the great designs which He had respecting him; a mind of a superior order, and one capable of acquiring every species of knowledge; a judgment at once penetrating and solid; a nature gentle, open, and obliging; great fondness for study; an extreme horror of vice, and especially of impurity; a lofty idea of the service of God, and a peculiar attraction for the interior life.

Mere child as he was, he practised interior recollection without knowing it. "I must always remain within myself," he used to say; "I must never altogether go abroad." This maxim, which he had learnt of the Holy Spirit without having been taught it by man, was graven so deeply in his heart, that, even thus early, he kept a continual watch over himself, and avoided nothing so much as an unguarded effusion.

The devotion which he had for the Holy Virgin made him desire to belong to the Congregation consecrated to her at the College of Bourges, where, it may be said, he passed the first noviciate of that religious life which he already contemplated.

The image of perfection which God had disclosed to him presented itself unceasingly to his mind under the most delightful attractions; and the desire which he felt for it often caused him, even in the midst of his recreations with his companions, such powerful transports, that his countenance appeared all on fire, his eyes sparkled, and he was compelled to leave the company, to go and abandon himself in secret to the movements of grace.

Having finished his humanities, and passed a year in rhetoric at Bourges, his father took him away to send him to Verdun, there to make a second year's study of rhetoric. He did so with much success; and after this, having asked permission to join the Company of Jesus, he was admitted therein, and entered the noviciate at Nancy on the 10th of December, 1605, being then in his eighteenth year.

God gave him grace to conceive from the first the true idea of that perfection which St. Ignatius proposes to his children. The life and conduct of this holy patriarch was the model which he undertook to imitate;

and he studied especially, after his example, to mortify the activity of his mind, and like him to subject all the movements of his heart to grace. And in this he very soon made such great progress, that those who had known him before were astonished to see that he had acquired in so short a time that tranquillity and evenness of mind which characterises perfect virtue.

After his noviciate, they made him enter immediately on his philosophical and theological studies at Pont-à-Mousson; a constant suffering which he experienced both in his head and stomach not permitting the superiors to employ him in the superintendence of the lower classes and the humanities, as was usual in the Company.

In the year 1616, the colleges of Champagne, Burgundy, and Lorraine, having been detached from the province of France, in order to their forming for the future a province of themselves, to bear the name of Champagne, F. Louis Lallemant remained in that of France; and made his solemn profession of the four vows at Paris on the 28th October, 1621. He taught the speculative sciences in several places; philosophy three years, mathematics four years, moral theology three years, and scholastic two years, at Paris. After this he was four years head of the noviciate, and master of novices, three years director of the second noviciate, prefect of the higher studies, and a few months rector of the college at Bourges.

Such was the course of his life, and the order of his employments; of which he acquitted himself so admirably, that he may be ranked among the most illustrious members of the Company. But although he was capable of every thing, it is nevertheless true that government and direction were the two offices for which he had received from Heaven the rarest talents.

The Holy Spirit, whose will it was to make of him an accomplished superior and director, and one capable of forming many others, had Himself acted as his master, and had instructed him in the spiritual life from his earliest years, as we have already remarked. He had attached him to Himself by that special devotion which He had inspired him with towards His own adorable Person. He had discovered to him all the most secret mysteries of grace. He had made him enter profoundly into the knowledge of His gifts, and had communicated them to him with that profuseness which He employs only in the case of souls which He intends to raise to the most eminent sanctity.

The fear of the Lord, which is the basis of all other gifts, and the foundation of the whole spiritual edifice, was always in him, as it is in the true children of God, grounded upon a solid humility, and accompanied with the other virtues which it introduces and preserves in souls, viz. innocence, purity, mortification, and disengagement from earthly things.

The knowledge which he had of his own nothingness, of the corruption of nature and its miseries, of the greatness of God, and the dependence of creatures upon the Creator, kept him in a continual abasement before His Sovereign and Adorable Majesty. The mean opinion he had of himself made him love his own abjection; and the love of abjection led him to seek all occasions of humbling himself and being humbled, and to embrace with joy those which presented themselves. The spirit of annihilation shewn by the Son of God in His Incarnation was the model of humility which he proposed to himself; and the Sacred Heart of the Incarnate Word was the school in which he studied the practice of this virtue. In this school, and from this divine Master it was, that he learned that sublime lesson of humility, of forgetting self and remaining buried in his own nothingness, to such perfection, that he occupied himself with his concerns, and spoke of them, and thought of them, no more than if he was not in existence, unless necessity obliged him, or a manifest movement of grace led him to do so.

His exterior and whole deportment breathed humility. Every thing he did he did quietly, and without eagerness, as if he would have wished to hide it from himself; so humble was he, and so averse to ostentation. For the same reason, he was more willing to co-operate secretly in the good works of others, than to undertake them himself; and although he may not have appeared in their execution, he often had the largest share in them, either by having been the author of them, through his advice or exhortations, or by having given them the support of his own credit and authority; or by having contributed more than any one else to their success by his management and care. He considered that Superiors ought to act thus towards their inferiors, interesting themselves in their labours, assisting and favouring them in their holy enterprises, employing them on any occasions which present themselves of promoting the glory of God and the good of souls, without wishing to do every thing in their own persons, and burdening themselves with a multitude of external occupations, which commonly prevent them from applying themselves, as much as they ought, to the government of their house. He said that this way of acting on the part of Superiors is extremely winning to inferiors, and encourages them to do their duty well, seeing themselves assisted and seconded in their functions by those who stand to them in the place of God.

The spirit of filial fear which he had from his childhood, was the faithful guardian that preserved to him undefiled the robe of innocence which he had received in baptism, and the precious treasure of virginity. The Father who heard his general confession in his last illness—a very able man, and of singular discretion—declared that he would not fear asserting on his oath, if occasion needed, that he had never committed mortal sin; and that he was so chaste, that he seemed to have no part in the corruption of nature. He never suffered temptations or movements contrary to purity.

His great maxim was, that our advancement in perfection is in proportion to the progress we make in purity of heart; that this is the shortest and the surest way of arriving at divine union, and the infallible means of disposing ourselves for large communications from God. This he knew by his own experience; and there was nothing to which he more applied himself than to keep his soul pure, not willingly suffering the least spot which might be displeasing to the eyes of God. It was for this reason that he kept a continual watch over his own interior, that he examined so carefully all the movements of his heart, and confessed every day with the greatest exactness.

Daily confession was one of the points which he most strongly recommended to such of our fathers as he perceived to be touched with a particular desire for their own perfection. He advised them to present themselves every day at the tribunal of penance, in order to accuse themselves of the least imperfections in their life, and to give account of every thing that concerned their spiritual direction.

This was his own practice; and as he always brought to confession all the requisite dispositions, a lively faith in the presence of Jesus Christ in the persons of his priests, a perfect confidence in the power which has been given them, a humble and loving contrition for his faults, a sincere zeal to repair them and to make full satisfaction to God, he experienced sensibly the effects of the sacrament, the peculiar grace of which is purity of conscience.

He was so faithful to grace that he never committed a deliberate fault. As soon as he perceived the shadow of the least sin, he retreated from it with all his strength; and F. Rigoleu testifies, that in his recreations it was sometimes remarked that he was suddenly silent, in obedience to the light which shewed him some imperfection in what he was beginning to say.

So far from allowing his body any gratifications which could soil the soul, he thought constantly only how to mortify it in all its senses. It is certain that his corporal austerities exceeded his strength; and in the judgment of his most intimate friends their severity considerably shortened his life.

As for interior abnegation, which is the most noble part of the spiritual sacrifice, he practised it perseveringly with an extreme rigour, combatting all his inclinations, or subjecting them to the Spirit of God. So that by a complete victory over his passions, he had arrived at that happy state of death, in which nature, being perfectly subjected to grace, offers no more obstacles to the divine life which the Holy Spirit desires to communicate to the soul.

He loved poverty as much as the world ordinarily eschews it. From the time that he bound himself to follow Jesus Christ, he would make use only of such things as were absolutely necessary, the meanest, the most worn, and the least convenient in the house. The whole furniture of his room consisted only of a wretched little bed without hangings, a table, two chairs, a *priedieu*, a Breviary, a Bible, and three or four other books which he could not do without. He took a pleasure in being always in want of something, that he might keep himself in the constant exercise of poverty; hiding his wants and his little discomforts with more care than misers hide their treasures, for fear the charity of Superiors or officials should deprive him of the opportunity of enduring them. But the idea he entertained of evangelical poverty was not confined to the stripping himself of exterior things. He carried it to the highest degree of which it is capable, that is, to a complete detachment from all creatures, and that perfect nudity of spirit which, rising even above the graces and the gifts of God, seeks but God alone, looks but to God, and clings to Him only. This was one of the sublime points in his doctrine by the practice of which he had attained to pure love.

He was naturally possessed of great courage, and

that firmness of mind which is hindered by nothing in the execution and pursuit of its designs. But his principal strength proceeded from a gift of grace, which, arraying him in the Spirit of God, made him undertake every thing and suffer every thing, where the interest of God was concerned. To this he felt himself so powerfully moved that nothing could stop him, neither the difficulties of the enterprise, nor the labour it entailed, nor the opposition of the world, nor considerations of human prudence, nor fear of ill success. It was enough for him to know that this was what God desired of him, to engage him to embrace it, and to make him believe that he should accomplish it.

Although his health was none of the strongest, he did not spare himself the least, labouring unceasingly in his employment, and in all those works to which obedience and charity called him for the glory of God and the service of his neighbour. Fervour of spirit made up for feebleness of body, and so supported him that he seemed indefatigable.

Patience and gentleness are among the noblest effects, as they are also the most solid proofs of strength. Father Lallemant excelled both in one and the other. He suffered with so much sweetness, that to see him suffer, no one would have thought he was suffering any thing. As he was perfectly master of himself, no one ever remarked in him any unevenness either of mind or temper. He possessed his soul in perfect peace, and his countenance was always serene. He never at any time raised his voice.

That supernatural courage with which he was animated, made him ask of God, like St. Ignatius, to be contradicted and thwarted in his designs by all the world, not only to have the opportunity of suffering, but also that the success of his undertakings might conduce so much the more to the glory of God, as the difficulties were greater which he would have had to surmount in order to their accomplishment.

He entreated during three years to be sent out on some foreign mission, and especially that of Canada, although fewer conversions were made there than elsewhere; because it was more fruitful in labours and crosses, because it offered a less brilliant career, and contributed more than any others to the sanctification of the missionaries. This is what made him prefer it to all others; and failing to obtain permission to go there in person, he always exerted himself to procure fervent labourers for that mission, and to render it in France all the service that lay in his power.

His love of missions sprang out of that spirit of piety which made him look upon souls as images of God, bearing the fair stamp of His likeness, and redeemed by the Blood of His Son, and filled him with a sensible grief at their ruin, and a burning desire for their salvation. For it is the gift of piety which infuses into the heart of Saints that most tender love and zeal which they experience for God and for their neighbour. This it is which imparts to charity an attraction and a sweetness which otherwise it lacks. It is a gift as rare as it is precious, and one that is necessary for men of letters and evangelical labourers, to prevent study and the turmoil of active employment producing in them dryness of spirit.

Father Lallemant was filled with an unction of

piety which appeared in all his actions, and particularly in such as had immediate reference to God, as when he recited the Divine Office, celebrated Mass, administered the Sacraments; and even in the smallest things, as when he made the sign of the Cross, or took holy water. His manner of performing these acts betokened a depth of devotion as tender as it was solid.

He had no greater delight than entertaining himself familiarly with God, calling prayer his happiness on earth, and giving to it more time than to any other of his occupations. Sometimes he would thus employ several hours of the night, which he stole from sleep. One day, being alone with a friend before the fire, he confessed to him that he had no difficulty in raising his mind to God; that it was as easy to him as to cast his eyes on the dogs which supported the wood upon the hearth.

Nothing interested him which was unconnected with God. His whole interior occupation was to discover what were the designs of God in every particular thing; and when he had ascertained them, to give himself up to Him, to execute them according to the lights of grace imparted by the spirit of Jesus Christ.

He always sensibly experienced the direction of the Holy Spirit in prayer, even before he had arrived at that state which the mystics call passive or supernatural, because the soul in that state simply consents to the operation of God in a manner which is not natural to it. Thus, no sooner did he betake himself to prayer, than he found himself illuminated by a divine light, which laid open before him the subject and the points of his meditation, and suggested to him all its acts, as he testifies in one of his writings.

His great devotion was to the Incarnate Word. All the powers of his soul were engrossed with the thought of His adorable Person, His different states and mysteries. That of the most Holy Eucharist was the object of his special homage, and the most frequent subject of his conversation; when speaking of it he was carried out of himself. All his exercises of piety were directed to the Man-God, or had reference to Him; and the love of our Lord formed the ground of his every action. Nothing made virtues appear more amiable in his eyes than the considering them as deified in Jesus Christ. Seeing them in this light, those which are naturally the most repulsive, or the most difficult, had for him the greatest attraction.

Every thing bearing the mark of the Son of God, every thing connected with Him, or in immediate contact with Him, was infinitely dear to him; hence he cherished an inconceivable tenderness for the Blessed Virgin and St. Joseph, and maintained a most familiar and loving intercourse with such among the angelic choir as are especially devoted to the Incarnate Word and His most holy Mother.

It was observed that he every day recited a portion of the Rosary; but he honoured the Blessed Virgin far more by the exalted sentiments of veneration, respect, love, and confidence, which he entertained for her, than by exterior practices.

He was gifted with an extraordinary grace for inspiring every body with a devotion to St. Joseph; and his advice to persons who desired to enter on the ways of spiritual perfection was, to take as their model of humility Jesus Christ, as their model of purity the Blessed Virgin, and as their model of the interior life St. Joseph. It was after these divine patterns that he laboured at his own perfection; and it was easy to perceive how happily he had wrought them out in his own person.

Every day, in honour of St. Joseph, he observed four short exercises, from which he drew wonderful profit. The two first were for the morning, and the two others for after dinner. The first was to raise himself in spirit to the heart of St. Joseph, and consider how faithful he was to the inspirations of grace; then turning his eyes inward on his own heart, to discover his own want of fidelity, he made an act of humiliation, and excited himself to perseverance. The second was, to reflect how perfectly St. Joseph reconciled the interior life with his external occupations. Then, turning to observe himself and his own occupations, he perceived wherein they fell short of the perfection of his model. By means of this exercise he made such progress, that towards the close of his life he remained in an uninterrupted state of interior recollection; and the attention which he paid to external things, instead of weakening his union with God, served rather to strengthen it. The third was, to accompany in spirit St. Joseph, as the spouse of the Blessed Virgin, and to meditate on the wonderful knowledge which he had enjoyed of her virginity and maternity, in consequence of the humble submission with which he received the announcement of the Angel respecting the mystery of the Incarnation. By this exercise he excited himself to love St. Joseph for his love of his most holy spouse. The fourth was, to figure to himself the adoration and homage of love and gratitude which St. Joseph paid to the Holy Child Jesus, and to beg to participate therein, that he might adore and love this Divine Infant with all the sentiments of the deepest reverence and the tenderest love of which he was capable. He wished to carry with him to the grave some tokens of his devotion to this great Saint, and requested that an image of his beloved patron might be put with him in his coffin.

It was observed on many occasions that St. Joseph never refused him any thing he asked; and whenever he wished to induce persons to honour him, he used to assure them that he did not possess a single grace which he had not obtained through his intercession. Thus he acted in the case of F. Paul Ragueneau and F. James Nouet, who were regents of the lower classes at the College of Bourges. At the time he was rector, observing in them excellent dispositions to virtue, he took particular pains with their spiritual advancement. As the Feast of St. Joseph approached, he sent for them both, and promised that they should obtain every thing they asked through the intercession of this great Saint, if they would exhort their scholars to be devout towards him, and to do something more than ordinary on his feast-day. The two young regents engaged to do as he said, and brought all their scholars to communion on that day; they then went to communicate to the father rector what each wished St. Joseph to obtain for them. F. Nouet asked for grace to speak and write worthily of our Lord. But the next morning, on seeking F. Lallemant, to tell him that upon due reflection he was anxious to ask for another grace, which he thought more conducive to his perfection, the Father replied that it was too late to ask for another grace, that the first had been already granted, and that he had pledged himself only for that one. This grace was conspicuously displayed throughout the whole course of F. Nouet's life. His sermons and his writings are proofs of it, and above all, his great work on our Lord Jesus Christ, which cost him the labour of many years, and which he finished only a short time before his death. With regard to F. Ragueneau, who recounted all this to Madame Marin, a Benedictine religious of Mont Martre, he would not say what favour he had asked of St. Joseph from F. Lallemant. It was apparently some interior grace which his humility obliged him to conceal, like so many other favours and precious gifts which he had received from Heaven. For he was a perfect religious, of great largeness of mind, remarkable discernment and solidity of judgment, an heroic courage, and capable of the greatest achievements, a holy simplicity, a wonderful confidence in God, and most perfect experience in spiritual things; a man completely detached from all temporal interests, and one who breathed only the love of God and zeal for souls. He was one of the first missionaries of New France; and I was informed by F. Joseph Poncet and F. Francis le Mercier, two holy religious who had been his colleagues in his apostolical labours, that there was no one who rendered more service to the Church of Canada, or more justly merited the title of an apostle. Returning afterwards to France for the purpose of acting as procurator to his beloved mission, he then displayed that rare talent for direction with which God had endowed him. Providence conducted to him an immense number of devout souls, and especially such as were being led by extraordinary ways; and he devoted himself with a boundless charity to assist them both by word of mouth and by letters. Persons wrote to him from all quarters, and his replies carried the light and unction of the Holy Spirit into the hearts of those to whom they were addressed. He died a holy death at Paris, on the 3d of September, 1680, at the age of 75. It were much to be wished that some one would undertake to collect his letters with a view to publication. But let us return to F. Louis Lallemant.

He agreed in opinion with those who believe that when the Incarnation of the Son of God was communicated to the angels, besides the homage which all the faithful amongst them paid to the Man-God, there were some who devoted themselves especially to Him and the Virgin Mother of whom He was to be born; that they habitually attended upon both one and the other during their mortal life; and that one of their offices is to inspire souls with a devotion to them, and to assist in every way such as most religiously practise it. On this account he paid particular honour to these holy angels, and entered into a spiritual alliance with them to honour and love Jesus and Mary, to make them known and loved by all the world, and to promote the increase of their glory. He never said Mass without beseeching the angels of the Incarnate Word to accompany him to the altar; and when he commenced reciting his Office, he invited the angels who form the court of the Blessed Virgin to unite with him in chanting the praises of God.

From the time that he formed the design of entering the Company of Jesus, he began to regard St. Ignatius as his father, entertaining for him the sentiments of a son, and having recourse to him with confidence in all his needs.

He possessed the gift of piety in its fulness, and it wrought in him all those effects which it habitually produces,—a filial submission to his Superiors, a paternal kindness towards his inferiors, and a fraternal charity for all the world.

It is piety which perfects obedience, making a man see only God in his Superiors, and feel towards them as a child. F. Lallemant was a man of this disposition; and his delight was to regulate his employments and all his conduct by obedience, as the true interpreter of the will of God. To enable himself to do this with more perfection, he asked for nothing, refused nothing, not even allowing himself the liberty of liking or disliking, always ready to do what was most laborious or the least to his taste, as soon as he perceived what his Superiors wished, without waiting till they gave him an express command.

Obedience was what he especially enjoined upon his novices, and he made them take this virtue for their particular examination five or six months together. "Do not think it irksome, my brethren," he used to say to them, "if I keep you so long on obedience. If you can make yourselves perfect in it, be assured you will be in the direct and certain way to holiness."

His exactness in observing the rules sprang from the same principle, because they marked out to him in detail what God desired of him; he regarded them with peculiar veneration, and kept them with that spirit of love which is the characteristic of perfect religious.

But the point on which his spirit of piety displayed itself most conspicuously was in his behaviour towards his equals and inferiors. In this one may truly say that he could hardly have been surpassed.

Charity in him displayed all those qualities which St. Paul ascribes to it. Nothing could be more patient, more gentle, more humble, more disinterested, more condescending, or more obliging.

His excellent disposition, his amiable and engaging manners, his singular modesty, his composed deportment, a mixture of sweetness and holy gravity, that heavenly expression which breathed in his countenance and in his words, gave him a ready entrance into all hearts. It sufficed to listen to him once, to make men eagerly desire to hear him and converse with him.

He knew so well how to accommodate himself to those whom Providence directed to him, to bear with their defects, to seek opportunities of serving them, and to gain access to their minds, that in the end, by this holy condescension and by this patience, he acquired a complete influence over them.

At whatever moment he was applied to, however occupied he might be, he received every one that came with a smiling countenance and an open heart; and he seemed never to have any thing else to do but to listen to those who wished to speak to him, without ever betraying in his manner any signs of weariness.

F. Rigoleu remarks in one of his letters, that some of the Fathers who made their second noviciate under this holy director at the same time with himself, were at first rather opposed to his views, but that he so won upon them by his sweetness, kindness, and humility, that before three months had elapsed, there was not a single one who did not yield himself implicitly to his guidance, one and all without exception declaring that they had never met with such a Superior.

However, God not seldom so permitted it that some of those who, as his Superiors, ought to have treated him with more kindness, or who, as his inferiors and disciples, were bound to shew him more respect and submission, should somewhat forget themselves in their conduct towards him and be a cause of trouble to him. But far from shewing resentment at this, or making any complaint, he rejoiced at it, and was the more willing to take pains to serve them. His revenge confined itself to desiring more ardently their spiritual progress; and he declared one day, in confidence, to a friend, that this desire was so strong within him that he was consumed by it, and could scarcely endure its violence. In fact, they who knew him best were persuaded that the burning zeal with which he was inflamed contributed no less to shorten his life than the rigour of his penances.

A short time after he was rector of the College of Bourges, a brother who performed the office of baker came to him one day, and rather rudely complained of having too much to do, desiring him to see to the matter, and put some one else in his place. The Father listened to him calmly, and promised to relieve him. He then went himself quietly into the bakehouse, and began kneading dough with all his might.

The brother, when the first heat of his excitement was over, was very much surprised, on returning to the bakehouse, to find there the father rector doing his work for him. He immediately threw himself at his feet and begged his pardon, full of confusion for his fault, and overcome with the sweetness and the humility of so compassionate a Superior.

It was thus he acted on similar occasions, employing lenity with so much prudence, that all hearts readily conceded to him all he wished. He used to say, that experience taught him every day more and more, that rule should be exercised in the Company with extreme mildness; that the Superiors ought to study how to make themselves obeyed rather from love than from fear; that the way to maintain regularity is not by rigour and penances, but by the fatherly kindness of Superiors, and their diligence in attending to the wants of their inferiors; and in preserving and increasing amongst them the interior spirit and prayer.

His great ability drew to him as much the esteem and confidence of souls, as his tender charity won their affections. Besides the natural lights of a superior understanding and a true and sound judgment, as well as those which he had acquired from a profound study of theology and personal experience, he was wonderfully illuminated with those infused lights which God gives to His ministers, either for their own direction or for that of others.

He was learned in the science of the Saints, as he has himself described it in his instructions on the Holy Spirit. What he says on this subject shews plainly enough that he must be numbered among those men who have been the most deeply versed in the spiritual life. He used to discourse concerning it divinely; and the Fathers who made their third year's noviciate under his direction were wont to admire in him that rare talent of infused science, that rich and varied knowledge of supernatural things, which, it was evident, could come only from his union with God, of which it bore the marks. For he had no leisure for study, and spent so much of his time in prayer and in talking to his novices, that he had scarcely any left for preparing the exhortations and conferences, which he gave every day; nevertheless they were so full and so beautiful, that any one would have said he had passed his whole time in composing them.

The oldest and most eminent of the Fathers were so delighted with his discourses, that they would have preferred going without a moment's recreation to being deprived of the advantage of hearing him speak of spiritual things. A very able Father declared he had never conversed with this holy man without carrying away from the conversation some fresh light, either as to the meaning of Scripture, of which he had a profound knowledge, or on some point of theology or spiritual science.

F. Julian Hayneuve, who, by his writings as well as heroic virtues, has deserved universal respect and veneration, when rector of the noviciate at Rouen, at the time that F. Lallemant was director of the Fathers who were passing through their third year's probation in the same place, from a desire to be one of the disciples of so accomplished a master, assisted as though he had been a novice at all the exhortations and instructions, which he declared were full of a light and an unction which he met with no where else.

It is impossible to conceive what influence his discourses exercised and what impression they produced upon souls. That heavenly gift, which St. Paul calls the grace of speech, was conspicuous in him, whether exhorting or warning, encouraging or consoling. It was often observed that a single word from his lips would calm a troubled soul or convince an obstinate intellect.

Some have considered with much reason that F. Louis Lallemant held the same place among the Jesuits of France, which F. Alvarez occupied among those of Spain. He certainly united in an eminent degree, as did that celebrated director of St. Theresa, the knowledge and the practice of mystical theology, and, like him, numbered among his disciples the most spiritual and interior men whom the Company has ever had amongst us. It has since been remarked, that all those who made their first or second noviciate under him, were commonly distinguished above others by a religious deportment, which corresponded with the excellent lessons they had learnt from him, and especially by the love of recollection and the interior life.

He himself acknowledged that God had given him a particular talent for the direction of those belonging to the Company, and that He made known to him His designs in their regard, the impediments which they threw in the way, and the road by which they had to walk in order to arrive at perfection. He declared that the holiness to which the members are called surpasses all imagination; and that could any one behold the graces which God has prepared for each of them, he would conclude they were destined only for a St. Ignatius or a St. Francis Xavier.

He had, as it were, an habitual gift of discernment and counsel, by the light of which he was enabled to distinguish in every thing what was the best, the most suitable to time and place under existing circumstances, the most conducive to the end which was aimed at, and the most agreeable to God. It was in accordance with this light that, seven or eight years before his death, he made that generous vow, so far above human weakness, of doing in all things that which he deemed most perfect.

In this, however, he acted with so much discretion, that in choosing what he esteemed the best, he did not reject what was less good, provided it was exceedingly good.

He used to say, that what we ought to endeavour to imitate in the conduct of Saints is not that which strikes us as most splendid in the rare examples of their virtues, but their constant fidelity in following grace in all things, even the least; and that if we were as courageous and as faithful as they were, we should become equal to them in merits, although we neither did nor suffered the same things as they did and suffered. His method of governing was wholly supernatural. The spirit of policy had nothing to do with it. He lamented over those communities in which the Superiors were guided by this spirit; which is, he said, the destruction of obedience and of the confidence which inferiors ought to have in those who stand to them in the place of Jesus Christ, in order to lead them to God.

He never did any thing hastily, nor took a single resolution without consulting the Holy Spirit; considering an eager zeal, which forestalls the movements of grace, and a too impetuous fervour, which does not give sufficient heed to the interior light, one of the defects which most hinders the operation of God in spiritual persons, and robs the evangelical workman of the fruits of his functions and of the labours of his ministry. Never throughout his whole conduct was there observable any fault against prudence.

The highest lights which souls enjoy come from the gifts of understanding and of wisdom. The Holy Spirit communicated them in their fulness to F. Louis Lallemant, as He has done to the greatest masters of spiritual doctrine; and it would be difficult to find any one who had penetrated more deeply into the understanding of the mysteries of our religion, and especially that of the Man-God. He might say with St. Paul, that he had received grace to make known to the world the unsearchable riches of Christ.

He did not stop, as is commonly done, at the outside, and what may be called the body, of the mysteries of the Incarnate Word and of the actions of the Saints. The gift of understanding enabled him to penetrate the spirit of them, and revealed to him the admirable dispositions of the interior of Jesus Christ, of the Blessed Virgin, and all the Saints. To this it was that he chiefly applied himself. The lofty idea which he entertained of the most Holy Virgin was founded on the knowledge he had gained of her incomparable perfections, and of the marvels which were wrought in her from the moment of her immaculate conception, and during the whole course of her life, but especially when she was raised to the divine maternity in the mystery of her Annunciation. He considered that she was exempted not only from original sin, but also from the debt of its contraction. Of all the Saints, St. Joseph and St. Ignatius were the two of whom he had the largest and most distinct knowledge. It seemed as if the latter had given him his spirit, and had obtained for him from God the power of communicating it to his children. He used to say, that what had been manifested to the world of the virtues and graces of this great Saint, and what his biographers had observed of them, was almost nothing in comparison with the interior perfection which lay hidden in the depth of his soul.

He had a particular grace for explaining Holy Scripture, and penetrating its various senses. He was ever reading it, and made it almost his sole study. But it was rather by means of prayer, than by consulting commentators. Prayer was his resource in all the difficulties he encountered in reading the Word of God; and he would sometimes during the space of a whole year petition our Lord to enlighten him on the meaning of some passage.

The gift of understanding is not limited to divine things, although they are its first and principal object. It extends also to human actions, and to things of this world, with the view of ascertaining the designs of God in them, and how far they conduce or are opposed to His glory. But it is only pure souls, and such as are detached from all self-interest, recollected within themselves, and intimately united to God, that are capable of this divine penetration. As he looked only to God and sought Him alone in all things, the presence of God, and the purity of his own intentions, served him as a torch to penetrate through the artifices and disguises of the human mind, to disentangle the designs and interests of God from among the affairs and intrigues of men, and to distinguish in each thing what there was of God, and what of the creature.

He was wont to say, that they who keep a strict watch over themselves, and take pains to observe and regulate all their internal movements, acquire a peculiar capacity for obtaining an insight into the secrets of hearts; either because God is pleased to reward with this favour the diligence with which they have studied their own interior, or because experience of what they feel in themselves teaches them to form an accurate judgment of what passes in others.

No wonder, then, that he penetrated as he did the depths of men's hearts, and discovered even the most secret thoughts which they wished to hide from him.

One of our own members has deposed, that once, when confessing to him, the holy man told him of a secret sin which he was omitting to accuse himself of; and that another time he revealed to him the thoughts which he was revolving in his mind, and detailed all the circumstances of a temptation with which he was assailed.

Another had sought him with the intention of disclosing to him some secret wound of his soul; but as he entered his room, overcome with shame, he suddenly changed his mind, and began talking of some other subject; when the Father, knowing the evil he was concealing, answered as distinctly to the point on which he had been afraid to speak, as if he had opened all his heart to him.

One day, seeing a young religious approaching him at a distance, who, for some human consideration or other, was afraid of appearing in his presence, and sought different pretexts to avoid meeting him, he called him to him, and told him all that was passing within him, as if he had seen it with his eyes. The young man, greatly surprised that the Father should have penetrated his thoughts, candidly acknowledged his weakness, and recovered at once his former confidence.

In this way F. Lallemant preserved several of his spiritual children from the evil into which they were about to fall; some who were wavering in their vocation he confirmed, others who were beginning to relax he excited to renewed fervour.

The gift of wisdom perfects that of understanding, giving it an unction and a sweetness without which all the knowledge it imparts would be dry and insipid.

It was by the way of wisdom that F. Lallemant received the lights of understanding. He experienced the fulfilment of our Lord's promise to His disciples. The unction of the Holy Ghost was his teacher; and the heavenly visions, the sweetnesses, the divine consolations with which he was often favoured in prayer and at the altar, seemed to place as it were in broad light the most obscure truths of faith, discovered to him the sense of Scripture, and unfolded before him that which is most hidden in the mysteries of our religion.

One night our Lord awoke him, and told him it

was the hour at which the mystery of the Incarnation was accomplished; that He was about to confer upon him some small participation of that grace which was bestowed on the Blessed Virgin in that great mystery, bidding him therefore dispose himself for its reception. He arose, and began to pray; and in the fervour of his prayer he felt himself interiorly, as it were, invested and wholly penetrated with the Man-God, by an intimate union, which purified him both in soul and body after an inexplicable manner. At the same time the Blessed Virgin appeared to him, and calling him her son, assured him she loved him tenderly, and exhorted him to be especially devout to the Sacred Humanity of her Son, which, said she, is almost forgotten by all the world. He ventured to ask two favours of her: the first, that he might always be mindful of her, for it was to him a cause of pain if sometimes he let pass any noticeable time without thinking of her; the second, that he might never be separated from that Adorable Humanity to which he had consecrated his heart. The Blessed Virgin promised him both favours; and, in fact, he ever after enjoyed equally the presence of the Son and of the Mother.

Some time after, finding himself assailed by a temptation to distrust and doubt of his salvation, he repulsed it by the remembrance of the assurance which the Mother of God had given him, that he should never be separated from the Sacred Humanity of her Son. But afterwards, reflecting on the reliance which he placed on this assurance, he was seized with a fear that there was something of presumption in it. While he was in this uncertainty, the Blessed Virgin appeared to him, and relieved him of his fears, pointing out to him that his confidence was not presumptuous, inasmuch as he relied not on himself, but on the grace which had been promised him; that this kind of promise is always conditional, and supposes that they to whom it is given will not be wanting in fidelity; that should he happen to fail in this, he would certainly be lost, notwithstanding the favour which she had obtained for him from God.

During the third year of his noviciate our Lord gave him a second Angel of a superior order to be his teacher and guide in the spiritual life.

One of his two Angels, or some Saint, used to awake him sometimes at night, and invite him to pray; but more often it was our Lord Himself, or St. Ignatius, who conferred this favour upon him.

St. Ignatius miraculously cured him of a disorder which he had when a student in philosophy; and during his second noviciate he obtained for him from God a complete deliverance from an habitual headache, which for nine years had troubled him at his studies.

One day, being attacked by an importunate and violent temptation, he betook himself to prayer, when St. Theresa appeared to him, and putting the enemy to flight, restored peace to his soul. The same temptation afterwards returning, he had recourse to prayer as usual, and beheld St. Ignatius and St. Theresa, who, chasing away the devil, freed him for ever after from that sort of attack.

One day, as he was praying to God in the church of the noviciate at Rouen, he was visited by St. Joseph, and received favours from him which are not known, any more than the great number of other heavenly visits by which he was instructed in his doubts, consoled in his troubles, strengthened in his labours, and encouraged in those enterprises with which God inspired him for His glory.

It is known for certain that he had several revelations of the state of the souls in purgatory. He witnessed their sufferings, learnt the cause of them, and often had the consolation of beholding the pomp of their triumphal entrance into heaven; how some Saint, St. Ignatius for example, presented to the Blessed Virgin the soul of one of his children, released from its sufferings; how the Blessed Virgin presented it to our Lord; in what manner Jesus Christ received it; the welcome which the Angels and the Saints gave it, and how its angel-guardian accompanied it to the throne of glory on which the Saviour placed it. In his prayers, spiritual readings, and studies, he was ordinarily favoured with consolations and sweetnesses of grace; and the unction of the Holy Spirit distilled from his lips, and made itself felt in his words.

It may be well supposed with what perfection he practised in his own person that which he so much recommended to others, entire self-abandonment to the guidance of the Holy Spirit. He had given himself up to it from childhood, and the whole course of his life was but one continual reliance on the direction of this Divine Spirit, who, having filled him with His gifts, made him correspond to all His movements with wonderful facility.

The Holy Spirit was his master in mystical theology. He did not learn it from men; and although he had for his directors religious of great virtue and capacity, he never derived from them the advantages which F. Seurin and F. Rigoleu found in him, and which made them what they were. The same Divine Teacher was his guide in those sublime ways of the spiritual life in which he made such marvellous progress. The interior law which the Holy Spirit had graven on his heart was his principal rule. His whole life was supernatural. His sentiments, his words, his actions, seemed to flow from a depth wholly filled with God. Not a fault was perceivable; in him the interior and the exterior perfectly corresponded. His inner life was all hidden in God with Christ; and the Spirit of Jesus sensibly manifested itself in his outward life as in a mirror, so that it was impossible to look at him without feeling touched with devotion and disposed to recollection.

He passed without contradiction for one of the most perfect Jesuits of his time, being animated with the true spirit of St. Ignatius, and closely resembling that holy patriarch. The superiors of religious orders, and especially the Carmelites and the nuns of the Visitation, and indeed all the most spiritual persons in the places where he resided, maintained a holy intercourse with him, and consulted him as an oracle of the Holy Spirit, whether for their own personal direction, or to assist them in guiding the souls of which they had the charge.

All his disciples had so high an idea of his virtue, that I never met with a single one who did not invariably speak of him with admiration. F. John Joseph Seurin and F. John Rigoleu, in particular, felt for him all the respect and veneration with which Saints are regarded; and their writings testify how perfectly they copied in their own minds and hearts the teaching and the sanctity of their master.

His renown travelled even into foreign countries, and his sanctity was miraculously revealed to Mother Louise of the Ascension, a poor Clare, then residing at Carion in Spain, and filling the whole world with the fame of the marvels which grace was operating in her. The holy man was shewn to her in spirit, as also the degree of perfection to which he had been raised. She desired to contract a holy friendship with him, and, taking the opportunity of some persons going to Rouen, begged them to salute in her name F. Louis Lallemant, of the Company of Jesus, and to recommend her to his prayers.

It might have been thought desirable that God should prolong a life which seemed so greatly to promote His glory. But the counsels of God are inscrutable. His Superiors perceiving that his excessive labours in conducting the noviciate at Rouen were effectually ruining his health, removed him from thence, and made him prefect of high studies in the College of Bourges, and afterwards rector of the same. But all the time he was there he did nothing but languish and sigh after death, regarding it as the passage from this state of corruption, in which the law of sin reigns within us in our own despite, to that blessed state of holy liberty where the clear vision of God renders those who are in the enjoyment of it incapable of sinning for all eternity. Feeling the approaches of death, he took in one hand a crucifix, and in the other an image of our Lady, looking first on one, then on the other, speaking lovingly to them, and regarding them in turn with marks of confidence and tenderness which melted to tears all who were present. In these pious sentiments he sweetly rendered up his soul to his Creator on the 5th of April, being Maunday Thursday, in the year 1635, aged about forty-seven years, twenty-nine of which were passed in the Company.

When the news of his death was spread through the town, the sentiments of respect and veneration with which he was regarded were heightened; every body spoke of him as a Saint, and people flocked in crowds to the college, to pay honour to his body. Some touched it with their rosaries, others cut off a lock of his hair, or a fragment of his clothes; every one was eager to possess some relic of him, and all pressed to kiss his feet or his hands; the greater part with a devotion so tender that they could not restrain their tears.

An Augustine Father, who was preaching the Lent in the cathedral, after his sermon upon the Passion of our Lord on Good Friday, made a short eulogium of the deceased, exhorting his hearers to be present at his funeral, which was to take place that evening, not so much, said he, to aid him with their prayers, as to beseech him to assist them with his own, in the hope that they might enjoy his patronage in heaven, and the whole town find in him a protector and a powerful mediator with God. And in fact, not only the people, but the clergy, the religious, and the persons most distinguished both for birth and station, assisted at his funeral, and testified the conviction they entertained of his sanctity and of his power with God.

There have been several revelations of him in glory,

and many have believed that they received particular favours through his intercession.

He was tall of stature, and of a majestic bearing; his forehead was broad and calm, his beard and hair dark auburn; his head already approaching to baldness; his face oval and well proportioned; his complexion dark; and his cheeks generally tinged with that heavenly fire which inflamed his heart; his eyes, which were full of an engaging sweetness, expressed the solidity of his judgment and his perfect evenness of mind. I have heard it said by those who knew him, and who were the most capable of judging, that it would be difficult to find a man of nobler appearance and more composed in all his movements, or one whose exterior betokened greater devotion and recollection; the very sight of him was enough to attract every one's respect and affection.

The most faithful portrait that could be drawn of the interior dispositions of his soul is to be found in the collection of his *Spiritual Doctrine and Maxims*, here given to the public as F. Rigoleu composed it. It is a gift which I present to such souls as aspire after interior recollection, and particularly to the religious of the Company of Jesus, who will find therein all the perfection proper to their state.

The Spiritual Doctrine

OF

FATHER LOUIS LALLEMANT,

OF THE COMPANY OF JESUS.

ALL that F. Rigoleu collected of the instructions of his director F. Lallemant concerning the spiritual life, may be reduced to seven principles: viz. the consideration of the end—the idea of perfection—purity of heart—docility in following the leadings of the Holy Spirit—recollection, or the interior life—union with our Lord—and the order or steps of the spiritual life.

FIRST PRINCIPLE.

THE CONSIDERATION OF THE END.

CHAPTER I.

GOD ALONE CAN MAKE US HAPPY.

§ I.

There is a void in our heart which all creatures united would be unable to fill. God alone can fill it; for He is our beginning and our end. The possession of God fills up this void, and makes us happy. The rivation of God leaves in us this void, and is the cause of our wretchedness.

Before God fills up this void, He puts us in the way of faith; with this condition, that if we never cease to regard Him as our last end, if we use creatures with moderation, and refer to His service the use we make of them, at the same time contributing faithfully to the glory which it is His will to draw from all created beings, He will give Himself to us to fill up the void within us, and make us happy. But if we are wanting in fidelity, He will leave in us that void which, left unfilled, will cause our supreme misery.

§ II.

Creatures desire to take the place of our last end, and we ourselves more than all, we desire to be our own last end. A creature says to us, "Come to me; I will satisfy thee." We believe it, and it deceives us. Then another and another holds the same language to us, deceives us in like manner, and will go on deceiving us all our life long. Creatures call to us on all sides, and promise to satisfy us. All their promises, however, are but lies; and yet we are ever ready to let ourselves be cheated. It is as if the bed of the sea were empty, and one were to take a handful of water to refill it. Thus we are never satisfied; for when we attach ourselves to creatures, they estrange us from God, and cast us into an ocean of pain, trouble, and misery—elements as inseparable from the creature, as joy, peace, and happiness are inseparable from God.

§ III.

We are like jaded epicures, who taste a dish, then leave it, and immediately stretch out their hand to another, to leave it also in its turn, finding nothing to their liking. We seize upon every manner of thing, without being able to satisfy ourselves with any. God alone is the sovereign good who can make us happy; and we deceive ourselves when we say, "Were I in such a place, had I such a situation, I should be satisfied. Such an one is happy; he has what he desires." Vanity! Were you Pope, you would not be content. Let us seek God; let us seek God only. He only can satisfy all our desires.

§ IV.

Of old the devil disguised himself as God, presenting himself to the heathen in idols as the author and the end of every thing in the world. Creatures do much the same thing. They disguise themselves as God, cheating us into the belief that they will satisfy us by giving us wherewithal to fill our souls. But every thing they give us serves only to increase our emptiness. *Now* we do not feel it; it is only truly realised in the next life, where the soul, separated from its body, has an almost infinite desire to see itself filled with God, and the disappointment of this causes it to suffer a pain in a manner infinite.

§ V.

At the hour of death we shall know how miserably we have let ourselves be deceived and deluded by creatures. We shall be astounded that for things so low and vile we should have been willing to lose that which is so great and precious; and our punishment for this foolish conduct will be, to be deprived for a time of the sight of God, without which nothing can satisfy the soul. The desire it has to see Him and possess Him is as much beyond conception as the punishment caused by such desire when it is unsatisfied.

This is why we must resolve generously to renounce all designs of our own devising, all human views, all desires and hopes of things that might gratify self-love; and, in short, every thing that might hinder us in promoting the glory of God. This it is which, in the words of Scripture, is called "walking before the Lord," "having an upright soul," "walking in truth," "seeking God with all our heart." Without this we shall never be happy.

§ VI.

Why do we cling to creatures as we do? They are so limited and so void of any solid good, that all the pleasure and satisfaction we may promise ourselves from them is but a vain imaginary happiness, which only famishes instead of filling us, because our appetite being infinite, it can be satisfied only in the possession of the sovereign good. Add to which that creatures endure but for a while and soon leave us, or we are ourselves compelled to leave them.

And as for men in particular, do we not know that they love only themselves, and in all things seek but their own interest? The little property, credit, authority which they possess, they economise for themselves; and if they had all manner of goods in abundance, they would not act otherwise. Every thing which they do not purely for God, they do from self-love; and in any thing which they do for others, they never lose sight of themselves. They are our benefactors and our faithful friends only so far as they find their own account in it. What reliance, then, can we place on the favour and the friendship of men?

CHAPTER II.

OUR HAPPINESS DEPENDS ON OUR PERFECT SUBMISSION TO GOD, WHO OUGHT TO REIGN ALONE IN OUR HEARTS.

§ I.

Our true greatness consists in our submission to God. We depend upon God in three ways. First, we cannot so much as exist but by Him. Secondly, we cannot have the means of arriving at Him, but from Him. Thirdly, we cannot take possession of our end and sovereign good but by Him. Herein the ancient philosophers deceived themselves, seeking their happiness in themselves and in human things.

§ II.

God alone has right of sovereignty over hearts. Neither secular powers, nor the Church herself, extend their dominion thus far. What passes there depends not on them. There God alone is King. It is His own proper realm. There He establishes His throne of grace. This interior kingdom it is that constitutes His glory. Our perfection and our happiness consist in the subjection of our heart to this empire of God. The more our heart submits to Him, the more perfect and the more happy shall we be.

§ III.

The supernatural government of one heart in which He reigns, is the object of more special care to God than is the natural government of the whole universe, and the civil government of all empires. God sets value on the heart alone; if only He see that subjected to His power—if only He possess that, He is content. So, again, it is God alone that can satisfy our heart. The heart is a void, which can be filled only by God.

§ IV.

The delight of God is to converse with hearts; there is the place of His rest; and so likewise God alone is the centre of hearts, and they ought to find their rest only in God, and to have no movement but for God.

O blessed interior life, which causes God alone to live in hearts, and which causes hearts to live but for God alone, and to take no pleasure save in Him! Blessed the life of that heart wherein God reigns, and which He possesses fully! A life separated from the world, and hidden in God; a life of love and holy liberty; a life which causes the heart to find in the kingdom of God its joy, its peace, true pleasures, glory, solid greatness, goods and riches, which the world can neither give nor take away.

§ V.

We imagine that a man must pass a sad and melancholy existence when he gives himself to recollection and the interior life. The very reverse is the case. Happiness even on this earth consists in possessing God; and the more we renounce ourselves to unite ourselves to God, the more we cease to be miserable, and the more happy we become. But the devil takes advantage of our ignorance and our weakness, to plunge us into constant errors and infirmities, whence we must needs extricate ourselves, if we would be capable of the sovereign happiness of this life, which consists in seeing God, and in enjoying the gift of His holy Presence, without which the highest seraphim would be wretched. A soul which, contemplating God incessantly, should hold itself ever ready to execute His will, would be blessed.

SECOND PRINCIPLE.

THE IDEA OF PERFECTION.

PERFECTION may be considered either in the general, or in the particular, that is to say, as it is peculiar to the Company of Jesus.

SECTION FIRST.

OF PERFECTION IN GENERAL.

CHAPTER I.

THE FIRST ACT OF A SOUL SEEKING PERFECTION.

ARTICLE I.

How we ought to seek God in all things, and to seek but Him alone.

§ I.

To seek God truly, we must represent Him to ourselves, 1, as the first principle of nature and of grace; 2, as the Preserver of all creatures; 3, as the sovereign Lord who governs every thing and disposes every thing by His providence. Thus we ought to regard all events, even the smallest, as flowing from the will of God and His good pleasure.

To seek God is to wish for nothing and to desire nothing but that which He wills, and which He ordains by His providence. We ought to consider how in God there are, as it were, two acts with reference to us. One by which He wills to bestow upon us such and such graces to conduct us to such a degree of glory, if we are faithful to Him. The other, by which He wills not to bestow upon us further graces, nor to raise us to a higher degree of glory. Few have sufficient courage and fidelity to accomplish the designs of God, and by their co-operation to reach the point of grace and of glory which God desires for them. We ought to regard the will of God, His judgments, and the decrees of His providence, with so much esteem, love, and submission, as to desire neither more grace nor glory than that which He is pleased to give us, even were it in our power to have as much as we would. We must confine ourselves to these limits, out of the unbounded respect which we ought to have for the dispositions of divine providence.

§ II.

Another excellent way of seeking God is to have no other object in all things but the glory of God.

This maxim, applied to literary studies, teaches us to seek to know only that which tends to the greater service of God. The devil has beyond comparison more knowledge than we have, but we surpass him in this, that we can refer our knowledge to the greater glory of God, which the devil cannot do.

The same maxim may be applied to all our employments and to all things generally. We ought to be so detached from ourselves, our own interests, our own tastes, our own individual inclinations and designs, as to be in a disposition to renounce every thing for the sake of the service of God, and of that which may help us to seek and to find God; for nothing is desirable in itself but God, and all else is desirable only with reference to God. So that to seek that which does not lead us to God, to bestow care upon it, or to take a pleasure in it, is an error and delusion.

When we desert this rule, and prefer that which is most agreeable to ourselves to that which most conduces to the glory of God, it is as if a king were to sell his kingdom for a glass of water;—the greatest folly in the world, seeing that every thing is but vanity, every thing is but a lie, which has not God for its object. And hence it follows, that every day we suffer immense losses; for we lose as much glory for ourselves as we ought to have procured for God when we had the power of doing so.

To act in all things for the greater glory of God, this is the noblest end imaginable. All that God Himself can give to the highest seraph without this is less than this; neither is it possible for God to raise a creature to a sublimer end than this; even were that creature a thousand times more perfect than the highest seraph.

Let us, then, seek God in all things, and make every thing serve as instruments of His greater glory; prosperity and adversity, consolations and dryness of spirit, yea, our very sins and imperfections. Every thing is available to those who know how to seek God, and to find God in every thing that happens to them.

§ III.

There is still another way of seeking God, which it is difficult to understand unless it be put in practice. It is not only to seek His will and His glory, not only to seek His gifts and His graces, His consolations and sweetness of devotion, but to seek Himself, to repose in Him alone, and to find no sweetness save in Him. Otherwise, if we make His favours and sensible sweetnesses our object, we expose ourselves to great dangers, and shall never reach the end at which we aim. Whereas, when it is God Himself and Him only that we seek, we rise above all created things, and esteem the crowns and glories of the whole universe—nay, a thousand worlds and every thing that is not God—even as nothing.

Our greatest care and our constant study ought to be to seek God in this way; and until we have found Him, we must not so much as stir abroad to seek to serve our neighbour, except in the way of experimental essays. We must be like hounds held at half leash. When we have arrived at the possession of God, we shall be able to give our zeal a greater freedom, and then we shall do more in one day than we have hitherto done in ten years.

§ IV.

When a soul has no longer any affection but for God, when it seeks but God, and is united to God, and feels no pleasure but in Him, when it finds no rest save in Him alone, nothing can cause it any pain. Thus the Saints, though persecuted by men, and assaulted by devils, laughed it all to scorn. It was but the outside that felt the blows, the interior was in peace.

Until we attain to this state, we shall always be miserable. Let the body be decked out with a thousand jewels, if the soul have departed, it turns to corruption, and is but a corpse loaded with infection. In like manner, let the soul possess all the advantages that can be desired, if it has not God, every thing else it has cannot prevent it being wretched.

When creatures display their attractions in order to tempt us, the best way to secure ourselves from being surprised is to retire at once into God, to sigh after God, to gain a sweet savour of God by some devout and holy thought, instead of stopping to contend and dispute against the allurements of the temptation, which has more in it of perplexity and danger. We ought to pursue the same course at the first pressure of sufferings, crosses, and adversities.

Our study must be to seek God, and our end to fill ourselves with God. We shall only perfectly attain to this after we have thoroughly purged ourselves from our sins. However, we must be always tending to it, and for this end we must avail ourselves of all creatures as means, without yielding our heart to them.

§ V.

A great misfortune it is to us to be able to find our satisfaction in creatures, when we ought to feel for them only contempt and aversion. We set great value upon some advantageous or desirable appointment; we are eager to obtain it; and when we have succeeded, we are gratified. A very nothing is sufficient to content us, as if God were not our happiness.

We must not fix our eyes or our hearts even upon the supernatural gifts of God. It is Him alone we ought to seek; it is in Him alone that we ought to rest. Out of Him every thing is nought. "God is my portion for ever."

"Our Father director," adds F. Rigoleu, "recommends nothing to us so much as to seek God simply in all things, without stopping at any thing out of God, not even His gifts."

ARTICLE II.

We must give ourselves wholly to God.

§ I.

It is a great help to perfection to serve God with a generous soul, and with a full and unreserved heart. If you compare the life of the lukewarm with that of the fervent, if you reckon up their happy and their unhappy days, you will find that the first will have spent many more sad hours than the second.

§ II.

Consider two religious: one who from the very first gives himself up to God, and resolves to spare nothing to secure his sanctification; another, who walks at a slow pace, and has not the courage to rise superior to more than half his difficulties. Compare the life of the one with the life of the other—I say the whole life, and not a mere portion of it,—and you will find that the lukewarm will have suffered much more than the fervent. "Affliction and unhappiness are in their ways," says the royal prophet, speaking of those cowardly souls who do not give themselves up generously to God; "the way of peace they have not known."

This term 'ways' denotes the inward disposition of one who, resisting God, feels in his interior only the torment and galling restraint of conscience. He is content only in appearance and on the surface, not in the centre of his soul, where the fervent have *peace*, which, according to the Hebrew, signifies the abundance of all good.

In short, there is a base infidelity in contenting ourselves with some small degree of perfection we may have acquired, since we are called to a state in which we may hope every thing from God, if we correspond faithfully with the grace of our vocation.

§ III.

We spend whole years, and often a whole life, in bargaining whether we shall give ourselves wholly to God. We cannot make up our minds to so complete a sacrifice. We reserve to ourselves many affections, designs, desires, hopes, pretensions, of which we are unwilling to strip ourselves in order to put ourselves in that perfect nudity of spirit which disposes us to being fully possessed by God. These are so many ties by which the enemy holds us bound, that he may prevent our advancing in perfection. We shall be sensible of the cheat at the hour of death, when we shall see that we have let ourselves be amused by trifles, like children.

We fight against God for whole years, and resist the movements of His grace, which urge us interiorly to rid ourselves of a part of our miseries, by forsaking the vain amusements which stop our course, and giving ourselves to Him without reserve and without delay. But burdened with our self-love, blinded by our ignorance, deterred by vain apprehensions, we dare not take the step; and for fear of being miserable, we continue in our misery, instead of giving ourselves fully to God, who desires to possess us, only to set us free from our miseries.

We must renounce, then, once for all, all our own interests and all our own satisfactions, all our own designs, and all our own choices, that we may henceforth be dependent only on the good pleasure of God, and resign ourselves entirely into His hands.

ARTICLE III.

How subtlety and dissimulation keep us far from God.

§ I.

"The Holy Spirit, who is the teacher of wisdom, is averse to all disguise," says the wise man. We shall never make progress unless we walk sincerely before God and before men. Mankind are full of endless deceit. We disguise ourselves habitually from ourselves and from others. It is one of the faults which we are least willing to acknowledge. We ought never to make excuses or palliate any thing. These duplicities and artifices of self-love keep us far away from God.

§ II.

A subtle soul, and one that employs policy and craft in dealing with its neighbour, forms scarcely a single design, conceives scarcely a single thought, which is not a sin, its habitual object being only to deceive others. Such conduct is one continued lie. It is in perpetual opposition to God, and seems to deny implicitly His providence over hearts.

§ III.

We must never use stratagem or policy when treating with superiors, either respecting the arrangement of our employments, or on any other subject, or indeed on any occasion whatsoever; for all this is but that fleshly wisdom condemned by our Lord. "The wisdom of the flesh is death. The wisdom of the Spirit is life and peace."

CHAPTER II.

THE PRINCIPAL MEANS OF PERFECTION.

ARTICLE 1.

The Sacraments are the principal means of acquiring perfection.

§ I.

THE chief exercises of perfection are the Sacraments, when we bring thereto the necessary preparation; and yet, strange to say, this it is which seems most to be neglected.

The Sacraments bestow graces which tend to produce in us the effects that are peculiar to each: confession, a great purity of heart; communion, a close union with God, and a fervour of spirit in all our actions.

§ II.

It is a matter of moral demonstration, that nothing conduces more to the progress of souls than confession and daily communion, provided we have made at the beginning three or four good confessions to lay the foundation of a good conscience; for the more you frequent these Sacraments, the more grace you receive for participating in their effects. Now the effects of these two Sacraments, purity of heart and fervour of spirit, are the best preparation with which we can approach to receive them.

§ III.

A soul which before communion should find itself weak, languishing, and in darkness, and after communion finds itself enlightened, fervent, and vigorous, cannot doubt the fruits of its communion; the effect of the Sacraments being to confer upon souls their own special grace, which is called sacramental. So after a good confession, the soul is greatly enlightened to know its own interior, it is filled with humble and loving contrition, and enjoys peace and repose of conscience. After a good communion, it experiences a sweet savour of God, and fresh strength to employ itself in His service.

ARTICLE II.

The use of penances.

The mean we ought to observe in penances is neither, on the one hand, to do so much as to injure health, nor, on the other, so little as to allow the rebellion of nature to be felt too strongly.

When we have arrived at a high perfection, we can do much with considerable ease; and by a special favour of God, we may even perform heroic penances, such as the Saints have done.

The most hurtful are those which deprive us of sleep, albeit God bestows on the most perfect the grace to sleep but little.

Thus the measure of penances varies with different persons, different constitutions, ages, conditions, times, and needs.

CHAPTER III.

THE EXERCISE OF THE VIRTUES THAT ARE MOST NECESSARY TO PERFECTION.

ARTICLE I.

Of faith.

§ I.

FAITH being, next to the clear vision of God, the most excellent participation of the uncreated wisdom, it must not be based upon natural reasons nor our own human inventions. Nevertheless such reasons may serve to subdue the repugnance and opposition of our mind, to rid us of our dulness, and to dispose us to believe, though they cannot be employed as a support to that which we believe by faith; for faith implies the whole authority of God, and is founded on His sovereign and infinite wisdom, which makes it impossible for Him to be deceived, and on His infinite fidelity, which makes it impossible for Him to deceive us.

§ II.

Some tremble at the sight of the truths of faith, and are unwilling to reflect upon them; not that they doubt them, but they avoid the thought of them, because they have not used themselves to it. This is a great error, and at death the devil will be able to assault them on their weak side.

§ III.

As it is faith which makes perfect that knowledge which prompts the will to act, and as, according to St. Thomas, it resides partly in the will, it facilitates the exercise of all virtues. For a knowledge of the faith touching temperance, for example, will make me perform an act of temperance more easily than the simple propriety of this virtue, and at the same time it will render my act supernatural.

We must endeavour, therefore, to ground ourselves more and more firmly in faith, walking always in its light, putting it in the place of those reasonings in which the human mind is always prone to indulge upon all kinds of subjects, and making it serve as the guiding torch and principle of all our actions. An act of the will grounded on faith is worth more than ten sentiments that have their source in the spiritual taste.

§ IV.

When God desires to make Himself perfectly master of a soul, He begins by gaining the understanding, communicating to it a high degree of faith. Thence He descends into the will, then into the memory, the imagination, and the concupiscible and irascible appetites, possessing Himself little by little of all these faculties. Next He passes to the senses, and the bodily movements, and in this manner He succeeds in completely occupying the interior and the exterior; and all this by means of faith, which comprises in an eminent degree all virtues, as theologians say, and is the first spring of their action. This is why we must render the exercise of faith familiar to us, and guide ourselves by it in all our actions.

§ V.

It is truly sad to see how, in religion, some, and often even the majority, guide themselves only by human reason and natural prudence, scarcely using faith, except so far as not to go against it. They apply themselves to the perfecting of reason and good sense, without taking the trouble to increase in faith. It is exactly as if a man were to take great pains with the education of his slave, and neglect that of his son.

§ VI.

Nothing better proves how blind and feeble, in the matter of moral perfection, human reason is by itself and without faith, than the little progress it made among all nations before the coming of Jesus Christ into the world. The Romans seem to have been the wisest and the greatest of all pagan people. Holy Scripture ascribes the ascendency and power they acquired to their wisdom and patience; and St. Augustine considers that God gave them the empire of the world as the reward of their virtue. Yet what was their wisdom, and to what did it tend? How much vanity and how much corruption was mixed with their purest and most solid virtues!

ARTICLE II.

How much our want of confidence displeases God and injures ourselves.

§ I.

One of the things in which we most dishonour God is our want of confidence in Him; and this fault arises from our not sufficiently considering what has been bestowed upon us in the incarnation, and what a God made man has done for men. "For God so loved the world as to give His only-begotten Son; and seeing that He spared not even His own Son, but delivered Him up to death for us all, what will He not give us after having given us Him?"

That the son of a king should be willing to die to expiate the crime of a subject whom he loved, or that a king should be willing to give the life of his son for a favourite—this would be an instance of admirable mercy and goodness. But that this son should be willing to die, and this father be willing to give the life of his son for their special mortal enemy, is an excess of mercy and goodness inconceivable. Yet this it is that God has done, giving His Son to human nature, His enemy, not only to save it, but also to raise it to the throne of the Divinity. This it is that the Son of God has done, who, when He might have saved men by a word, by a single tear or a single sigh, willed to merit for them the grace of salvation by a life of so much labour and poverty, and by a death of so much agony and shame.

And after this shall we have no confidence in so much mercy? Shall we refuse to hope that a Redeemer so full of goodness, who has ransomed us at the price of His own Blood, will deliver us from our sins and imperfections?

Distrust is extremely displeasing to God, above all in souls which He has prevented with extraordinary graces. It was in punishment for a slight distrust that Moses entered not the land of promise. He died in sight of that land so often promised, and so ardently desired; but he entered not, and God would not let Himself be turned by any prayers.

§ II.

We wrong God when we say, "When shall I attain to indifference? when shall I gain the gift of prayer?" As if God were needy or grudging of His gifts, as if He had not Himself undertaken the work of our perfection. Let us only follow His will, let us co-operate with His graces, let us study purity of heart, and rest assured that He will not be wanting to us.

§ III.

Many will never arrive at a high perfection, because they do not hope sufficiently. We must have a strong and solid hope, grounded on the mercy and infinite goodness of God, and on the infinite merits of Jesus Christ. "Thou only, O Lord, art the sustainer of my hope."

§ IV.

We must hope and expect great things from God, because the merits of our Lord belong to us; and to hope much in God is to honour Him much. The more we hope, the more we honour Him.

ARTICLE III.

On humility.

§ I.

St. Lawrence Justinian says that we do not know what humility is, unless we have it in our heart. It is only those who are humble in heart that are capable of understanding it. Therefore our Lord said, "Learn of Me, because I am meek and humble of heart." To acquire humility, we must, in the first place, never omit any outward actions in which we may be able to practise it according to our condition, and on such occasions as present themselves; and we must ask of God true feelings of humility, that we may perform well those exterior acts of this virtue which sometimes are done in a spirit of vanity. In the second place, we must make frequent interior acts of humility, acknowledge our own nothingness and wretchedness, love our own abasement, exercise continually a rigorous judgment, and inwardly pass sentence upon ourselves and upon every thing we do.

We must never reprove any one without being previously convinced, and acknowledging before God, that we do far worse ourselves, and are more guilty than him whom we are about to reprove.

When we enter upon the duties of any office, as that of regent, preacher, or superior, we ought to prepare ourselves for it by some practice of humility, mortification, or charity; such as visiting prisoners or the poor in hospitals, serving in the kitchen, &c.

§ II.

Offices of humility and charity are the best, because humility preserves within us the peace and the gifts of God, and charity keeps us occupied about our neighbour.

Let us be humble, patient, mortified, united to God, and He will bless our labours: their success depends absolutely on the blessing of God; for without it all our talents and all our exertions are nothing.

§ III.

God ever reserves to Himself dominion over the gifts with which He favours us. He desires to have the sole glory of them. It is not for the display of our excellence that He confers them upon us; it is to manifest His own. We have not, neither ought we to have, more than the simple use of them solely for the glory of God, and not for our own interest. And this must be understood of all kinds of graces, gifts, and privileges, and even of natural talents and endowments.

In the good we do, and in the good we possess, God leaves to us the profit and advantage, reserving to Himself the glory; He will not have us attribute that to ourselves.

We are not content with this allotment; we take God's share to ourselves; we desire to have the glory as well as the profit of our possessions. This injustice is a kind of blasphemy; for nothing is due to nature, considered in itself—and thus we ought to consider it —but vileness and abasement. It is to that we ought incessantly to tend and aspire with a desire and a thirst insatiable, since therein consists our true greatness; all else is but presumption, vanity, illusion, and sin. So much so, that they in whom this desire of abjection is most ardent are the greatest in the sight of

God. It is they who, above all others, walk in the truth, and they are so much the more like unto God, as with Him they seek only His glory. This is His own property; glory belongs to Him alone. As for us, all our estate is nothingness; and if we attribute any thing to ourselves, we are robbers. If we love the esteem and applause of the world, we are fools; we feed ourselves with wind.

§ IV.

We commonly form to ourselves a false idea of humility, imagining it to be something degrading to us. It has the very contrary effect; for as it gives us a true knowledge of ourselves, and is itself unmixed truth, it brings us near to God, and consequently it confers true greatness upon us, which we seek in vain out of God.

Humiliation degrades us only in the estimation of men, which is nothing; it raises us in the estimation of God, in which true glory consists.

Upon such occasions, so trying to nature, we must reflect, that if men behold us despised, defamed, and made a mock of, God looks upon us as exceedingly exalted by the very things which lower us in the eyes of men. Jesus Christ rejoices to see us wearing His livery, and the angels envy us the honour.

§ V.

Some one will say, "I cannot persuade myself that I am a greater sinner than others. If I break one rule, I see others who break many; if I am guilty of certain faults, I see others who are guilty of greater."

The difficulty we feel in conceiving this humble opinion of ourselves arises from our being as yet so very unspiritual. We shall have it when we are more advanced. In all arts and sciences there are secrets which are known only to those who are adepts in them. So in spiritual science, which is the most excellent of all, inasmuch as it is purely supernatural, there are maxims the knowledge of which belongs only to the Saints, who are doctors in this divine science. A St. Francis of Assisi, a St. Francis Borgia, were most eminent masters in humility. They esteemed themselves, not after a manner of speaking, but sincerely and from the bottom of their heart, the greatest sinners in the world. They were inwardly persuaded of that which their lips declared.

ARTICLE IV.

Of the love of crosses.

§ I.

St. Ignatius the Martyr had the love of crosses and of self-annihilation so deeply graven in his heart, that being condemned to be devoured by wild beasts in the amphitheatre, he desired that the lions, after tearing his body in pieces, might also consume his bones; that nothing might remain of the holocaust which he had consecrated to God in order to prove himself His worthy disciple. He would have deemed himself happy could he have been so completely annihilated in his torments as to leave not a particle of his body visible to the eyes of the world. "The world," said he, "will see my body no more:" he exulted with joy at the thought.

§ II.

As our Lord wrought the redemption of the world only by His cross, by His death, and the shedding of His blood, not by His miracles or preachings, so likewise the evangelical labourers apply the grace of redemption only by their crosses, and by the persecutions they·suffer. So much so, that no great fruits can be expected from their ministry, if it be not accompanied by contradictions, calumnies, injuries, and sufferings.

Some think they do wonders because they preach powerful discourses, well composed, well prepared, and delivered with grace ; because they are the fashion, and are welcomed every where. They deceive themselves ; the means on which they rely are not those which God makes use of to do great things. Crosses are needed to effect the salvation of the world. It is by the way of the cross that God leads those whom He employs to save souls, apostles and apostolic men, a St. Francis Xavier, a St. Ignatius, a St. Vincent Ferrer, a St. Dominic.

§ III.

We must not look upon our crosses and afflictions in the light of evils which are the cause to us of suffering, or as mortifications which lower us in the eyes of the world ; but we must look at them, after the example of our Lord, in the eternal counsels of God, in the decrees of His providence, and in the designs of His love towards us ; in the Heart of Jesus Christ, who has chosen them for us, and presents them to us as the material of those crowns which He is preparing for us, and as a trial of our courage and fidelity in His service.

§ IV.

In the beginning of the spiritual life, we must not ask sufferings of God ; we must think rather of purging our conscience, devoting ourselves to acquire purity of heart, the knowledge of our own interior, and recollection. From thence we rise to peace of soul, thence to communion with God, next to infused virtues, and finally to the gifts of the Holy Spirit. Then it is that God inspires us according to His designs and will ; leading some by labours, as St. Francis Xavier ; others by sufferings, as St. Ludwine; others by contradictions and persecutions, as St. Ignatius: but of ourselves we must not make any particular choice, otherwise we shall always be in trouble; not possessing as yet sufficient virtue to endure crosses, it would be to undertake to carry a giant's load without the strength to do it. When, however, at the call of God, we enter into states of toil, suffering, and humiliation, then neither will labours overwhelm us, nor persecutions disturb us, and often even great austerities will not destroy our health.

SECTION SECOND.

OF THE PERFECTION PECULIAR TO THE COMPANY OF JESUS.

CHAPTER I.

WHEREIN CONSISTS THE PERFECTION PECULIAR TO THIS COMPANY.

ARTICLE I.

The end of the institution of the Company of Jesus, and the means of arriving thereat.

GOD the Father has given the Company of Jesus to His Son, to love Him and to honour Him; and our institute imitates and honours every portion of the life of Jesus Christ. For if some fail in this duty, it is their own individual fault, not that of the institute.

As the end which our Company has in view is the greatest and sublimest possible, being the very same with that of the Son of God Himself when on earth, so also the means to attain that end are most excellent, seeing that our institute embraces all such as are supernatural, as prayer, sacraments, preaching; and all those that are natural, as talents, intellect, sciences, as well as the method of teaching them : but the latter must be used in subordination to supernatural prudence, and derive their strength and virtue from the highest exercise of prayer.

This it is in which we fail, if we do not take care; for want of supernatural prudence, we set too much value on natural and human means, we give too much application and study to them, and too little to such means as are supernatural and divine. Hence it is that we reap so very little fruit from our employments; and this single fault is enough to spoil every thing else, nothing being able to subsist without grace and an interior spirit.

It is marvellous to see a religious of the Company continuing long in a state of imperfection, possessing as he does among us so many means of arriving at perfection; it is quite inconceivable how many graces he must have wasted, and how sadly he must have abused them, particularly if he has lived many years in the Company.

From the moment we relax in the way of perfection, and wish to satisfy ourselves with an ordinary degree of virtue, we fail in the end after which we ought to strive as religious, viz. our own perfection; and that at which as Jesuits we are bound to aim, viz. the greater glory of God, which we are obliged to promote by studying our highest perfection, and that of our neighbour.

An excellent person observed to one of our Fathers at Paris, that he was not surprised at the zeal, the fervour, and the sanctity of Father Suffren, but that he was astonished we were not all so many Fathers Suffren. What good might not be done by a regent who had the interior spirit of this holy man!

That motto of St. Ignatius, *Ad majorem Dei gloriam*, signifies that in the matter of perfection and sanctity we must never set any limits to our designs, and must never say, "It is enough, I am satisfied, I want no more;" since by the very obligation of our calling we must aspire after the perfection of the apostolical life, and a height of virtue altogether evangelical.

ARTICLE II.

The Company belongs to Jesus Christ as Saviour.

St. Ignatius passionately desired to be admitted into the family of our Lord. He besought the Blessed Virgin to obtain him this favour, and then he asked it of the Eternal Father. His prayers were heard. One day, as he was on his way to Rome, he entered a chapel, and as he was engaged in prayer, the Eternal Father appeared to him with Jesus Christ bearing His cross, together with the Blessed Virgin and a troop of Angels and Saints. The Eternal Father presented Ignatius and his companions to His Son, and commended them to Him. The Son of God received them graciously, and promised to assist them at Rome in the execution of the design they had formed of dedicating themselves to apostolic ministrations. Thus it is in His quality of Saviour that Jesus Christ received the Company into His service, to employ them in promoting the salvation of souls; and He gave it His Name to signify that He associated it to the office which that sacred name imports.

As for us who are the children of St. Ignatius, we ought to consider ourselves as belonging to the Saviour, being members of His household and devoted to His service, and for the love of Him to the service of souls.

With this end in view, let us make three acts of generous zeal: 1. A desire to have been able to serve and honour our Lord in such manner as is worthy of Him from the first moment of our existence. 2. A regret at having lost so much time which we might have employed in knowing Him, loving Him, and serving Him. 3. An offering and a fresh consecration of ourselves to His service, in union with the love which the Eternal Father and the Holy Spirit bear Him, and the honour and adorations which the Blessed Virgin, the Angels, and the Saints have rendered Him, render Him incessantly, and will continue to render Him for ever and ever. Let us offer Him our body, to be used and consumed in the fulfilment of His designs; every moment of our life, even to the last, to be employed in His service; our soul, resigning it to the disposal of His providence; our death, desiring it may come from the excess of our labours for His glory; our resurrection and our beatific state, to love Him and to bless Him throughout eternity.

ARTICLE III.

St. Ignatius the model of the perfection of the Company.

St. Ignatius excelled equally in the active life and in the contemplative; and it may be said that there have been many Saints distinguished pre-eminently for one only of the perfections which he united in a sovereign degree. What austerity could be greater than that which he practised in the first years of his fervour? What more singular gift of chastity than that with which the Blessed Virgin favoured him from the time of his conversion? What voluntary poverty more rigorous than that which he observed so long and during such numerous journeys, living only on alms as a beggar? What greater humility than his condescending, on two occasions, to learn the rudiments of the Latin tongue amongst children, when he was already of an advanced age? What patience more heroic than that which he displayed amid so many persecutions? What supernatural prudence more perfect than that which is so conspicuous in his whole conduct and in his constitutions? What zeal more ardent and more unbounded than his? What evenness of spirit more constant and unchangeable? What prayer more sublime? What intercourse with God more intimate?

At the sight of this model of perfection, which we children of this holy patriarch ought to imitate, well may we be confounded, considering the little virtue we have acquired, and the little good we have done, in so apostolic a state. As for those who, like seculars, allow themselves to be captivated by the false brilliancy of this world's fleeting charms, they know not their wretchedness. What confusion will be theirs in another life, unless they take heed!

CHAPTER II.

OF THE DIFFERENT DISPOSITIONS OF RELIGIOUS WITH REGARD TO PERFECTION.

AMONG religious there are three different kinds. The first never refuse their senses any thing. Are they cold? they warm themselves. Are they hungry? they eat. Does it come into their mind to take some amusement? they take it without reflection, always bent on pleasing themselves, scarcely knowing in practice what self-mortification is. As for their functions, they discharge them, to be clear of their obligation, without interior spirit, without relish, and without fruit.

These are in danger of mortal sin: and sometimes,

even, they are actually in sin; though they are not aware of it, because they never enter seriously into themselves, and only very superficially examine the state of their conscience.

In this complete forgetfulness of themselves, a multitude of objects passes every day through their thoughts, and their heart being carried out of itself, and intoxicated, as it were, with the whirl of outward things, in its absence, the mind is continually deceived by the illusions of nature and of the devil, whose suggestions it follows blindly.

Such religious may often be in far greater danger than seculars themselves. For the latter know that they sometimes fall into mortal sin; they are distrustful of themselves, and their fears make them cautious. But the former, trusting to their state, and buoying themselves up on the false presumption, that in religion it is rarely that a man sins mortally, live on in a deceitful security, which causes them to fall from very carelessness; and to stifle the remorse of conscience, they invent to themselves lies which flatter them in their error. Such a state is perilous, because they do not perceive their own falls.

The second avoid the excesses of the first, and deny themselves all such satisfactions as they do not deem necessary; but they let themselves be deceived under the appearance of good. They form some design which falls in with their own inclination, and then they seek for high motives to colour their choice and justify their conduct. With regard to their functions, they execute carefully all that belongs to the exterior, but with little interior application and recollection, giving too much liberty to their senses, and neglecting to keep guard over their heart.

These are full of imperfections and venial sins, and

often are in danger of sinning mortally. For as they are weak, and derive but little strength from within, they let themselves be vanquished on occasions where victory would be easy, were the interior well guarded.

The third, as being perfect, have renounced all desires, are indifferent to every thing, satisfied with every thing, and have no other will than the good pleasure of God. They unite together outward exactness and inward application; they keep watch over their own heart, preserve their peace of soul, and practise recollection as much as obedience permits.

These last receive three signal favours from the three Persons of the Most Holy Trinity: from the Father, a strength as if invincible in action, in suffering, and in temptations; from the Son, rays and splendours of truth, which shine without ceasing into their soul; from the Holy Spirit, a fervour, a sweetness, and a consolation full of joy.

CHAPTER III.

THE MOTIVES THAT INDUCE US TO LABOUR AT OUR PERFECTION.

ARTICLE I.

The desire of our own salvation.

THE salvation of a religious is inseparably connected with his perfection; so that if he ceases to attend to his spiritual advancement, he draws nearer and nearer to his destruction and ruin. If he is not utterly lost, it is because God, willing to save him, mercifully prevents him before his fall. All the masters of the spiritual life agree in this maxim, that not to advance is to fall back. But as some have already made a certain progress, they are often a considerable time before they are aware they are losing ground, because this takes place imperceptibly.

ARTICLE II.
The order of a well-regulated zeal.

Our first care as well as our chief study must be our own perfection, which should be preferred before every thing; then making a due distribution of what we have to spare of active exertion and mental energy, we shall apply ourselves to the service of our neighbour under the influence of a true zeal regulated by prudence. Whoever acts otherwise may rely upon it, that though he wears the habit of the Company, he possesses none of its spirit, seeing that our rule and our profession oblige us to set more value on those means of perfection, which, as instruments, unite us to God, the First Cause, from whom every movement should proceed, than on all other exercises. Thus all else must be regulated in subordination to that which is first, viz. the interior.

An apostolical vocation like ours demands the renunciation on our part of all friendships, all studies, all pursuits, which neither assist us on our own way to God, nor enable us to lead our neighbour to Him.

ARTICLE III.
The fruit of our labours.

God does not employ the imperfect in the execution of His great designs, and this lest they should ruin their own souls. For were He so to employ them, they would take occasion to wax proud, and their vanity would prove their destruction. But do you labour effectually at your perfection; cleave to God; seek only to please Him, and then, were you even in a desert, should He wish to make use of you, He will know how to find you; and He will make you work wonders, even though your state and your vocation would not naturally lead you to the functions of the apostolic life. In the time of St. Bernard, how many bishops were there, how many prelates and doctors distinguished for their knowledge and prudence; nevertheless God did not cast His eyes upon them. He went and took the Abbot of Clairvaux in his solitude, to employ him in the highest affairs of the Church. And of what a variety of good works was not the blessed Mary of the Incarnation made the instrument!

ARTICLE IV.

How many persons are interested in our perfection.

It furnishes us with a powerful motive to fervour to consider how many persons are interested in our perfection.

1. Our Lord, who gave His blood and His life to purchase for us the perfection to which God destined us, and who would not that the fruit of His death should be lost.

2. The Blessed Virgin, who procures us so many graces to make us perfect, and looks forward to the day when we shall be her crown and her glory.

3. Our good angels, who labour with so much zeal to lead us along the path of perfection, that they may have us for companions in a blessed eternity.

4. St. Ignatius and our holy patrons, as well as the other friends we have in heaven, who so ardently desire that we should walk in their steps, and assist us so powerfully with their intercession.

5. The souls in Purgatory, who would receive so much more assistance from us if we were more perfect.

6. Religion, which we should serve so much better, if we were more closely united to God.

7. The Church, to which we should be of so much

greater service, if we had arrived at the degree of sanctity to which we are called.

How many souls will God shew us hereafter, whom He would have saved by our means, had we been perfect instruments of His glory! How many whom we should have aided in sanctifying themselves, had we ourselves been saints! How many others, who will have remained long in Purgatory, and who, by our assistance, would have obtained their freedom sooner, had we possessed a greater degree of merit before God!

Who can set a limit to the fruit which our ministrations might have produced, had they been animated with a perfect charity! The souls we should have won to God would have won others, and these others again through a long course of years. If such have not been their effect, the fault is ours; we must render account thereof to God; but we are so blind, that this we do not understand.

CHAPTER IV.

THE MEANS OF PERFECTION PECULIAR TO OUR COMPANY.

ARTICLE I.

In what way the exercise of prayer in the Company should be practical.

MEDITATION is an inward discourse tending to make perfect the will, and to render it holy: thus it is not purely speculative, like that of philosophers; it is practical, and that in two ways: first, in that it serves to give a better direction to the will, and to regulate the other powers of the soul; secondly, in that it produces different interior acts, and operates as a spring for the formation of external acts, according to the model proposed for imitation.

The exercise of prayer peculiar to the Company is practical in both these ways; and he who should pretend that it was not sufficient for it to be practical in the first way, and that it must be so also in the second, would be in error; because it would follow from such a view, that contemplation was not suited for the Company, which is false.

It is an error in prayer to constrain ourselves to give it always a practical bearing. We excite and disquiet ourselves in resolving how we shall behave on such and such occasion, what acts of humility, for example, we shall practise. This way of meditating by consideration of virtues is wearisome to the mind, and may even possibly produce disgust. Not but that it is well to do this when we pray, to foresee occasions and prepare ourselves for them; but it should be done with freedom of mind, without refusing to yield ourselves to the simple recollection of contemplation when we feel ourselves drawn to it. For then our Lord, in the course of one single meditation, will endow a soul with some particular virtue, and even with many virtues, in a far higher degree than would be acquired in several years by these external acts. St. Paul the Hermit had the virtue of patience, and that of charity towards his neighbour, although he never exercised them. It is sufficient, then, quietly to embrace such opportunities as offer for practising any virtue, humility, for example, and to endeavour also without eagerness to perform acts of the same, leaving the rest to prayer.

We should regard as practical, and not purely speculative, such exercise of prayer as disposes the soul to charity, religion, humility, &c., although the affection remains within the soul, and does not express itself in outward acts.

ARTICLE II.

The obedience and exact observance of the rules peculiar to our Company, and the motives thereto.

"The Company of Jesus," says Suarez, "is the strictest of all religious orders, although it is not the most austere." In fact, it is impossible for the monastic discipline to be more stringent; every thing therein depending on the sole will of a superior as respects employment, residence, and the details of our conduct; all which is a great blessing to us, and conduces powerfully to our perfection.

The ways of God within us are those graces which He bestows upon us, when we are in the state to which He has destined us, and in the place which He has marked out for us. To these God so attaches the graces by means of which He would lead us to heaven, that whilst we remain therein, He bestows them on us in abundance; but if we quit them, He generally withdraws Himself from us, until by His mercy we return to them again.

That superiors should not be well affected towards us matters not; God will always so dispose our employments, that the one He has destined for us shall infallibly fall to our lot. For though He sometimes permits, in punishment of our sins, that superiors should fail either in charity or in prudence in their behaviour towards us; yet when we shall have confessed the faults which have drawn this chastisement down upon us, and have done penance for them, God in His mercy will recompense us double for the disadvantage we may have incurred. So that we must be under no anxiety to have superiors who are friendly to us, or to be in favour with them; neither must we speak to them to obtain the employments we desire, or employ others to speak in our behalf.

We ought to resign ourselves once for all without reserve into the hands of God's providence; and if we are ill treated by superiors or others, first of all, to feel assured we have well deserved it, if not in this instance, at least on other occasions; secondly, to enter into ourselves, and if we are in fault, ask God's pardon; thirdly, to consider the injustice with which we feel we have been treated as simply coming from God, who permits it for our good, and designed to permit it before our superiors or the other persons in question had any thought of so treating us; fourthly, to adore with all humility and from the bottom of our heart, this will of God and disposition of His providence, and submit ourselves thereto with perfect resignation; considering that what on the part of men is an effect of their hatred or envy in order to our humiliation, on the part of God is a means which His goodness employs to exalt us to a higher degree of glory, if we are but faithful to Him. We see this in the example of Joseph, and in that of Jesus Christ Himself. Let us learn, then, to serve our Lord with an entire abandonment of ourselves.

A religious who observes his rules and practises obedience may say, "I do what an Angel would do, were he in my place; what the Blessed Virgin would do, and Jesus Christ Himself." What an assurance to have! How full of comfort is the thought!

We ought to hold ourselves so disengaged in the midst of our devotions and all our actions, that we may be always ready to quit every thing when obedience or charity summons us elsewhere. If, for instance, at the time which we have fixed for saying the rosary of our Lady, an opportunity occurs of hearing a confession, or doing our neighbour some other service, we must leave that exercise of devotion to attend to this occasional work of charity.

CHAPTER V.

ZEAL FOR THE SALVATION AND PERFECTION OF OUR NEIGHBOUR.

ARTICLE I.

Motive for zeal.

"HE that hath the substance of this world, and shall see his brother in need, and shall shut up his bowels from him, how doth the charity of God abide in him?" 1 John iii. 17.

These words of the beloved disciple of Jesus Christ are to be understood also of spiritual goods, and should fill with trembling many religious and ecclesiastics, who having received so large a share of the riches of the science of salvation and of the full knowledge of grace, see millions of souls perishing in ignorance of the truths of faith, without being touched by their misery, and without imparting to them of their abundance.

This consideration affected most powerfully the heart of St. Francis Xavier, as he testifies in some of his letters.

ARTICLE II.

What use we ought to make of knowledge, after the example of St. Ignatius.

St. Ignatius, when he was already full of the Spirit of God, applied himself to the study of letters, with the view of giving weight and authority to the functions of the apostolic life, to which he felt himself called. Already he possessed that heavenly science, which was all he needed to teach others the ways of salvation. But his zeal and prudence convinced him of the necessity of joining to this infused science, that which is acquired in the schools, because without this he would not have been permitted to employ himself in instructing his neighbour.

Are there not some among us who do the very reverse? While they are still devoid of the interior spirit, do they not devote themselves to study in a manner altogether human, without uprightness or purity of intention, without moderation, perhaps from motives of vanity, contemplating already the employments which their pride covets, and looking upon knowledge as a means of attaining the object of their ambition, an ambition altogether opposed to the spirit of St. Ignatius, and the end to which the studies of the Company are directed?

And what will be the fruit of knowledge acquired out of vanity, for ends so far removed from the greater glory of God? St. Ignatius employed acquired science to give authority to the infused science which he had received from Heaven. Alas, are there not those to be found, who, unprovided with the gifts of grace, employ their natural talents and knowledge to gain the esteem of men!

ARTICLE III.

The means by which the reputation and influence of the Company are to be maintained.

The means to be employed to maintain and increase the reputation and influence of the Company are humility, the practice of Christian virtues, zeal for souls; not the visits and the friendship of the great of this world.

St. Ignatius desired Father Laynez and the others, his first companions, to tell their faults to each other daily, to wait on the poor in the hospitals, and teach the catechism to children. F. Laynez, Provincial of the Company at Rome, did, in fact, employ himself in teaching the catechism, when St. Ignatius sent him the second time to the Council of Trent, to take part therein as one of the Pope's theologians. F. Antony Araoz, by adopting a different course in Spain, was near ruining the Company.

To maintain the authority of the Company in the classes and in the other offices, without being willing to endure any humiliation, is to work its destruction.

It is incredible what good our functions would effect, if they were watered with the blessings which contradictions and humiliations draw down from heaven. St. Ignatius suffered an incalculable amount of contempt and persecution in the exercise of his zeal. St. Francis Xavier, when departing for the Indies, would not accept any offers that were made him; and when it was represented to him that he would lower his dignity of apostolic legate, if he was seen washing his own linen and preparing his own meals, he replied that he fully hoped to be able to wait on himself, and wait on others, without dishonouring his character, or impairing the authority which the Holy See had entrusted to him; that it was this human respect, and these false ideas of propriety, which had reduced the Church to the state in which they then saw it. Let a regent take an affront from one of his scholars without displaying any feeling of irritation; God will be honoured by this act of patience, and will not fail to repair, in the presence of the scholars themselves, the injury inflicted on this good religious.

The Company must be maintained and perfected by the same means by which it was established, that is to say, by such as are supernatural. Accordingly, we must not desire that our Fathers should be cardinals or confessors to kings. It would be an insult to our Lord to look to the countenance of princes as a support to a work of which He is Himself so visibly the Author; and to expect its preservation from the favour of the powers of this world. God, and its own virtues, will preserve the Company.

CHAPTER VI.

DIVERS COUNSELS.

ARTICLE I.

Advice to a teacher of young religious on their coming out of the noviciate.

THE glory of God demands that as soon as ever our brethren have completed their noviciate, they should be taught to walk in the ways of that holiness which is peculiar to our Company. This is the object of the following counsels.

1. He who is entrusted with their direction must first ascertain what progress they have made in the interior life, and whether they have really begun to enter thereon, or whether their advancement still consists only in avoiding the ordinary sins of young persons, together with a certain exactness in carefully performing their spiritual exercises of prayer, reading, and examination of conscience. Generally speaking, they have not made much progress in prayer. Further, he must examine whether they be not ignorant of the ways of God, knowing no other perfection than that which they themselves practise, or whether they do not even perform their actions without any idea of perfection. In fine, he must learn, as far as is possible, the disposition of their soul: all this information being necessary, in order to judge in what way they must be directed, and to aid them in fulfilling the designs of God.

2. Treat them with a fatherly kindness, and try to win their heart by offering to assist them in every way, even as regards exterior things, procuring for them, if possible, whatever they need. Then, having secured their affection, let them perceive the ardent desire you feel for their perfection, how you long to see them wholly given up to God, and how anxious you are to contribute to this end with all your power.

3. Apply yourself to the unravelling their conscience, extricating them from that perplexity and darkness incident to souls that have not yet entered upon the ways of perfection. For this purpose it will be useful to read the treatise De Reformatione Vitæ, contained in F. Gaudier's book of Spiritual Exercises. If God shall cause some light to shine into their soul, however little it may be, it will be a great gain. Be on the watch for this; and reckon it much if, after earnest application, their mind becomes enlightened ever so little. God commences by small beginnings, to which a high value must ever be attached when the spirit of perfection has once been formed in a soul.

4. As soon as you perceive that they are beginning to emerge from their darkness, lead them on to great purity of conscience, as being the surest way, and the one best calculated to bring them to union with God. Allow them the frequent use of confession, since you have the power of doing so. Lay it down to them as a maxim not to conceal the least faults they may have deliberately committed, and even to confess every time they shall fall into such. Give them much encouragement in the alternations and changes to which they shall be subject. Blame them also sometimes with discretion when they are in fault, especially when the fault is of any moment; and apply this corrective in confession, that it may be more effectual. Never dismiss them,

however, without encouragement. This is a course which should generally be pursued with regard to souls that are as yet beginners, viz. always to temper the sharpness of reproof with the sweetness of exhortation; for such souls should be furnished with every possible aid.

5. Seek to animate them with a spirit of penance, and bring them to a resolution of never passing over any thing in themselves which is fitting matter of public self-accusation, earnestly recommending this practice to them. And with regard to bodily mortification, labour to inspire them with a high esteem and strong desire for it, so that they may ask you for much, and you may often grant them some, but little at a time, as, for instance, to take the discipline frequently, but only for the space of a *Pater* or an *Ave*. Make them to understand that the frequent practice of these little mortifications is of great use in keeping the flesh subject to the spirit, and the spirit subject to God; but take care to restrain them within strict bounds of moderation. For if you gave them full permission, the least temptation might create disgust for them; and they would then speedily come to have a horror of the spiritual life. And further, it is prudent, in granting them these permissions, to comport yourself in such a way as to give them the impression that you concede what they ask with reluctance. By this means you will obviate a thought which is apt to suggest itself to the minds of many, and is a great hindrance to their advancing in the way of God.

6. Inure them to much self-privation in all things. This will not be difficult, if from the first you can contrive to free them from certain little attachments which are natural to us, as preferring one room to another, fondly retaining certain pictures, either on account of

their beauty, or from affection for the givers. Shew them clearly the great advantages enjoyed by those souls which are attached to nothing. Induce them to be contented, according to the rule, with whatever is meanest in the house; let them accustom themselves to ask for it, and rejoice to fare the worst of all. Provide them, so far as prudence allows, with opportunities of practising this self-renunciation; and when you meet with one whose mind is strong enough to endure it, subject him to trials of a rather sharper nature.

7. Beware of shewing a preference for some over others. Treat all with equal affection and sweetness, rendering them with a tender charity all such services as the rule and obedience will allow. Be assured that you will have done more towards their perfection if you have won their heart, than if, without that, you had given them all the best instructions possible. By such means you will oblige them to regard you in turn with a filial love and confidence which will make them open their whole heart to you, and freely give up to you all little private preferences. Above all, it is important that you should never listen to their mutual complaints, or pay the least attention to the reports they may bring you. Nothing is more detrimental to peace and the union of charity, which you are bound to preserve among them, than accusations of this sort.

8. Keep them employed in such moderation as neither, on the one hand, to excite them to great eagerness in study, nor, on the other, to leave them too much leisure. Never set them a task to be done in any limited time, as in a day or a week. Next to sin and the passions, nothing is so injurious to a soul as eagerness in study; and this is occasioned when haste is required to finish some work in a given time. While

you think to push forward these poor children in knowledge, you will cramp the Spirit of God within them, and force them to leave His ways to throw themselves into those of nature, and into a state at once profane and opposed to their vocation. God desires to possess them without hindrance, and in perfect liberty; and His whole work is directed to detach them from time and the things of time, in order to unite them to Himself, and to bind them absolutely to the sole interests of His love and service.

9. Take care they do not form particular friendships, either with the members of our own house, or with externs. As long as they have such engagements, they will never make any progress in virtue. For this reason you must make them break off at once all those little intimacies which tend to produce attachments of this kind. If, however, you should observe that some who have a true desire of perfection are benefited by the conversation of particular persons, you must not hinder them from private conversation, provided that the individuals with whom they contract this intimacy are really capable of being of use to them in the way of improvement.

10. Endeavour to make them entertain a great respect and much deference for each other; as though they were princes, who, entertaining a tender mutual affection, were nevertheless to converse together but this once in their life; or as though it was our Lord Himself with whom they were speaking. This sort of intercourse, decorous and religious, and this spirit of holy courtesy, are extremely pleasing to God, and banish from society many of the puerilities and faults into which people commonly fall when they follow their natural inclinations.

Such is pretty nearly the sum of those general principles which may dispose them to be led by the Spirit of God. In the next place, observe carefully in what direction the attraction of grace would lead them. Whether it is to a spirit of penance, or to a horror of one of their own vices, or to the love of some particular virtue; and as soon as you have ascertained the designs of God in this regard, second the operations of His grace, and give them the necessary instructions for combating this vice or practising this virtue. Then, when they are sufficiently instructed, bid them after communion note down in writing to what acts of this virtue they feel themselves most drawn, or what acts of this vice they would desire to combat. Always attach importance to whatever they shall make known to you as communicated to them by God, unless you presently discover therein some temptation or some deceit of the enemy.

Sometimes it will not appear that these souls are making progress; and then it is necessary gently to inquire into their practices, and see what preparation they make before their prayers, as well as before confession and communion: they must be exhorted to some holy exercise, to devotion to our Lord, to the Blessed Virgin and St. Joseph, and to their angel-guardian; they must be reminded from time to time of what you have thus recommended them to do; and when occasion offers, it would be well always to insinuate some word or other, to encourage them more and more in the holy work they have undertaken.

ARTICLE II.

Advice to the Fathers of the third year for the time of their noviciate.

§ I.

The third year of noviciate is so important, that only God and the Fathers who have the direction of it know how necessary it is, not only for the perfection, but for the salvation of our members; and good reason indeed has our Father General for refusing to dispense any one from passing through it.

It is a year's retreat, and must be spent in silence and recollection. Whoever enters upon it without a thorough determination to continue therein of his own free will, and to avoid all occasions of talking, conversing, and distracting his mind, will never make much progress, because it is necessary to keep aloof from all occasions, so long as virtue is still weak.

After this year of retreat, we shall pass the rest of our days in the employments of the exterior life; therefore we cannot apply ourselves too much meanwhile to the exercises of the interior life.

Most Saints and religious who arrive at perfection generally undergo two conversions; one by which they give themselves up to the service of God; the other by which they devote themselves entirely to perfection. This is observable in the Apostles, when our Lord called them, and when He sent down upon them the Holy Spirit; in St. Theresa and her confessor, F. Alvarez, and in many others. This second conversion does not take place in all religious, and it is owing to their own negligence. The time of this conversion in our case is generally the third year of noviciate. Let us, then, animate ourselves at this time with a new courage, and let us not be sparing of ourselves in the way of God's service, because it will never be more difficult to us than it is now. As time goes on, it will become gradually easier, and difficulties will be smoothed away. For as we purify our hearts more and more, we shall also receive graces in greater abundance.

§ II.

There are three things to the acquirement of which

we must particularly apply ourselves in the Company. The first is the love of our Lord, whom we must acknowledge as our founder, St. Ignatius being only His deputy. The second is a sincere contempt of ourselves, which should make us seek to have the refuse of every thing and the last place everywhere, and give up all desire for honourable employments, great successes, and the esteem of men. If we have no ambition to rise above a state of ordinary virtue, and have no true love or wish for our own abjection, we shall never be fitted to receive the great graces which God would bestow upon us, if He did not find this obstacle in us. To have this love and this desire of contempt, we must seek them at their source in the Heart of Jesus Christ, often entering therein by recollection, to contemplate the Word Himself and His Most Sacred Humanity in a state of self-annihilation. And if some should say, that there is danger lest such a habit of recollection should interfere with the active duties of zeal to which our vocation obliges us, I reply that the very reverse is the case, and that it is certain that a man of prayer will do more in one year than another will do in his whole life. We must be continually asking these three things of God and our Lord Jesus Christ, and of St. Ignatius, especially during the octave of his feast.

§ III.

We must apply ourselves all our life to three things. The first is the love of God. Many even of those who pass for excellent religious, spend their time in the employments of God's service without scarcely ever, or at least in a very slight degree, raising their attention to God Himself. Alas, what is every thing that may occupy us out of God, as compared with God Himself! Every thing which is not God is nothing. The thought of a God is something so exalted, that if a man had done and suffered for the glory of God, every thing that all mankind have done and suffered from the beginning of the world, all would still be nothing to offer to a Being of so much majesty. This is what Saints have felt. The second is a constant contempt of ourselves, our actions, and every thing that concerns us, together with a holy hatred of every thing in us which is opposed to God. The third is a horror and a detestation of sin and of every thing that leads us to sin, looking upon ourselves habitually as a sink and a sewer of all evils.

Two things there are to which we must devote our constant attention all our life long. The first is, to purge ourselves more and more from venial sins ; the second, to seek God, as well by prayer, employing therein all the time we have to spare, as by fervour and fidelity in acquitting ourselves of the duties of obedience, not tolerating in our heart any passion, any affection, any desire for other places or other employments, but those to which obedience binds us. To reach this point, it is absolutely necessary to have the gift of prayer.

§ IV.

Three things there are which are peculiarly incumbent upon us during the whole course of our spiritual life. The first is, to be perpetually cultivating purity of heart by vigilance in discovering and mortifying our passions. The second, to devote ourselves more and more to the knowledge and love of our Lord, without which we can never attain to any solid or exalted spirituality. The third, not to spend our time in contemplating and dwelling with complacency on the lights and sentiments which God gives us ; because favours of this kind produce their effect the moment we receive them, and it is useless, therefore, to stop to consider them; to do so, serves only to nourish self-love. We ought to refrain from making reflections on what God operates within us, except to strengthen ourselves in the good with which He inspires us; and that we may stand confounded at the favours which He confers upon us, in order to practise that self-abnegation which He asks of us, viz. that we set our hearts on God only, and not on His gifts.

"What the Father director constantly recommends to us," says F. Rigoleu, "is purity of heart, recollection, and prayer; to avoid venial sins; to burden ourselves with few exterior occupations, unless obedience obliges us to undertake more; to devote ourselves to such exercises of humility as are the meanest and the most despised, and to cherish always a great disengagement of mind."

ARTICLE III.

Advice to Fathers of the third year, on completing their noviciate, for their conduct during the rest of their life.

The year which immediately follows our third year's noviciate is full of danger, especially the first three or four months. It is the critical time, on which the rest of our life depends. The fervour and regularity which we display are distasteful to those who have not so tender a conscience. Sometimes we have not the courage resolutely to uphold the cause of perfection; we are afraid of displeasing men, we get weary of going against the stream, we relax, we fall, we rise and fall again, and at last we encounter more powerful obstacles, which little by little ruin all the good designs we have formed; so that after a certain time we find that we have relapsed into our former state, and then we follow, as before, the usual course of the imperfect.

After our third year's noviciate, it must be our principal care to preserve ourselves in great purity of heart, by avoiding the smallest venial sins; and in great disengagement of spirit, by mortifying every kind of irregular affection and attachment to creatures, even to the extent of not desiring more graces than it pleases God to bestow upon us.

Let us often examine the state of our heart, and see whether it be quite free from all eagerness, all disquietude, all disorderly movement. When we find ourselves burdened with too many occupations, let us ask the Superior to relieve us at least from some portion for a time. Let us give up such as are not enjoined us; let us watch ourselves at this time more narrowly, and fortify ourselves more diligently by prayer and by our other exercises of devotion and penance.

"The following," says F. Rigoleu, "are the points which he used to urge upon us most frequently and most earnestly."

1. Purity of heart, which is acquired by a strict watchfulness over our interior, and by daily confession, to which we must attach much importance. For the oftener we confess, the more we purify ourselves, the grace proper to this sacrament being purity of conscience. Thus every confession, besides the increase of habitual grace and spiritual gifts, imparts also a fresh sacramental grace, that is to say, a new title to receive from God both actual graces and the aids necessary for emancipating ourselves more and more from sin.

2. A full and unreserved fidelity towards God, giving Him always the best affections of our heart, not introducing subtlety and double-dealing into our intercourse with Him, not seeking to walk in His ways by by-paths, serving Him as much as possible with a whole heart, making God alone the end of all our designs and all our undertakings. Saul had not sinned more grievously than David; and yet God rejected Saul and for-

gave David, because David, although a sinner, had an upright heart, and Saul did not deal sincerely with God.

3. A desire and hunger after our perfection, a determined will to be constantly tending towards it with all our strength;—let this be always our chief object and our greatest care. Let us bear in mind that this care is more of the essence of religion than vows themselves; for it is on this that all our whole spiritual progress depends. Herein consists the difference between true religious and those who are so only in appearance and in the sight of men. Without this care to advance in perfection, the religious state does not secure our salvation; but nothing is more common than to deceive ourselves on this point. We say we are striving after perfection, and in reality we are not striving after it at all.

4. A diligent endeavour to make progress in prayer, and to become solidly spiritual; and to this end, to free ourselves as far as lies in our power from the embarrassment of such exterior things as may be matter of our own choice; to avoid too great familiarity either with our own members or with strangers, particularly children, and still more especially women; to give ourselves much to recollection, and prepare ourselves carefully for the Holy Sacrifice of the Mass; to strive to draw therefrom all the fruit which it is fitted to produce; not to shorten the time allotted to the thanksgiving, which, well made, may repair much that is defective in our penances.

Not to relax in the practice of penance. A sincere and pure observance of our vows, without burdening our consciences with certain things opposed to their spirit, whence arise great scruples at the hour of death. On the contrary, it is a great consolation in this extremity, when we are about to appear before God, to have nothing to reproach ourselves with on the subject of our vows, and to see that we have strictly observed them; their end being, as some have considered, to retrench every thing which might hinder us in tending to and reaching perfection itself.

6. To follow the leadings of the Holy Spirit, His will, His inspirations, according as they become known to us, concerning ourselves about nothing else. For if we make a good use of such light and knowledge as we possess, God will favour us therewith more abundantly in a more excellent degree; and thus we shall be enlightened in proportion as we are faithful in co-operating with grace.

7. Never to attribute or appropriate to ourselves the favours which God bestows upon us, nor glorify and exalt ourselves thereupon, any more than for the success of our occupations and labours, as a speech, a tragedy, a declamation, or a sermon. God leaves us the profit of these things, but the glory He reserves to Himself; it is due to Him, and it is insufferable vanity in us to take it to ourselves.

8. When we come out of our year of retreat, let us take care not to appear to wish to teach or reform others. Let us do, on our part, whatever we can, and desire to do infinitely more. Let us speak discreetly on the subject of exalted perfection with those who are capable of it. Let us not be anxious to put forward, at first, the best that we know; for in this there would be vanity, and it would be profitable to no one.

It is of the utmost importance in the Company to be firmly persuaded that no dispensation from our vows is valid before God without a legitimate cause, and unless it be such as can pass the judgment of God. So much so, that every Jesuit who obtains such a dispensation without just cause is actually an apostate before

God, although in the sight of men, and, as the phrase is, *in foro externo,* he is justified.

ARTICLE IV.
Advice to preachers.

§ I.

If a preacher be not a man of prayer, he will never produce much fruit, because his discourses, in the matter of design, thoughts, style, action, and on account of the imperfect views and mixed intentions with which all will have been done, will be full of sins, at least such as are venial.

The advantage to the hearers depends very greatly on the holiness of the preacher, and his union with God, who can give him in a quarter of an hour's prayer more thoughts, and thoughts better calculated to touch hearts, than he would derive from a year's reading and study.

People weary themselves to death with labouring to compose fine sermons, and nevertheless scarcely any fruit results. How is this? Because preaching is a supernatural work, as much as the salvation of souls, which is the end proposed; and the instrument must be adapted to this end. Now it is not knowledge, nor eloquence, nor other human talents, but holiness of life and union with God which make us fitting instruments to effect the salvation of souls. Most preachers have sufficient knowledge, but they have not sufficient devotion or holiness.

§ II.

The true way of acquiring the science of the Saints, and possessing matter wherewithal to fill a sermon, an exhortation, or a spiritual conference, is to have recourse, not so much to books, as to inward humility, purity of heart, recollection, and prayer.

This was the practice of the holy Fathers who explained Scripture; the holy scholastic Doctors who taught theology with most success; the holy preachers who announced the Gospel with the greatest fruit.

When a soul has attained to perfect purity of heart, God Himself acts as its instructor, one while by the unction of spiritual consolations and interior delights, at another by sweet and touching illuminations, which teach it how to speak to the hearers' hearts better than study or other human means can do. It is thus that God has dealt with the apostolic labourers of our Company. Father Edmund Auger, for example, although overwhelmed with business, and having scarcely any leisure for study, electrified all France with his preaching, by which he wrought wonderful conversions.

This path, being the shortest and the easiest for producing fruit in souls, is the one we ought to follow, abandoning that which is longer and more difficult, viz. such great application to study as dries up the spirit of devotion. But we cannot rid ourselves of our self-sufficiency, or trust entirely to God.

§ III.

A preacher must speak well, and not neglect elocution. The reverence which is due to the word of God demands this of him. He must avoid, however, too studied an elegance of style, lest the ear of his audience should stop short at mere words and eloquence, which would hinder the whole fruit of the sermon. He would thus preach himself and not Jesus Christ.

When he has acquired a good style, his whole attention must be directed to this one object, viz. that grace may enliven what art and nature have formed, and that the Spirit of God may reign in his whole discourse as the soul animates the body.

To this end he must ask the Holy Spirit to suggest such thoughts as He knows to be calculated to move the hearts of his hearers.

He must neither love, nor value, nor commend any thing save Jesus Christ and what belongs to Him; he must not seek to be himself loved, commended, or esteemed by any body, nor have any other object in view than to make our Lord be known and loved, and draw the whole world to His service.

§ IV.

It is a fearful sight to see men who are called to the apostolic life carrying ambition and vanity into the sacred ministry of preaching. What fruit can they produce? They have gained what they have been pursuing for the space of six or seven years. They have accomplished their end at the cost of innumerable sins and imperfections. What a life! What manner of union with God! How is it possible that God should make use of such instruments? Hence come dissatisfaction, vexation, disquietude, fatal falls. One man falls in this way, another in that. One man into scruples and torments of conscience which allow him no repose. Another into complainings against superiors and rebelliousness of spirit, which renders the yoke of obedience intolerable to him. A third abandons the Company. Their unhappiness arises from their not having entered upon their employment by the way of obedience.

ARTICLE V.

Advice for various employments in the Company.

§ I.

The Company being a supernatural state, in order that the means which it employs and the end at which it aims may be mutually proportioned, its government must also be supernatural. Hence, superiors who are guided only by natural prudence are often deceived. Josue was deceived by the Gabaonites because he asked not counsel of the Lord. Every superior must act on supernatural principles; and so, in his degree, must a regent and a director.

§ II.

It is the interior spirit, and not regulations, which requires to be increased in the Company. The multiplication of rules springs out of human prudence, which relies more on its own inventions than on such means as are supernatural and divine. It is very injurious to true regularity, which must proceed from interior principle, and be based on the love and desire of perfection. For this great number of regulations, in addition to the rules, disgusts the mind, and leads to their being slighted so much the more readily, as they are not always uniform, some being often not in harmony with others. St. Ignatius also lays greater stress on the interior law which the Holy Spirit writes in the heart, than on the constitutions and exterior rules.

In giving the Exercises to a spiritual person, it is necessary above all things to consider what particular state of grace his soul is in, that we may accommodate ourselves thereto. We must do the same in our own case at the commencement of our retreats; and, generally speaking, it is of great consequence to ascertain what state of the spiritual life those souls are in which we have to direct, seeing that God commonly proportions His graces to the state of the soul; so that if it be in a state of penance, He bestows upon it graces of penance; if it be in a state of union, He bestows upon it graces of union.

The advantage of a retreat entirely depends on the attention paid by the director to ascertain what is passing within the soul to which he is giving the Exercises; and for this reason he ought, if possible, to hold communication with it several times a day, and see what grace, nature, and the devil are working within it, and aid it according to its needs.

Two extremes must be avoided in the direction of spiritual persons. One is, the giving too easy credence to souls who, from reading the marvellous operations of grace in the Saints, at feeling the least sensible sweetnesses, imagine they are already being favoured with the like. Dangerous vanity! The other is the keeping minds down too low, and never allowing them to rise to the height of perfection to which God calls them. There are directors who will not listen to any mention of contemplation, or heavenly visitations, or extraordinary favours. Illusion most prejudicial to the advancement of souls!

§ III.

In deciding cases of conscience, more dependence must be placed on the lights of the Holy Spirit, which constitute the science of Saints, than on human reasoning. They who in this matter rely on parity of reasoning often fall into error. It is allowable, for instance, to slay a man who tries to rob you of your goods ; then it is allowable to slay one who seeks to rob you of your reputation by calumny. Such reasoning is not sound: in cases still more parallel one conclusion does not follow from the other. In matters of morality it is sufficient that two cases should differ, for us not to judge of the one as of the other, however little diversity there may seem to exist between them.

§ IV.

If in our classes we appear to treat the children of the rich with peculiar attention on account of their advantages of fortune, we shall do very wrong ; we shall inflict a very great injury on the children themselves, for we shall foster in them that spirit of pride which wealth inspires ; and we shall scandalise the others, who will perceive that we allow ourselves to be dazzled, like the rest of mankind, by the splendour of this world's greatness, for which we are bound by our profession to feel and to shew nothing but contempt and aversion.

THIRD PRINCIPLE.

PURITY OF HEART.

CHAPTER I.

ITS NATURE AND ITS PROPERTIES.

ARTICLE I.

In what purity of heart consists.

PURITY of heart consists in having nothing therein which is, in however small a degree, opposed to God and the operation of His grace.

All the creatures there are in the world, the whole order of nature as well as of grace, and all the leadings of Providence, have been so disposed as to remove from our souls whatever is contrary to God. For never shall we attain unto God until we have corrected, cut off, and destroyed, either in this life or in the next, every thing that is contrary to God.

ARTICLE II.

How necessary purity of heart is to us.

§ I.

The first means towards the attainment of perfection is purity of heart; by it alone a St. Paul hermit, a St. Mary of Egypt, and so many other holy solitaries attained thereto. Next after purity of heart come the precepts and spiritual doctrine to be found in books; then direction and faithful co-operation with graces bestowed. This is the high road of perfection.

We must devote our whole care to the purifying of our heart, because there lies the root of all our evils.

To be able to conceive how requisite purity of heart is to us, it would be necessary fully to comprehend the natural corruption of the human heart. There is in us a very depth of malice, which we do not perceive, because we never seriously examine our own interior. If we did, we should find therein a multitude of desires and irregular appetites for the honours, the pleasures, and the comforts of the world unceasingly fermenting in our heart.

We are so full of false ideas and erroneous judgments, of disorderly affections, passions, and malice, that we should stand confounded at ourselves, could we see ourselves such as we are. Let us imagine ourselves a muddy well, from which water is continually being drawn: at first, what comes up is scarcely any thing but mud; but by dint of drawing, the well is gradually cleansed, and the water becomes purer, until at last it is as clear as crystal. In like manner, by labouring incessantly to purge our soul, the ground of it becomes gradually cleared, and God manifests His presence by powerful and marvellous effects which He works in the soul, and through it, for the good of others.

When the heart is thoroughly cleansed, God fills the soul and all its powers, the memory, the understanding, and the will, with His holy presence and love. Thus purity of heart leads to union with God, and no one ordinarily attains thereto by other means.

§ II.

The shortest and the surest way of attaining to perfection, is to study purity of heart rather than the exercise of virtues, because God is ready to bestow all manner of graces upon us, provided we put no obstacles in their way. Now it is by purifying our heart that we clear away every thing which hinders the work of God. When all impediments are removed, it is inconceivable what wonderful effects God produces in the soul. St. Ignatius used to say, that even Saints put great obstacles in the way of God's graces.

§ III.

Without an abundant supply of grace, we shall never do any excellent acts of virtue; and we shall never obtain this abundant supply, till we have thoroughly purged our heart. But when once we have reached this perfect purity of heart, we shall practise those virtues, an opportunity for which is furnished us; and with respect to others, an opportunity of which may not occur, we shall possess the spirit, and so to say, the essence of them, which is what God principally requires; for it is very possible to perform an act of some particular virtue without possessing its spirit and essence.

§ IV.

Of all the exercises of the spiritual life, there is none against which the devil directs more opposition than the study of purity of heart. He will let us perform some exterior acts of virtue, accuse ourselves publicly of our faults, serve in the kitchen, visit the hospitals and prisons, because we sometimes content ourselves with all this, and it serves to flatter us and to prevent interior remorses of conscience; but he cannot endure that we should look into our own heart, examine its disorders, and apply ourselves to their correction. The heart itself recoils from nothing so much as this search and scrutiny, which makes it see and feel its own miseries. All the powers of our soul are disordered beyond measure, and we do not wish to know it, because the knowledge is humiliating to us.

ARTICLE III.

The order to be observed in purity of heart, and the different degrees of purity.

§ I.

The order to be observed in cleansing the heart is, first, to note all venial sins, and correct them; secondly, to observe the disorderly movements of the heart, and amend them; thirdly, to keep watch over the thoughts, and regulate them; fourthly, to recognise the inspiration of God, His designs, His will, and encourage ourselves to the accomplishment of them. All this must be done calmly, joining therewith a true devotion to our Lord, which comprises a lofty conception of His greatness, a profound reverence for His person and for every thing belonging to Him, as well as the love and imitation of Him.

§ II.

There are four degrees of purity, and to these we may attain by a faithful co-operation with grace. The first is, to free ourselves from actual sins and the penalty due unto them. The second, to get rid of our evil habits and disorderly affections. The third, to deliver ourselves from that original corruption which is called *fomes peccati*, the aliment of sin, which is in all the powers of our soul, and in all the members of our body, as is manifest in children, who have the inclination to evil before they yet have the power of actually committing it. The fourth, to shake off that weakness which is natural to us, as creatures taken out of nothingness, which is called *defectibility*.

The first degree is attained mainly by penance. The second, by mortification and the exercise of the other virtues. The third, by the sacraments, which operate within us the grace of our renewal. The fourth, by our union with God, who being our beginning and the source of our being, can alone strengthen us against the weaknesses to which our nothingness of itself draws us down.

A soul may attain to a degree of purity at which it has such complete dominion over its imagination and its powers, that they have no longer any exercise, except in the service of God. In this state it can will nothing, remember nothing, think of nothing, hear nothing, but what has to do with God; so that if in conversation, vain and frivolous discourse were held, it would have to recollect itself, for lack of ideas or images whereby to understand what was said, or to retain the remembrance of it.

CHAPTER II.

THE THINGS FROM WHICH WE MUST CLEANSE OUR HEARTS.

ARTICLE I.

Venial sins.

§ I.

WE conceive of venial sin only as of a light word, a vain thought, an act of little consequence. This is a great illusion; since it is of faith that God punishes a venial sin with supernatural sufferings, longer and keener than the most terrible torments of this life. From whence the conclusion follows, that the malice of venial sin is greater, beyond compare, in the judgment of God than it is in the idea of men.

Venial sin is an evil so great, that it obliges a God of infinite goodness—who would have been willing to remain upon the cross for the love of men even for centuries—to condemn a soul He loves to the bitterest of all sufferings when it appears before His tribunal with the stain of this sin upon it; for the greatest torment we can conceive a soul enduring, when separated from the body, is to be deprived for ever, or for a time, of the sight of God. And this it is that venial sin deserves, which has not been expiated by penance during this life. Such is the light in which we ought to regard it.

Now we look at our sins only under their physical

aspect, which attracts us, or under their moral aspect, of which we scarcely form a conception. We must contemplate them in their effects, and consider that they prevent our union with God, and banish us from Him for ever in this life, if we continue in them. We must view them as opposed to that which is God's peculiar possession, that is to say, His glory, as well as to our own spiritual advancement, and to the designs of His providence with respect to us, which they interrupt and thwart.

§ II.

That which happens to seculars in the matter of mortal sin, we religious experience with respect to venial. In seculars passion quenches the light of faith, as well as that of reason. Inordinate affection corrupts the judgment, and they then fall into the greatest disorders. The Jews had sufficient light to know that Jesus Christ was God; envy blinded them, and they put to death the Messiah whom they expected. Socrates, Plato, Trajan, might have known by the simple light of nature the abominable crimes to which they abandoned themselves. Their brutal passion blinded them. Nothing is more plain than the obligation of making restitution when we have unjustly deprived our neighbour of his goods; and yet every day we see how avarice quenches all the lights, natural and supernatural, which demonstrate this obligation. Men do not make restitution, and they never will make it. Attachment to worldly goods has so corrupted their judgment, that they have no longer light to see its necessity.

It is in the same way that we harden ourselves in a multitude of habitual venial sins. Vanity, sensuality, attachment to our own little comforts, stifle within us the lights of grace, which enable us to see the evil of this class of faults. Those who, from tenderness of conscience, pursue another course, we regard as scrupulous persons. And to flatter ourselves in our blindness, we palliate, by a thousand specious pleas, the passion that blinds us. We invent for ourselves some good intention, and this done, we carelessly pass by all the movements of grace.

§ III.

The multiplication of venial sins is the destruction of souls, causing the diminution of those divine lights and inspirations, those interior graces and consolations, that fervour and courage, which are needed to resist the assaults of the enemy. Hence follow blindness, weakness, frequent falls, an acquired habit of insensibility of heart; because, when once an affection to these faults is contracted, we sin without feeling that we are sinning.

A man who takes no pains to avoid venial sins, though his labours of zeal in behalf of his neighbour be crowned with ever so brilliant a success, is in peril of being lost; for it is impossible for him, living as he does, not to fall sometimes into mortal sin, even without knowing it. But he is none the less guilty of the sins which he commits in this ignorance, because it is, as it were, wilful.

§ IV.

They who carefully avoid venial sins, generally preserve a constant feeling of devotion, and possess within them a moral certainty that they are in a state of grace. On the contrary, they who allow themselves to commit venial sins without scruple feel no unction of solid piety, and the Holy Spirit gives them no assurance that they are in a state of grace.

§ V.

In case of falls, we ought, as soon as ever we are sensible of them, to offer to God an act of interior adoration, to return to Him with love, to beg His forgiveness with confidence, and begin again to do what is good, without giving way for an instant to despondency or disquietude.

ARTICLE II.

The passions.

§ I.

Clement of Alexandria calls the passions the devil's *characters;* as if the devil, by means of our sins and evil habits, our disorderly affections and passions, imprinted his mark upon us. He alludes to the imperial badge worn by soldiers, which St. Augustine calls the " character of malice."

So long as we are in subjection to passions, we are the slaves of Satan, who makes them act at will, pretty much as the performer does the notes of the organ on which he presses. To this end he excites the humours of the body and the phantoms of the imagination. He awakens the remembrance of certain objects, and represents the image of them before the mind in such manner as he knows is calculated to arouse the passion which he desires to put in action ; and unless we are on our guard, he generally succeeds in his design. Often he is permitted to irritate the humours of our body in such a way, that we become disagreeable to others as well as to ourselves.

§ II.

They who are perfect have such dominion over their passions, that they rule them as they will. In them they are, in some wise, as they were in our Lord, in the Blessed Virgin, and in certain of the Saints, rather *propassions* (in the place of passions) than really passions ; that is to say, they are movements of the inferior appetite resembling those of the passions, but subject to reason, and excited only at its command, and by the impulse of grace directing the reason.

The imperfect are now joyful, now sad, according as their passions are calm or disturbed; for sadness and anxiety arise solely from the affections, which, when unmortified, produce these alternations of peace and disquietude.

They who aspire to perfection find the tyranny of the passions intolerable, and endeavour to free themselves therefrom by labouring constantly to mortify them. But worldly people, who live in a state of perpetual slavery, do not even sigh after liberty. They love their chains, and, as Job says, "they find their delight among the briers and thorns that lacerate them."

§ III.

Concupiscence and the passions insensibly extinguish the infused and supernatural lights of the understanding, so that in the end they succeed in stifling them entirely. Hence it is that we see minds of a high order extremely blind nevertheless in spiritual things. A man enjoys strong sight, but it does not therefore follow that he has a strong mind; the two faculties are quite distinct. Such as are led by passion to make a profession of heresy (as was done by a certain German prince to pique Charles V.,) are at the beginning heretics only by humour and passion, retaining in their soul a conviction opposed to the errors of the false religion which outwardly they profess. But in course of time, as passion strengthens and sins multiply, all that remained of the light of faith is lost, the understanding is darkened, and they become altogether heretics.

Thus, in matters which concern perfection, all disorders commence by means of a passion or irregular affection for some object. Little by little it corrupts the understanding, and this again at last lets itself be so won over as no longer to pronounce judgment save in favour of that passion which has possession of us.

We contemplate some object, an employment, for example, which we think would suit us, or which would give us a distinguished position. Passion is aroused; we love, we desire this employment. At first the understanding, illuminated by the lights of grace, resists the desire, and condemns it; but passion growing stronger, and the lights of grace being gradually extinguished, the understanding no longer makes any resistance. It yields to the disorderly inclinations of the will; it approves them; it discovers reasons to justify them; and, corrupted by the will, it helps in its turn to corrupt it, proposing to it false maxims in order to sanction its irregularities.

ARTICLE III.

The fund of pride there is in us.

§ I.

Pride is the love and desire of our own superiority. It is of all our vices the most hidden, the most deeply rooted, and that of which the occasions are the most frequent. These are occurring every hour; either with respect to the goods and advantages which we possess and from which we draw matter for self-complacency, exaltation of ourselves above others, and desire to be esteemed and praised, or with respect to the evil and the faults that are in us, and which we try to conceal, to disguise, to diminish, to excuse, and are unwilling even inwardly to acknowledge. In one day we are guilty of more than a hundred acts of pride.

This vice in religious is of a different character to what it is in seculars. In the latter, pride finds its object and its matter in worldly goods and exterior advantages, wherein they desire to excel; but in religious, pride is what it was in the rebel angels, it attaches itself to their personal superiority and spiritual goods. It is a great evil, and the source of all evils.

§ II.

To become like to God we must renounce all resemblance to the devil, which consists in pride, vanity, and presumption; as also all resemblance to brutes, which consists in the passions, and the disorderly movements of the sensual appetite.

Every vice produces in the soul four evil effects: 1. it clouds and blinds it; 2. it defiles it; 3. it disquiets and harasses it; 4. it enfeebles it. But of all vices, that which specially darkens the mind is pride; and that which specially defiles the heart is pleasure.

We are naturally always disposed to let ourselves be captivated by the splendour of honours and the applause and esteem of men, and by the allurements of pleasure and gratification of our senses, because we suffer grace to have but very slight dominion over our mind. For the same reason, if any one says a word about our faults, we cannot endure it. It will excite in our heart fifty movements of anger, vexation, bitterness, and impatience.

Strange injustice of the human heart! God has forgiven us venial sins innumerable; and when we have confessed them, even after such frequent relapses, He has given us interior consolations, as a sign and pledge of our reconciliation; and yet we cannot forget a disobliging word which has been said to us, or a slight affront which has been offered us; we continue to preserve the remembrance of it, and wait only for an opportunity to testify our displeasure. This comes of the foolish esteem and false love which we entertain for ourselves. We think more of our own interests than those of God; pride blinds us.

The malice of our proud heart is manifested also in

this, that if any one has the least defect, although he may excel in every thing else, we pass over all the perfections he possesses, and fasten upon the one defect; we think of it, we talk of it, we take occasion thereupon to reckon such person our inferior, and inwardly to exalt ourselves above him; so that, in fact, we rank in our own estimation above every body in the world.

§ III.

We are extremely averse to acknowledge those faults in us which are opposed to the virtues which we believe ourselves to have acquired; although, as a matter of fact, we are very evidently guilty of such. But our proud spirit cannot stoop humbly to acknowledge them, because such acknowledgment is contrary to the idea we entertain of ourselves, and shocks the vain-glory with which we flatter ourselves.

We are so full of deceit and vanity, that, even though we cannot but perceive that we do not possess certain virtues, yet should we accidentally perform some acts belonging to them and receive praise, on that account we immediately allow ourselves to be persuaded that we really possess these virtues, and flatter ourselves with this false opinion, like those madmen who fancy themselves kings; for we believe ourselves to be what we are not.

§ IV.

Unless we are most strictly faithful to grace, we do every thing, even the most sacred acts, with a view to our own individual excellence; so that if we say Mass, if we betake ourselves to prayer, if we make our spiritual reading, or perform other exercise, all that we look to therein is our own spiritual superiority. Such motive is an improper one. What we ought to aim at is to tend towards God, and to unite ourselves to Him by these holy exercises. This last motive regards only the glory of God. It is conformable to the will of God. It is pure and disinterested. It is pleasing to God.

§ v.

We sometimes feel too sensitively those occasions of discontent which are given us by superiors, or by the community at large. What state of life is there in the world in which from time to time we do not suffer some annoyance? If we are refused something which others are not bound to grant us, leave of absence, for instance, we murmur and make loud complaints. What can be more unreasonable? a little humility, a little self-mortification would save us a great deal of pain.

§ vi.

God tries hearts, and sometimes He withdraws His graces because He perceives how much pride there is in us. He foresees that if He gave us more consolations and lights, if He granted us such and such favours, we should become still prouder. Already we are on the brink of the precipice, and to prevent us falling, He withholds from us graces which would be the occasion of our falling; thus He refused to deliver St. Paul from that importunate temptation of impurity, lest his heart should be puffed up with vanity. It was not that St. Paul was proud, but God would prevent his becoming so.

§ vii.

The littleness of our heart is inconceivable. Does God grant us the least consolation, a single tear of devotion, we make it a ground for exalting ourselves wonderfully in our own eyes. And yet what is it? it is not a thousandth part of what God is ready to give us. Let us imagine a poor man who has received a penny from the hand of some great noble, going away exulting with joy, without staying to partake of the great man's bounty, who is willing to shower on him handfuls of gold. This is exactly what we do.

ARTICLE IV.

We must not neglect our least imperfections.

§ I.

We ought to pay the strictest attention to the least movements of the spiritual life within us, seeing that God makes more account of them than of all the occupations and all the actions of our natural life.

To have stifled in our heart the stirring of a passion, or of one irregular inclination, to have rooted out of the soul one single imperfection, is a greater gain than if we had obtained possession of a hundred thousand worlds for a whole eternity.

Should we have accomplished nothing else, by labouring a whole day like a common porter, than delivering ourselves from an idle thought, we ought to reckon ourselves well rewarded for our trouble.

§ II.

Certain things which are trifling in themselves are nevertheless of great importance in the case of religious. Thus, to walk carelessly through the streets, to allow ourselves some indulgences at table with seculars, to laugh loud before externs; these are slight faults in themselves, but important in their consequences, because seculars draw the conclusion that those in whom they witness such things have not much devotion, and hence they go on to lose the respect which they had for the Order. Or, again, to say something to the disadvantage of a house, or of the superior of a house, to one who is to go and reside there, is a considerable fault, because it deprives the religious of that indifference which he ought to have with respect to place, and which is a point of great moment. This defect is only too common.

§ III.

We must carefully suppress certain volitions, or incipient acts of the will, which we are continually making with respect to different objects which excite in us feelings having the character of imperfection, as of pride, envy, bitterness, sensuality; because, from these incipient acts proceed such as are formal; and from a simple volition we easily pass to a full and deliberate consent of the will. However, in the matter of devotion, these incomplete acts of the will are good, as Suarez observes.

ARTICLE V.

Of the denial of our inclinations in order to put ourselves in a state of holy indifference.

§ I.

We commonly harbour in our soul some one thing which mars the whole interior life; this may be some ill-regulated affection, some project, some preference as to place, or desire for a particular employment or office. We must study to acquire a complete indifference, and protest that we seek nothing in this life, except to possess God as much as it is possible for us to possess Him, and that all else is matter of indifference to us.

We are wrong in complaining, as we do sometimes, of not having sufficient occupation where we are. Such complaint proceeds from our not being sufficiently detached from our own inclinations and our own will. We have not a perfect indifference as respects all employments; we have private ends of our own. We wish to be employed in certain offices, to which we limit our desires; as preaching, for instance, or directing a congregation in such and such a town; and when these particular occupations are not allotted to us, we seem to have our hands tied, we fancy ourselves without employment. This is all illusion. He who has a will disposed for any good indifferently, of whatever kind it be, and forms no private design of his own, will have only too much to do. First of all, there is prayer, which by itself might form the whole employment of a religious; but they who have made no progress in prayer during youth will never devote themselves to it in their old age. Then, visiting the hospitals and the prisons; catechising, which is a ministration so peculiarly belonging to the Company, and one which St. Ignatius and our first Fathers performed with so much zeal; giving exhortations to nuns, and missions to country parishes for one or two days, &c.

You aspire to such and such an employment; you wish, for example, to have a certain class in a particular college. Suppose you obtain it by interest, or by importunity. It is true, your own will has found its satisfaction; but all the labour of this class will at least prove fruitless to you; in vain will you offer it to God by subsequent good intentions. It will not be pleasing to Him, because it is not conformable to His will. This is not at all what He desired of you. All the favour you can expect from God, under such circumstances, according to His ordinary dealings, is not to allow some great fall to happen to you in the said employment; unless, acknowledging your fault, you put yourself sincerely in the disposition to take another occupation, and, informing your superiors of the whole matter, resign yourself absolutely to their will.

§ II.

It is of no use your protesting that you are indifferent to every thing; if you prize certain distinguished employments, you are not so. So long as you set this value on them, your pretended indifference is nothing short of hypocrisy.

It is not possible to acquire indifference, unless, in the first place, we have a due esteem for the interior life, and sufficient acquaintance with it to rank it above every occupation. Secondly, unless we despise all the distinction connected with exterior functions, all the gratification to be found in them, and all the advantages they hold out. Without this, we may indeed attain to a species of indifference, but even this only with difficulty and effort. It will never be lasting, because, after all, the heart cannot refrain from loving something. But if we love and value as we ought the interior life, we shall be for ever indifferent to all the employments of the exterior life, because the former, when we have it, has, beyond comparison, more attractions and more delights than the latter. It is extremely important that we should be thoroughly convinced of this, for as we can induce seculars to despise riches only by shewing them how they may acquire other goods more solid and more lasting, in like manner we shall never despise the satisfaction we may promise ourselves from exterior employments, until we are similarly convinced that we shall find more solid good in the self-recollection of the interior life.

Without the gift of prayer, we shall never reach a perfect, general, and lasting indifference. We may, it is true, be in a measure indifferent to certain things and for a limited time, but our indifference will be neither complete nor peaceable, it will always be accompanied with uneasiness, and have much repugnance to combat.

§ III.

We ought to be so indifferent as to be more readily disposed to those things for which we feel the most aversion, and ask for them of God and our superiors.

He who cannot as yet bring himself to this is far removed from true indifference.

Some entertain no plans, but they hope for such an employment or such an advantage; they must rid themselves of this also, or they cannot attain to a perfect indifference.

We ought to live in a state of complete abandonment of ourselves to the will of God, the decrees of His providence, and the calls of obedience, sacrificing to God all our aspirations, and all those human hopes which we are ever ceaselessly entertaining, especially in youth. The young live on the hope of the future, the old on the memory of the past.

Let us consider that there is nothing more vain than hopes of this kind, and that they mostly deceive us; that of fifty, scarcely three come to any thing, God taking pleasure in confounding them, because they are so many usurpations of His rights; in fine, that to labour for success is to diverge from the ways of Providence, and to quit the road which God has marked out to us from all eternity.

ARTICLE VI.

How we ought to comport ourselves with respect to divine graces, and with what self-abnegation we must receive them.

§ I.

Self-abnegation in the case of beginners consists in withdrawing from the occasions of sin, in mortifying their passions, their own will and private judgment. In those who have made some progress in the spiritual life, it consists in not attaching themselves to the gifts of God. For although we acknowledge we hold every thing from God, we nevertheless act as if the graces which are the gift of His pure mercy, were our own by nature; as if we could keep and possess them in the same manner as we possess the presents which we have received from the liberality of men; which is false.

God, in order to prevent this appropriation of His graces, sometimes withdraws them, and takes from us that facility in the practice of virtues which He had given us; so that we shall seem to ourselves to have become again proud or sensual, and shall experience as much difficulty in humbling and mortifying ourselves as we felt at the beginning. But God acts thus only for our good; we must not interfere with Him; He has His own work to do at present, and we have to learn to endure the operation of His hand. *Ut simus patientes divina.*

He deprives us of His consolations and of sensible devotion in prayer and in our other exercises, to try our fidelity, and to reduce us to that perfect nudity of spirit in which those souls ought to be which the Holy Spirit would fill with His gifts. All that we have to do on our part is to keep our heart as pure as possible; carefully avoiding the least faults, and for the rest giving ourselves up wholly to God, and submitting to all the dispensations of His providence.

This rule applies not only to the time of our noviciate, but to our whole life; let us then have confidence in God, and be sure He will not be wanting to us.

§ II.

We appropriate to ourselves the good affections which God enables us to form, and attach ourselves to them with a sort of spiritual sensuality or secret vanity; we write them down, and would wish never to be without them.

Not that it is a bad custom to make a brief memorandum of them, for the purpose of recollecting them and making use of them hereafter; but to do so in a spirit of ownership is a dangerous abuse.

We are travellers; we must be always advancing towards our destination, and not stop for so small a matter. God has far greater favours in store for us; He is infinitely rich and infinitely bountiful; He never fails to impart His gifts to us in proportion as we are faithful in co-operating with them. Let us but employ those which He bestows upon us whilst we have them, and then pass on like a traveller who walks gaily along a beautiful road, nor, for all its beauty, lingers on his way, any more than he would elsewhere.

They who never cease reflecting on the lights and affections which grace bestows, are like a traveller who, from time to time, after taking a few steps forward, turns back to look at the road he has traversed, and loses his time in gazing at it with a vain complacency.

§ III.

Let us consider that the graces which God gives us are God's property, and not ours. We must practise poverty even in respect to these spiritual goods: the more we receive the graces of God with purity of heart and self-denial, the greater and more abundant will they be.

§ IV.

When God favours us with some light, immediately, at the very moment we receive it, it produces the effect which God intended, for it has wrought in the soul that disposition which He desired, viz. a greater capacity for divine union, which is the object for which all grace is bestowed.

We must not, then, after the manner of some, make action and practice the end of all the lights we receive, so as to esteem those thrown away which do not lead to some active result. It is enough that they gradually dispose the soul to union with God, which is the very end of all our works. For every thing we do in the exercise of virtue is bearing us on to this goal. When these lights and sentiments have passed away, we must not make efforts to recall them. If, however, God brings them back to the mind, it is well then to remember them; but hardly any but beginners should allow themselves to write them down.

§ v.

No sooner do we attach ourselves to any object out of God, than we give a handle to the devil, who, by means of such attachment, will not fail either to deprive us of freedom of mind, and fill our souls with disquiet, or to give us, or at least obtain for us, as far as in him lies, that on which we have set our affections, especially if it be some sweetness or sensible consolation, of which he will be most lavish in order to destroy us if he can.

When, then, a director perceives that the souls he is guiding have attachments of this kind, he must debar them the object of them for a time : when hereafter he shall see them in a state of indifference, he may permit them their customary use of it.

They who have been truly enlightened by the Holy Spirit direct their affection to God only, not attaching themselves even to the holiest things. Does God inspire them with some good sentiment, they receive it with thanksgiving and reserve, taking good care not to be deceived by admitting other thoughts, which the devil endeavours craftily to suggest to them. And when this divine sentiment has gone by, they no longer hanker after it, nor strive to retain it longer than God wills. They do not set about recalling the cause or the occasion which had excited it, as by repeating the same exercises, the same meditation, the same spiritual reading, with the view of experiencing a like sentiment; but they pass on, walking ever in perfect nudity of spirit; and thus they deprive the devil of the power and the opportunity of deceiving them by sweetnesses and sensible consolations and other extraordinary means, that he may afterwards lead them on to the precipice.

CHAPTER III.

THE CARE WE OUGHT TO TAKE TO PRESERVE PURITY OF HEART IN ACTION.

ARTICLE I.

We must perform our actions with a pure intention.

WE ought to take the strictest care to perform all our actions with a pure intention. An action which in itself is good, becomes altogether bad when it is preceded or accompanied by an intention which is not pure ; and it is partly good and partly bad when, though preceded by a pure intention, it is afterwards accompanied by one that is impure ; as, for example, by vainglory, which insinuates itself insensibly.

The principal enemies with which purity of intention has to contend are vanity, pleasure, self-interest, and aversion. This is why, at the commencement of our actions, as on going to table, or to recreation, we must overcome our repugnances and renounce our own gratification, so as in nowise to act from any of these impure motives, being ever disposed to do what we are about to do with the aim of pleasing God, even when we do not find our own pleasure or profit therein. And in the progress of our actions we ought to use great circumspection to keep them clear from every defilement that may mingle with them, whether it be external, such as want of modesty ; or internal, such as private self-seeking.

ARTICLE II.

We ought to act on supernatural principles.

Our heart is unceasingly attracted towards good; but it is always some natural good, unless the Holy Spirit gives it a higher aim. We ought, then, to watch all the movements of our heart, in order to follow only those which come from the Holy Spirit.

The holy Angels never performed those actions which we call purely natural; they renounced for ever their self-love from the pure motive of the love of God; and whilst they were in a state of probation, they performed only acts of faith, hope, charity, and other supernatural virtues. Thus it is that they merited the possession of God, and were rendered eternally blessed.

We ought to imitate this fidelity of the Angels, acting always on supernatural principles. But we are wholly immersed in our own nature, and most of our actions are either merely natural, or proceed partly from grace, and partly from nature. Scarcely any are wholly of grace and perfectly supernatural.

CHAPTER IV.

MENTAL CAUSES OF THE CORRUPTION OF THE HEART.

ARTICLE I.

Error and false maxims.

WE never have vices or imperfections, without, at the same time, having false judgments and false ideas, which are the cause of these disorders in our conduct; for the understanding and the will are the two sources of malice, as also of goodness, in creatures endowed with free will. Thus the imperfect have their minds full of practical judgments grounded on the false ideas which they conceive in accordance with the inclinations of corrupt nature. This it is that keeps us in such a pitiable state. The little good that we do so blinds us, that we imagine we have attained to a sufficient height of virtue, and the good opinion we entertain of ourselves makes it most difficult for us to correct ourselves of our faults. The common people followed our Lord. He said to them, " Blessed are the poor in spirit ;" and these good souls humbly received His doctrine. The Pharisees, the doctors of the law, the chief priests, did not follow Him, vainly imagining that they were in possession of something far higher than the doctrine He preached.

ARTICLE II.

Ignorance.

They who do not follow the guidance of the Holy Spirit, remain all their life involved in those three kinds of ignorance of which St. Lawrence Justinian speaks.

The first is what he calls *nescientia veri et falsi*, an inability to distinguish between what is true and what is false.

This ignorance is found in those who, taking no pains to watch the movements of their own interior, are unable to distinguish in themselves the different operations of God, of nature, and of the devil; so that having to choose, as often happens, between two contrary sentiments, they take the false for the true, an idea of their own imagination, or a suggestion of the enemy, for a divine inspiration; their own inclination for an attraction of grace. They freely allow themselves every thing which does not appear to them to be wrong, every thing which in their judgment is sanctioned by reason and good sense. This is their sole rule; and they follow the maxims of faith only in that moderate and qualified form which their reason approves. To maintain themselves in the enjoyment of this liberty, they put forward some such pleas as these: that they wish to avoid scrupulosity; that they are unwilling to weary their minds, or become theoretical, or act without a due regard to common sense.

It is dangerous for those who are called to a high degree of perfection to confine themselves to the guidance of reason and good sense, or to place more reliance on these than on the lights of the Holy Spirit.

For, in the first place, there is no mind so penetrating, no judgment so solid, which the devil cannot deceive. Secondly, such guidance is defective, because in many matters reason is too short-sighted, neither does it suffice for guidance in all cases. Thirdly, such guidance is purely natural; it is of a low order; it is limited in itself, and confines within a narrow scope the designs of God, which are high and of a vast extent. Fourthly, it usurps the rights of the Holy Spirit, making human reason the judge and ruler of divine inspirations and calls, instead of itself being in subjection thereto, and leaving to the Holy Spirit to control and dispense His own graces.

The second kind of ignorance is called by St. Lawrence Justinian *nescientia boni et mali*, an inability to discern between good and evil. This is, properly speaking, the not knowing how to preserve that just moderation and mean, wherein virtue consists, between the two extreme vices which are opposed to it; which knowledge can be obtained only by the direction of the Holy Spirit.

Moral virtues degenerate into vices when we carry them beyond a certain point, which point is not always the same, the least circumstance in matter of time, place, or persons being capable of changing it. Reason may sometimes hit it, but not always; it may easily be deceived in making this judgment. It is the Holy Spirit who teaches us to discern infallibly this true mean, and to persevere therein when it is found. He it is who teaches how to practise mortification without going to an excess injurious to health, or sparing ourselves under pretext of discretion; to lean now to the side of tenderness, now to that of rigour; and to give ourselves to prayer and penance at one time more than another.

Hence we conclude, first, that out of the true Church no moral virtue can possibly be possessed in its perfection: secondly, that what is good at one time is not so at another, and that thus many things which formerly were practised in the discipline of the Church are not so at present; that many of the canons of ancient councils are now no longer in force, on account of the changes that have taken place from age to age: thirdly, that we cannot for this reason accuse the Church of laxity, as do the inventors of new opinions, who extol only the ancient Church, and its customs and usages, which they appear to wish to restore, not considering that the same Spirit who governed the Church of old governs it now, and accommodates His ways to the times and the different dispositions of the faithful.

The third kind of ignorance is called *nescientia commodi et noxii*, an inability to discern between what is beneficial and what is injurious. This is displayed when from among such things as are really good in themselves we are unable to distinguish which are more or less conformable to the designs of God. Thus St. Paul, when he was assaulted with that importunate temptation in the flesh, knew not whether it were expedient or not that he should be delivered from it; he entreated, therefore, that it might depart from him; and the Holy Spirit revealed to him that the temptation was providentially ordained for the glory of God.

Hence it follows that this ignorance may sometimes be met with even in the holiest persons, at least as respects some particulars, although, generally speaking, in their actions and occupations they perceive what they ought to do and what is the better part, and have the light of the Holy Spirit to enable them to know the will of God, pretty much as we have the light of the sun to reveal to us the objects before our eyes. Secondly, that even were all the intellect and good sense now distributed amongst men concentrated in one individual, he would not be able to judge in such and such contingency what is best for us, and what enters into the order of providence in our regard. The very Angels could not tell; for who can know what God desires of us, whither He is leading us, and by what road He would lead us? the interior ways of the just being as various as their countenances. Thirdly, that the power of this discernment appertains, like the preceding, to the Holy Spirit, who fathoms the very depth of the heart of God, and knows all His designs and all His will, manifesting them to the souls which give themselves up wholly to His guidance.

CHAPTER V.

EXTERNAL CAUSES OF THE CORRUPTION OF THE HEART.

ARTICLE I.

The harm that results from particular friendships and the conversation of the imperfect.

PARTICULAR friendships and frequent and familiar conversation generally tend to detraction, petty intrigues and cabals, complainings, ridicule of each other, infringement of the rules, waste of time, and other like faults.

We ought to cultivate an universal charity, and converse with all indifferently in time of recreation; we must neither avoid nor seek out individuals, nor form a particular intimacy with any one, without having first so far tried him as to have reason to hope we may profit by his good example to make progress in virtue.

It is advisable, however, to have some one in the house in whom we may place confidence, and whose advice we may ask when in doubt; he will recommend the matter to God, and then give us his opinion with sincerity.

ARTICLE II.

The faults we ought to avoid in conversation.

§ I.

We should take heed that our conversation be not puerile, and that in our mutual intercourse we are not wanting in gravity, respect, and courtesy; we should be careful not to fall into the habit of contradicting each other, or of making excuses when we are blamed; we should beware of talking too much, and neglecting to talk of spiritual things, and indulging in unguarded effusions, and in our conversations and recreations filling our mind with a multitude of subjects, which serve only to produce uneasiness and dissipation of spirit.

We ought never to remit our self-recollection, or forget for a moment the presence of God; but maintain constantly a modest and humble demeanour, talk little, and only of such things as are profitable; defer one to the other; and break ourselves of that spirit of contradiction which disposes us to take exception at another's opinions.

§ II.

Our conversation ought to be courteous and obliging, mild and pleasing, tempered with a modest cheerfulness and gravity, accommodated to the humours of others, without contradiction and carping, jesting and raillery, levity and flattery, free from the compliments and manners of the world, accompanied with discretion and simplicity, full of edification, animated by the Spirit of God, and seasoned with the holy unction which grace imparts to such souls as are fully possessed by it.

§ III.

Both in conversing and in paying visits we should take care that our heart and our mind do not stop short at exterior things, and limit themselves thereto. Whatever may present itself to our senses, we ought inwardly to say, " Away, away ; this is not what I seek ; what I seek is union with God ; it is God only that I desire."

ARTICLE III.

Of unprofitable visits and conversation.

§ I.

A large proportion of the visits that are made serve only to cause distractions. They who in this matter act only on natural principles will not gain upon seculars in a whole month as much as they who are guided by supernatural motives will in a day.

§ II.

We must mortify as much as possible a curiosity for hearing news, and the itching desire to retail it. Nothing is more opposed to the interior spirit, or more dissipating to the heart. As a fish dies when it is taken out of the water, because it is no longer in its element, so the spirit of recollection is lost amidst these worldly conversations for the same reason,—it is out of its element.

§ III.

How astonishing to see (as nevertheless sometimes

happens) a monk or a nun whom God has withdrawn from the entanglements of the world, and placed in religion as in an earthly paradise, where they may nourish themselves with the bread of angels, the fruit of life, the hidden manna; where, in recollection, in prayer, in the very rigours of penance, they may taste sweetnesses and consolations which fully satisfy the heart, where they may drink at their source the pure waters of grace; souls to whom God offers the joys of heaven, and who might find in God their happiness, even in this life,—amusing themselves, like people of the world, with pleasures which flatter the senses, taking delight in reading some profane book, seeking their satisfaction in visits, the news of the day, empty talk, familiar conversations, in which so many hours are wasted,— precious time, which they steal from their exercises of devotion, the duties of their occupation, and the calls of obedience;—and how is it that they can do this? what is the charm by which they thus suffer themselves to be deceived? *Fascinatio nugacitatis obscurat bona.* Trifles have power to fascinate a soul consecrated to Jesus Christ by ties so holy, by vows so many times renewed. Trifles prevent its knowing the good things which God has prepared for those who, by a generous self-denial, leave all to give themselves to Him.

What torrents of holy rapture did God pour into the soul of a St. Francis Xavier, when, after the toils and dangers of a journey of five or six thousand leagues, he said, that for one only of those divine consolations with which his soul overflowed, he would willingly expose himself again to the same sufferings; and that every one would do the like, had God given him to taste of the same sweetness!

FOURTH PRINCIPLE.

OF THE GUIDANCE OF THE HOLY SPIRIT, AND DOCILITY THERETO.

CHAPTER I.

THE NATURE OF DOCILITY TO THE GUIDANCE OF THE HOLY SPIRIT.

ARTICLE I.

In what this docility consists.

§ I.

When a soul has given itself up to the leading of the Holy Spirit, He raises it little by little, and directs it. At the first it knows not whither it is going; but gradually the interior light illuminates it, and enables it to behold all its own actions, and the governance of God therein, so that it has scarcely aught else to do than to let God work in it and by it whatever He pleases; thus it makes wonderful progress.

§ II.

We have a figure of the guidance of the Holy Spirit in that which God adopted in regard to the Israelites in their exodus from Egypt during their journeying in the wilderness towards the land of promise. He gave them, as their guide, a pillar of cloud by day and a pillar of fire by night. They followed the movements of this pillar, and halted when it halted; they did not go before it, they only followed it, and never wandered from it. It is thus we ought to act with respect to the Holy Spirit.

ARTICLE II.

The means of attaining this docility.

The principal means by which we obtain this direction of the Holy Spirit are the following :

1. To obey faithfully God's will so far as we know it; much of it is hidden from us, for we are full of ignorance; but God will demand an account at our hands only of the knowledge He has given us; let us make good use of it, and He will give us more. Let us fulfil His designs so far as He has made them known to us, and He will manifest them to us more fully.

2. To renew often the good resolution of following in all things the will of God, and strengthen ourselves in this determination as much as possible.

3. To ask continually of the Holy Spirit this light and this strength to do the will of God, to bind ourselves to Him, and remain His prisoners like St. Paul, who said to the priests of Ephesus, " Being bound in the Spirit, I go to Jerusalem;"—above all, in every important change of circumstances, to pray God to grant us the illumination of the Holy Spirit, and sincerely protest that we desire nothing else, but only to do His will. After which if He impart to us no fresh light, we may act as heretofore we have been accustomed to act, and as shall appear best for the time being.

This is why at the commencement of important affairs, as the opening of the Chambers, the assemblies of the clergy and councils, the assistance of the Holy Spirit is invoked by votive masses said in His honour.

4. Let us watch with care the different movements of our soul. By such attention we shall come gradually to perceive what is of God and what is not. That which proceeds from God in a soul which is subjected

to grace, is generally peaceable and calm. That which comes from the devil is violent, and brings with it trouble and anxiety.

ARTICLE III.

Objections against this doctrine of the guidance of the Holy Spirit.

Four objections in particular are brought against this interior guidance of the Holy Spirit.

The first is, that it appears to bear some resemblance to the inward spirit of the Calvinists.

To this we reply: 1. That it is of faith, that without the grace of an interior inspiration, in which the guidance of the Holy Spirit consists, we cannot do any good work; to say the contrary, is to be a semi-Pelagian. 2. The Calvinists would determine every thing by their inward spirit, subjecting thereto the Church itself and its decisions, and acknowledging no other rule of faith, having invented this false doctrine in order to elude the authority of tradition and councils and the holy Fathers; instead of which, the guidance which we receive from the Holy Ghost, by means of His gifts, presupposes the faith and authority of the Church, acknowledges them as its rule, admits nothing which is contrary to them, and aims only at perfecting the exercise of faith and the other virtues.

The second objection is, that it seems as if this interior guidance of the Holy Spirit were destructive of the obedience which is due to superiors.

We reply: 1. That as the interior inspiration of grace does not set aside the assent which we give to the articles of faith, as they are externally proposed to us, but contrariwise gently disposes the understanding to believe; in like manner, the guidance which we receive from the gifts of the Holy Spirit, far from interfering with obedience, aids and facilitates the practice of it. 2. That all this interior guidance, and even divine revelations, must always be subordinate to obedience; and in speaking of them, this tacit condition is ever implied, that obedience enjoins nothing contrary thereto.

For in the state of faith in which we live, we ought to make more account of the commandment of our superior than of that which our Lord Himself might have given us by an immediate revelation, because we are assured that it is His will we should act in this matter after the pattern of the Saints, who by submitting to obedience merited to be raised to a higher reward than they would have been had they paid exclusive regard to the revelations they received.

The only fear is lest superiors should sometimes follow too much the suggestions of human prudence, and for want of any other kind of discernment condemn the lights and inspirations of the Holy Spirit, treating them as dreams and illusions, and prescribing for those to whom God communicates Himself by favours of this kind, as if they were sick patients.

In such case we must still obey; but in His own time God will know how to correct the error of these rash persons, and teach them to their cost, not to condemn His graces without understanding them, and without being competent to pronounce upon them.

What renders them incapable of forming a right judgment is, that they live entirely in external things and in the hurry of business, and have but little spirituality about them, never having risen above the lowest degrees of mental prayer. And what induces them to pass judgment is, that they do not like to appear ignorant of things, of which, nevertheless, they have neither experience nor knowledge.

The third objection is, that this interior direction of the Holy Spirit seems to render all deliberation and counsel useless. For why ask advice of men, when the Holy Spirit is Himself our director?

We reply, that the Holy Spirit teaches us to consult enlightened persons, and to follow the opinion of others. It is thus He referred St. Paul to Ananias, that he might learn from him what he ought to do. In the consultations which usually take place in the Company, if the superior be a spiritual and interior person, the different opinions which are laid before him will give him light the better to know the will of God, and to discern what is most expedient in present circumstances.

The fourth objection is made by some who complain that they are not themselves thus led by the Holy Spirit, and that they know nothing of it.

To them we reply, 1st, that the lights and inspirations of the Holy Spirit which are necessary in order to do good and avoid evil, are never wanting to them, particularly if they are in a state of grace. 2dly, that being altogether exterior as they are, and scarcely ever entering into themselves, examining their consciences only very superficially, and looking only to the outward man, and the faults which are manifest in the eyes of the world, without seeking to discover their secret roots and to become acquainted with their own predominant passions and habits, without investigating the state and disposition of their soul and the movements of their heart, it is no wonder that they have nothing of the guidance of the Holy Spirit, which is wholly interior. How should they know any thing of it? they do not even know their interior sins, which are their personal acts produced by their own free will. But they will infallibly acquire the knowledge, if only they bring the necessary dispositions.

First, let them be faithful in following the light which is given them; it will go on always increasing.

Secondly, let them clear away the sins and imperfections which, like so many clouds, hide the light from their eyes; they will see more distinctly every day.

Thirdly, let them not suffer their exterior senses to rove at will, and be soiled by indulgence; God will then open to them their interior senses.

Fourthly, let them never quit their own interior, if it be possible, or let them return as soon as may be; let them give attention to what passes therein, and they will observe the working of the different minds by which we are actuated.

Fifthly, let them lay bare the whole ground of their heart sincerely to their superior or to their spiritual father. A soul which acts with this openness and simplicity can hardly fail of being favoured with the direction of the Holy Spirit.

CHAPTER II.

THE MOTIVES WHICH LEAD US TO THE PRACTICE OF THIS DOCILITY.

ARTICLE I.

That perfection and even salvation depend on docility to grace.

§ I.

THE two elements of the spiritual life are the cleansing of the heart and the direction of the Holy Spirit. These are the two poles of all spirituality. By these two ways we arrive at perfection according to the degree of purity we have attained, and in proportion to the fidelity with which we have co-operated with the movements of the Holy Spirit and followed His guidance.

Our perfection depends wholly on this fidelity, and we may say that the sum of the spiritual life consists in observing the ways and the movements of the Spirit of God in our soul, and in fortifying our will in the resolution of following them, employing for this purpose all the exercises of prayer, spiritual reading, sacraments, the practice of virtues and good works.

§ II.

Some exercise themselves in many commendable practices and perform a number of exterior acts of virtue; thus their attention is wholly given to the material action. This is well enough for beginners, but it belongs to a far higher perfection to follow the interior attraction of the Holy Spirit and be guided by His direction. It is true that this latter mode of acting yields less sensible satisfaction, but there is more of the interior spirit and of virtue in it.

§ III.

The end to which we ought to aspire, after having for a long time exercised ourselves in purity of heart, is to be so possessed and governed by the Holy Spirit that He alone shall direct all our powers and all our senses, and regulate all our movements, interior and exterior, while we, on our part, make a complete surrender of ourselves, by a spiritual renunciation of our own will and our own satisfaction. We shall thus no longer live in ourselves, but in Jesus Christ, by a faithful correspondence with the operations of His Divine Spirit, and by a perfect subjection of all our rebellious inclinations to the power of His grace.

§ IV.

Few persons attain the graces which God had destined for them, or, when they have lost them, succeed afterwards in repairing the loss. The majority lack the necessary courage to conquer themselves, and the fidelity to trade with advantage in the gifts of God.

When we enter on the path of virtue, we walk at first in darkness; but if we follow the leadings of grace faithfully and perseveringly, we shall infallibly attain a great light both for our own guidance and for that of others.

We wish to become saints in a day; we have not patience to await the ordinary course of grace. This proceeds from our pride and cowardice. Let us only be faithful in co-operating with the graces which God offers us, and He will not fail to lead us to the fulfilment of His designs.

§ v.

It is certain that our salvation in the Company, as in all other religious orders, depends absolutely on our interior correspondence with the guidance of the Spirit of God. Unless we follow our Lord with a perfect fidelity, we are in great danger of being lost, and it is impossible to say what harm we may do both to the Company and to the Church. Consider how many little attachments we have to venial sins! how many imperfections! how many designs and desires which are not in subjection to the movements of grace! how many useless thoughts do we every day revolve in our mind, not to mention thoughts of bitterness and vexation!

This hinders more than we can say the establishment of the kingdom of God within us, and is of infinite prejudice to our neighbour; because our Lord has made us His ministers of state, and has entrusted to us His Blood, His merits, His doctrine, the treasures of His graces; an office which, elevating us above the angelic nature, demands from us in the exercise of it the most perfect fidelity of which we are capable. And yet it is

...nishing to see with what negligence and unfaithfulness we discharge it.

§ VI.

But what is worst of all, is the opposition we make to the designs of God, and the resistance we offer to His inspirations; for either we do not wish to hear them, or we reject them when we have heard them, or, when we have received them, we weaken and impair them by a thousand imperfections of attachment to creatures, self-complacency, and self-satisfaction.

And yet the principal point in the spiritual life so entirely consists in disposing ourselves to grace by purity of life, that if two persons were to consecrate themselves to the service of God at the same time, and one were to devote himself wholly to good works, and the other to apply himself altogether to the purifying of his heart and to rooting out whatever within him was opposed to grace, the latter would attain to perfection twice as soon as the former.

Thus our greatest care should be, not so much to read spiritual books, as to pay great attention to divine inspirations, which are sufficient along with a little reading; and to be faithfully exact in corresponding with the graces which are offered us.

We should also frequently beg God to enable us to repair before we die all our past losses of grace, and to reach that height of merit, to which in His first intention He desired to lead us, which intention we have hitherto frustrated by our infidelities; finally, that He will forgive us those sins of which we have been the cause in others, and will also repair in them those losses of grace which they have incurred through our fault.

§ VII.

It sometimes happens that after receiving some good inspiration from God, we immediately find ourselves assailed by repugnances, doubts, perplexities, and difficulties, which proceed from our own corrupt interior, and from our passions, which are opposed to the divine inspiration. Did we receive it with an entire submission of heart, it would fill us with that peace and consolation which the Spirit of God brings with Him, and which He communicates to souls in which He meets with no resistance.

§ VIII.

The lights of grace come to us by degrees according to our interior disposition, and depart also in the same manner, leaving us in darkness. So that we have an alternation of day and night, and resemble in some wise the inhabitants of the polar regions, who have more or less of day in proportion as they are nearer to or farther removed from the pole. Now we ought to aspire after the enjoyment of a perpetual day; nor will it fail to shine into our soul, when, having thoroughly purified it, we shall continually follow the guidance of the Holy Spirit.

ARTICLE II.

There are but few perfect souls, because there are but few who follow the guidance of the Holy Spirit.

§ I.

The reason why we are so slow in arriving at perfection, or never arrive at it at all, is, that in almost every thing we are led by nature and human views. We follow but little, if at all, the guidance of the Holy Spirit, to whom it belongs to enlighten, direct, and animate.

The generality of religious, even of the good and virtuous, follow in the guidance of their own conduct, and in the direction of others, only reason and good sense; and in this many of them excel. The rule is a good one, but it is not sufficient in order to arrive at Christian perfection.

Such persons are guided ordinarily by the general opinion of those amongst whom they live; and as the latter are imperfect, although their life is not irregular, seeing that the number of the perfect is very small, they never attain to the sublime ways of the Spirit; they live like the generality, and their method of directing others is imperfect.

The Holy Spirit waits some time for them to enter into their own interior, and observing therein the operations of grace and those of nature, to dispose themselves to follow His guidance. But if they abuse the time and the favour He vouchsafes them, He abandons them at last to themselves, and leaves them in that darkness and that ignorance of their own interior which they have loved, and in which they henceforth live, amidst great perils to their salvation.

§ II.

We may say with truth that there are but very few who persevere constantly in the ways of God. Many wander from them perpetually; the Holy Spirit calls them back by His inspirations; but as they are intractable, full of themselves, attached to their own opinions, puffed up with their own wisdom, they do not readily let themselves be guided. They enter but seldom into the way of God's designs, and make no stay therein, returning to their own inventions and ideas, which deceive and delude them. Thus they make but little progress, and are surprised by death, having taken but twenty steps where they might have taken ten thousand, had they abandoned themselves to the guidance of the Holy Spirit.

On the other hand, truly interior persons who are guided by the light of the Spirit of God, for which they have disposed themselves by purity of heart, and which they follow with perfect submission, proceed at a giant's pace, and fly, so to say, in the ways of grace.

ARTICLE III.

The excellence of grace, and the injustice of the opposition we offer to it.

§ I.

We ought to receive every inspiration as a word of God, proceeding from His wisdom, His mercy, His infinite goodness, and capable of operating in us marvellous effects, if we put no obstacle in its way. Let us consider what one word of God has accomplished. It created the heaven and the earth, and drew all creatures out of nothingness to a participation in the existence of God in the state of nature, because it met with no resistance in nothingness. It would operate something more in us if we offered it no resistance. It would draw us out of our moral nothingness to a supernatural participation in the holiness of God in the state of grace, and to a participation in the beatitude of God in the state of glory. And for a little point of honour, for some office which gratifies our vanity, some little pleasure of a moment, a trifle, we prevent those great effects of God's word, of His inspirations and the impressions of His Spirit. After this, will you not confess that Wisdom was right in saying, " The number of the foolish is without end ?"

§ II.

If we could see in what way the inspirations of God are received in our souls, we should perceive that they remain, so to say, on the surface, without sinking any deeper ; the opposition they encounter in us preventing them from making their due impression. And this comes from our not giving ourselves up sufficiently to the Spirit, and not serving God with a perfect fulness of heart. Hence, in order for graces to produce their effect in the heart of sinners, they must enter in with noise and violence, because they meet with great resistance; but souls that are possessed by God they penetrate gently, filling them with that wonderful peace which always accompanies the Spirit of God. On the other hand, the suggestions of the enemy make no impression on good souls, because they find contrary principles ruling within them.

§ III.

One of our greatest evils is that we are so sensual, and so delighted with exterior things, that we esteem, we admire, we have a taste for nothing but what attracts attention and flatters our senses. And nevertheless, it is of faith that the least inspiration of God is a thing more precious and more excellent than all the whole world, seeing that it is of a supernatural order, and has cost the Blood and the Life of a God.

What a gross folly! we are insensible to the inspirations of God, because they are spiritual, and infinitely exalted above the senses. We make no account of them, we prefer before them our natural talents, occupations of distinction, the esteem of men, our own little conveniences and satisfactions. Monstrous illusion! of which, nevertheless, many are undeceived only at the hour of death.

§ IV.

We do great wrong to God in two ways. First, in that we confess, with truth, that we have need of the Holy Spirit and of His assistance, and yet take from Him the direction of our soul, and wish to manage His graces our own way, without depending on His holy guidance both in the use of them and in the conduct of our interior life. This is to usurp the rights of the Holy Spirit, and to arrogate to ourselves His office; for to Him alone it belongs to guide souls. Secondly, in that our inmost soul being destined for God only, we fill it with creatures to His prejudice; and instead of dilating and enlarging it indefinitely by the presence of God, we straiten it exceedingly by occupying it with a few wretched nonentities. This is what prevents our attaining to perfection.

ARTICLE IV.

The Holy Spirit exercises the office of comforter to faithful souls.

St. Athanasius remarks that throughout the Old Testament there is no mention made of the Holy Spirit under the name of Comforter, *Paraclitus*. The reason is declared in these words of our Lord: " If I go not, the Paraclete will not come to you: but if I go, I will send Him to you." It was necessary that the Incarnate Word should enter into glory, before He sent the Holy Spirit as Comforter.

The interior comfort which the Holy Spirit bestows is much more profitable than the bodily presence of the Son of God would have been. Therefore He said to His disciples, " It is expedient to you that I go."

The Holy Spirit comforts us especially in three things:

First, in the uncertainty of our salvation, which is terribly great, since all our senses, interior and exterior, all our powers, all our passions, all our actions, are to us principles of eternal condemnation.

This is one of the truths of faith, because without grace, in the state of corrupted nature in which we live, all is vicious within us, and most of our actions are bad and often damnable. Besides, all the objects which present themselves to us from without are allurements to sin; riches, honours, pleasures, all are full of snares.

Add to this, that we cannot merit final perseverance ; if the guidance and protection of God be wanting to us, as they were to Solomon and Tertullian, we shall perish like them. It is this uncertainty that has made Saints tremble. But in this affliction the Holy Spirit comforts us, being " the Spirit of adoption of the sons of God," and, as St. Paul says, "the pledge and assurance of the heavenly inheritance ;" a soul is rarely lost which has once received this pledge and enjoyed some experimental knowledge of God. The Holy Spirit bears inward witness to fervent and faithful souls, of what they are to God and what God is to them ; and this witness banishes their fear and forms their consolation.

Secondly, the Holy Spirit comforts us in the temptations of the devil, and in the contradictions and distresses of this life. The unction which He pours into souls animates them, fortifies them, aids them to win the victory; it sweetens their troubles, and makes them find their delight in crosses.

Thirdly, the Holy Spirit comforts us while we live in the Church here below absent from God. This is the cause of inconceivable torment to holy souls ; for feeling in themselves this, as it were, infinite void, which we all have in us and which all creatures are unable to fill, which cannot be filled but by the fruition of God,—these poor souls, so long as they are separated from Him, languish and suffer a prolonged martyrdom, which would be intolerable to them without the consolations which the Holy Spirit gives them from time to time. All such consolations as come from creatures serve only to increase the weight of their miseries. " I am bold to affirm," says Richard of St. Victor, "that a single drop of these divine consolations can effect more than all the pleasures of the world together. These latter cannot satisfy the heart ; and a single drop of that interior sweetness which the Holy Spirit pours into the soul, ravishes it out of itself, and causes it a holy inebriation.

CHAPTER III.

OF THE GIFTS OF THE HOLY SPIRIT IN GENERAL.

ARTICLE I.

Of the nature of the gifts of the Holy Spirit.

§ I.

SANCTIFYING grace requires many other qualities, both for its preservation and for action. These qualities are the theological virtues, the gifts of the Holy Spirit, the supernatural or infused moral virtues, the fruits of the Holy Spirit, the beatitudes, the moral virtues, natural or acquired.

The theological virtues hold the first rank, because they have direct reference to God, and unite us immediately to Him.

The gifts of the Holy Spirit come next after the theological virtues, because they are, as it were, their fulfilment, and serve to make them operate in a more excellent manner.

The supernatural moral virtues are inferior to the gifts of the Holy Spirit, because they dispose the soul only to the performance of ordinary good works; whereas the gifts dispose it to perform extraordinary actions.

The fruits of the Holy Spirit are nothing else than infused virtues, when we arrive at exercising them not only without pain or repugnance, but with joy and pleasure.

When these same virtues are fully developed, and have become perfect acts, they are called beatitudes.

The natural moral virtues hold the last place, because they perfect the soul only according to reason and not according to faith, and because they can be separated from sanctifying grace.

§ II.

The gifts of the Holy Spirit are habits, or permanent qualities, which God communicates to the soul together with sanctifying grace and the infused virtues, to fortify the natural powers, and to render them responsive to the movements of His Divine Spirit, and capable of exercising those acts of virtue, the most difficult and most noble, which are called heroic. There are seven gifts of the Holy Spirit; the gift of wisdom, which is the first in dignity, and the gifts of understanding, science, counsel, piety, fortitude, and the fear of God.

The first four enlighten and perfect the understanding; the last three perfect the will and the interior appetite. The gift of understanding is given us that we may penetrate more intimately into the truths of faith; the gift of wisdom, that we may perceive their causes and their fitnesses; the gift of knowledge, that we may judge correctly of human things; the gift of counsel, to direct the actions of a lively faith; the gifts of piety, fortitude, and fear, to bring the appetite into harmony with the reason illuminated with so many lights; piety, to soften our harshness towards others; fortitude, to strengthen us against our own weaknesses and cowardice; fear, to repress our pride and the irregularities of concupiscence.

§ III.

Isaias arranges the gifts of the Holy Spirit in excellent order; he joins together wisdom and understanding, because the one serves to dispose us for the other. The understanding penetrates divine things, to dispose the soul to relish them by wisdom. He joins together counsel and fortitude, because counsel is necessary for the direction of fortitude, which without it would be rashness. He joins together knowledge and piety, because knowledge without piety is dry and barren; and he assigns to fear the last place, as the base and foundation of all the other gifts.

§ IV.

Faith is not to be compared in excellence with gifts, because they contain it and are its perfection.

Faith is made perfect by the gifts of knowledge, understanding, and wisdom, which enable us to see distinctly and with more unction and relish what by faith we discern only obscurely and with repugnance. In this manner it is that truths and extraordinary knowledge are imparted in visions.

§ V.

Gifts do not subsist in the soul without charity, and in proportion as grace increases, they increase also. Hence it is that they are so very rare, and that they never attain a high degree of excellence without a fervent and perfect charity; venial sins and the slightest imperfections keeping them, as it were, bound down and preventing them from acting. Thus the way to excel in prayer is to excel in these gifts; and indeed the most sublime contemplation is scarcely any thing different, for it is by penetrating deeply into supernatural knowledge that the soul falls into ecstasy and swoons away.

ARTICLE II.

Of the effects of the gifts of the Holy Spirit.

§ I.

We have four kinds of lights to direct us in our actions. First, reason; which is very weak, and is not sufficient by itself to conduct us to our end. Some have compared it to *ignes fatui*, which shine in the night a little above the ground, and lead the traveller straight to rivers and precipices; for, after all, human reason unenlightened by faith is but a low thing, and can conduct us only to our ruin.

Secondly, faith; which, by attaching us to supreme truth, supplies us with a safe guidance secure from error.

Thirdly, supernatural prudence; which, being added to faith, makes us choose those supernatural means which are the most useful for attaining a supernatural end.

Fourthly, the gifts of the Holy Spirit; which, by principles more exalted, without reasoning, without perplexity, shew us what is best, enabling us to discern it in the light of God with more or less of evidence, according to the degree in which we possess Him.

§ II.

We may compare those who are led by the gifts of the Holy Spirit to a vessel running full-sail before the wind; and those who are led by virtues, not as yet by gifts, to a shallop propelled by oars with more labour and noise, and at much less speed.

§ III.

Those great conversions of kings and princes which excite admiration are the effects of the gifts of the Holy Spirit. God sometimes communicates to them efficacious impulses so powerful as to lead them to forsake all, and dedicate themselves to the cross. Such graces must needs be very strong to break so many attachments at a blow. This happens to them particularly at times when they meet with reverses, or on other occasions which Providence orders in their favour.

§ IV.

It is by the gifts of the Holy Spirit that Saints succeed at last in freeing themselves from the slavery of creatures; the plenteous effusion of these heavenly gifts effacing from the mind the esteem, the remembrance, the thought of earthly things, and banishing from the heart all affection and desire for them, so that they think, as it were, only of what they will, and are affected only by what they will, and in such degree as they will. They feel no longer the importunity of distractions, nor that disquietude and excitement which troubled them before; and all their powers being perfectly regulated, they enjoy a sovereign peace and the liberty of the children of God.

§ V.

We who as yet do not partake so abundantly of the gifts of the Holy Spirit must labour and toil in the practice of virtue. We are like those who make way by dint of rowing against wind and tide; a day will come, if it please God, when, having received the gifts of the Holy Spirit, we shall speed full-sail before the wind; for it is the Holy Spirit who by His gifts disposes the soul to yield itself easily to His divine inspirations. With the assistance of the gifts of the Holy Spirit, Saints reach such a height of perfection, as to accomplish without labour things of which we should not venture so much as to think; the Holy Spirit smoothing away all their difficulties, and enabling them to surmount every obstacle.

§ VI.

There is a great difference between the intelligence of a child and reason; between reason and faith; between an ordinary faith and that which is enlightened by the gifts of the Holy Spirit, or sublime contemplation. There is a still greater difference between such knowledge as we have in this life and that which we shall have in a state of separation from the body; and this again differs still more widely, beyond all comparison, from that of the blessed souls in heaven and of the lost souls in hell.

In childhood we know neither God, nor the immortality of our soul, nor the eternity of rewards and punishments. By reason we may learn something of these truths; by faith we know them with certainty; by the gifts of the Holy Spirit we touch them and taste them, but still indistinctly. In the state of separated souls we shall see them, as it were, unveiled. In heaven or in hell we shall have a clear evidence of them, a full experience for ever. Alas, what are we amusing ourselves with, and what pleasure can we take in the things of earth!

§ VII.

We should do well to accustom ourselves to notice in the Gospel the gifts of the Holy Spirit, and the actions which our Lord performed in accordance with these principles. The parables belong to the understanding. The discourse which Jesus Christ addressed to His disciples after the supper belongs to the gift of wisdom.

Any one illuminated, in however small a degree, by the divine light might easily discern in the records of Holy Scripture, in the Gospels, in the Acts of the Apostles, a sovereign wisdom in the conduct of the narrative; for the Holy Spirit mentions precisely what ought to be mentioned, omits what ought to be omitted, details at length what ought to be so detailed, agreeably to His own intention. In profane histories, on the contrary, it is easy to detect error of judgment, or corruption of heart and malicious design, on the part of the author. Falsehoods are blended with truth. Passion often predominates; and we may compare them to waters that are muddy and infected with the pestilential nature of the soil through which they have passed. It is in Holy Scripture alone that truth is to be found always pure and free from mixture at its source.

ARTICLE III.

Whence it comes that the gifts of the Holy Spirit produce so little effect in souls.

§ I.

It is asked, why the generality of religious and of devout persons who lead a tepid life form so few acts of the gifts of the Holy Spirit, since, as they are in a state of grace, they possess them.

The answer is, that this proceeds from their keeping them, as it were, bound down by contrary habits and affections, and that the numerous venial sins which they commit every day shut out those graces which are necessary in order to produce acts of the gifts of the Holy Spirit. God refuses them the succour of His graces, because He foresees that if He bestowed them upon them in their present disposition, they would be of no use to them, their will being held bound with a thousand chains which would prevent their yielding their consent.

When we have lived a long time in such tepidity, performing at the same time, nevertheless, many good works, the way of escaping from it is to cultivate purity of heart; this is the surest road. The devil lays no snares therein, for it is impossible he should prompt souls to purify themselves.

Let us apply ourselves in earnest and without intermission to this holy exercise, with a will determined to refuse God nothing which He asks of us in order to lead us to a higher perfection; thus should we be the sooner delivered from those chains which render the precious gifts of the Holy Spirit within us of no avail, and shall behold ourselves enriched with their fulness.

§ II.

It is astonishing to see so many religious, who, after having lived in a state of grace some forty or fifty years, saying Mass every day, and practising all the holy exercises of the religious life, and consequently possessing the gifts of the Holy Spirit in a very high physical degree, and corresponding with that sort of perfection in grace which theologians call *gradual* or physical increase,—it is astonishing, I say, to see these religious displaying nothing of the gifts of the Holy Spirit in their actions and in their conduct; their life is wholly natural; when they are blamed or disobliged, they shew their resentment at it; they exhibit so much eagerness for the praises, the esteem, and the applauses of the world; they take so much pleasure in them, and are so fond of their own comfort, and seek it so carefully, as well as every thing that flatters self-love.

There is no ground for astonishment in all this: the venial sins which they continually commit keep the gifts of the Holy Spirit tied up, as it were; so that it is no wonder that the effects are not visible in them. True it is that these gifts increase, like charity, habitually and in their physical being, but not actually, and in that perfection which answers to the fervour of charity, and adds to our merit; because venial sins being opposed to the fervour of charity, consequently prevent the operation of the gifts of the Holy Spirit.

If these religious cultivated purity of heart, the fervour of charity would increase in them more and more, and the gifts of the Holy Spirit would shine out in their whole conduct. But while they live in this way, without recollection or attention to their own interior, letting themselves follow the bent of their own inclinations, avoiding only the most grievous sins and neglecting little things, these gifts will never be very manifest in them.

It is past all conception, says St. Lawrence Justinian, how our heart becomes filled with sins unless we take care to be continually cleansing it. It is a filthy ditch, which always requires emptying. The most spiritual and most perfect are not free from this defect, but ever feel the infirmities and wounds of corrupted nature, which are never entirely cured.

§ III.

The reason why we are so little illuminated by the lights of the Holy Spirit, and so little guided by the motions of His gifts, is, that our soul is sensual beyond measure, and full of a multitude of earthly thoughts, desires, and affections, which extinguish within us the Spirit of God. Few give themselves wholly to God, and abandon themselves to the leadings of the Holy Spirit, so that He alone may live in them and be the principle of all their actions.

§ IV.

As all who are in a state of grace possess the gifts of the Holy Spirit, they sometimes make acts of the same; but it is only, as it were, in passing, and so rapidly that they are scarcely aware of them. Thus they remain ever in the same state, without sharing the bounty of the Holy Spirit, owing to the opposition He meets with in them.

CHAPTER IV.

OF THE GIFTS OF THE HOLY SPIRIT IN DETAIL.

ARTICLE I.

Of the gift of wisdom.

WISDOM is defined to be a knowledge acquired by first principles; for "the name *sapientia*, wisdom, comes from *sapor*, savour; and as it is the property of the taste to distinguish the flavour of viands, so," says St. Isidore, "wisdom, that is, the knowledge that we have of creatures by the first principle, and of second causes by the first cause, is a sure rule for judging rightly of every thing."

The gift of wisdom is such knowledge of God, His attributes and mysteries, as is full of flavour. The understanding only conceives and penetrates. Wisdom judges and compares; it enables us to see causes, reasons, fitnesses: it represents to us God, His greatness, His beauty, His perfections, His mysteries, as infinitely adorable and worthy of love; and from this knowledge there results a delicious taste, which sometimes even extends to the body, and is greater or less according to the state of perfection and purity to which the soul has attained.

St. Francis was so filled with this taste of wisdom, that in pronouncing the name of God or the name of Jesus, he experienced in his mouth and on his lips a taste a thousand times sweeter far than honey and sugar.

Thus it is to the gift of wisdom that spiritual sweetnesses and consolations and sensible graces belong. They are the effects of this gift; but when they are produced only in the inferior part of the soul, they may proceed from the devil, especially in such as are not perfectly purified.

There is this difference between wisdom and science, that the latter does not ordinarily produce that spiritual taste which the former communicates to the soul. The reason is, that science regards only creatures, although in reference to God ; but wisdom looks at God Himself, the knowledge of whom is full of attractions and sweetness. This also proceeds from charity, the perfection or fervour of which is the health of the soul ; for when the soul is once thoroughly healed of its infirmities and languors, and is in perfect health, it tastes God and divine things as though they were its own proper goods, without feeling the repugnances, disgusts, and difficulties, which it experienced heretofore on account of its weakness.

This taste of wisdom is sometimes so perfect that a person who is possessed of it, on hearing two propositions, the one formed by reasoning, the other inspired by God, will at once distinguish between the two, recognising that which comes from God by a certain natural relation, as it were, between itself and its object, " *per quandam objecti connaturalitatem,*" as St. Thomas says; pretty much in the same way as one who has eaten sugar, afterwards easily distinguishes the taste of sugar from that of other sweet things, or as a sick man knows the symptoms of his disorder by his experience and sensations as well as the physician does by his knowledge.

At first, divine things are insipid, and it is with difficulty we can relish them, but in course of time they become sweet, and so full of delicious flavour, that we taste them with pleasure, even to the extent of feeling nothing but disgust for every thing else. On the other hand, the things of earth, which flatter the senses, are at first pleasant and delicious, but in the end we find only bitterness in them.

A soul which, by mortification, is thoroughly cured of its passions, and by purity of heart is established in a state of perfect health, is admitted to a wonderful knowledge of God, and discovers things so great, that it loses its power of acting through its senses. Hence proceed raptures and ecstacies, which indicate, however, by the impression which they produce in those who have them, that they are not altogether purified or accustomed to extraordinary graces; for in proportion as a soul purifies itself, the mind becomes stronger and more capable of bearing divine operations without emotion or suspension of the senses, as in the case of our Lord and the Blessed Virgin, the Apostles, and certain other Saints, whose minds were continually occupied with the most sublime contemplations, united with wonderful interior transports, but without there being any thing apparent externally in the way of raptures and ecstasies.

As there are persons so wicked that they seem to have no taste but for evil, committing it in sheer wantonness of heart and for the mere sake of the pleasure they take in doing evil, which is the height of iniquity and the true mark of folly, according to St. Bernard; so there are souls so good that they have no taste but for what is good, and act in all things from no other motive but that of good. Goodness is itself the attraction that leads them to do good; and this is the peculiar effect of wisdom, which so fills the soul with a taste for goodness and the love of virtue, that it no longer feels any thing but disgust for other objects. A taste for what is good comes, as it were, naturally to it. St. Bernard admirably sets forth this doctrine in one of his sermons on the Canticles. "Wisdom," he says, "is the love of virtue; it is nothing else but a relish for what is good: when it enters into a soul, it overpowers the malice it finds there, and expels the taste for evil which malice had introduced into it, filling the soul with the savour of good which it ever brings with it. No sooner has it been admitted than it deadens the carnal feelings, purifies the understanding, rectifies the corrupt taste of the heart, and restores to the soul perfect health, which capacitates it for relishing the savour of goodness and of wisdom itself, which of all good things is the sweetest and the most excellent.

The vice opposed to wisdom is folly, which, after its kind, is formed in the soul in the same manner as wisdom, but by contrary principles; for wisdom refers every thing to the last end, which in morals is called the *altissima causa*, the supreme and primary cause. It is this it seeks, this it follows and relishes in all things. It judges of every thing by reference to this sovereign end. In like manner, folly takes as its end, its first principle, its *altissima causa*, either honour, or pleasure, or some other temporal good, having a taste for nothing else, and referring every thing thereto, seeking and valuing only that, and despising every thing else.

"The fool and the wise man are opposed one to the other," says St. Isidore, "inasmuch as the latter is possessed of the taste and the sense of discretion, in which the former is wanting." And this is why, as St. Thomas observes, "the one judges rightly of things that regard conduct, because he judges of them by reference to the first principle and the last end; and the other judges ill, because he does not take this sovereign cause as the rule of his sentiments and actions."

The world is full of this sort of folly, and the wise man declares that "the number of fools is without end."

In fact, the generality of mankind have a depraved taste, and they may justly be called fools, because they act like fools, placing their last end, at least practically, in the creature and not in God. Each has some object to which he is attached, and to which he refers every thing, entertaining neither affection nor passion except in connexion with it; and this is to be a fool indeed.

Would we know if we are of the number of wise men or fools, let us examine our tastes and distastes, either with respect to God and divine things, or with respect to creatures and the things of earth. Whence spring our satisfactions and our dissatisfactions? Wherein does our heart find its repose and its contentment?

This sort of examination is an excellent means of acquiring purity of heart. We ought to familiarise ourselves with the practice, examining our likings and dislikings frequently during the day, and trying little by little to refer them to God.

There are three sorts of wisdom condemned in Scripture, which are so many veritable follies. *Terrena*, earthly wisdom, when a man has no taste but for riches; *animalis*, sensual wisdom, when he has no taste but for bodily pleasures; *diabolica*, devilish wisdom, when he has no taste but for his own superiority.

There is a folly which is true wisdom before God. To love poverty, contempt, crosses, persecutions; this is to be a fool according to the world's esteem. And yet wisdom, which is a gift of the Holy Spirit, is nothing else but this same folly which has a taste only for what our Lord and the Saints delighted in. Now Jesus Christ, in every thing that He touched during His mortal life, as poverty, abjection, the cross, left a sweet odour, a delicious savour; but few souls have their senses sufficiently purified to perceive this odour and to taste this savour, which are altogether supernatural. The Saints have "run after the odour of these ointments," like a St. Ignatius, who took delight in seeing himself made a mock of; a St. Francis, who so passionately loved abjection, that he performed actions for the purpose of making himself ridiculous; a St. Dominic, who was more gratified at Carcassonne, where he was generally insulted, than at Toulouse, where he was honoured by all the world.

What taste had our Lord and the Blessed Virgin and the Apostles for the glories of the world and the pleasures of life? "My meat," said Jesus Christ, "is to do the will of Him that sent Me." The Apostles "went from the presence of the council rejoicing that they were accounted worthy to suffer reproach for the name of Jesus." "I please myself in my infirmities, in reproaches," says St. Paul.

To say that our Lord, when He might have redeemed us without suffering, when He might have merited every thing which He did merit for us without dying a death so infamous as the death of the cross, nevertheless chose the death of the cross for our salvation, is a folly according to human reason. But that which seems folly in God is wiser than the wisdom of all mankind.

How unlike are the judgments of God to the judgments of men! Divine wisdom is a folly in the judgment of men, and human wisdom is folly in the judgment of God. It is for us to see to which of these two judgments we will conform our own. One or the other we must take as the rule of our actions.

If we have a taste for praises and honours, so far we are fools; and the more relish we have for being esteemed and honoured, the more foolish we are. As, on the contrary, the more love we have for humiliation and the cross, the wiser we are.

It is monstrous that even in religion there should be found persons who have no taste for any thing but what makes them of importance in the eyes of the world; who do all their actions, for the twenty or thirty years of their religious life, only that they may attain some end which they have in view; who scarcely feel either joy or sadness except with reference thereto, or at least are more affected by that than by any thing else. As for all that regards God and perfection, it is insipid to them; they feel no relish for it.

This is a fearful state, and worthy of being deplored with tears of blood. For of what perfection are such religious capable? And what fruit can they gather from their labours among others? But, oh! what confusion will be theirs at the hour of death, when it shall be disclosed to them that, during the whole course of their life, they have neither sought nor relished any thing but show and vanity, like people of the world. Let such persons be ever so melancholy, only utter a word which gives them a hope of some advancement, however false it may be, and you will instantly see a change come over their countenance, and their heart expand with joy as at the news of some great success.

For the rest, as they have no taste for devotion, they treat its practices as follies, the amusement of weak minds, and not only guide their conduct by these erroneous principles of an earthly and devilish wisdom, but communicate their sentiments also to others, teaching them maxims altogether contrary to those of our Lord and the Gospel, the rigour of which they try to soften by forced interpretations that fall in with the inclinations of corrupt nature; supporting themselves by other passages of Scripture ill understood, on which they build their own ruin; as for example, "*curam habe de bono nomine*, be careful of your reputation;" "*corporalis exercitatio ad modicum valet*, bodily exercise is profitable to little;" "*rationabile obsequium vestrum*, let your service to God be a reasonable service," &c.

Now God, by an admirable disposition of His providence, ordained that St. Ignatius should be possessed of that wisdom for which he is famous throughout the world, and that even such as we have been describing should loudly proclaim it, in order that, having been also so devoted and signal a lover of poverty, contempt, and the cross, and having so strongly recommended the love of these things to his children, he might have the right one day to condemn and judge the guilty, shewing them how far they have strayed from the path of true wisdom.

The beatitude which answers to the gift of wisdom is the seventh : " Blessed are the peace-makers;" whether because wisdom orders every thing according to God, and peace consists in this good order ; or because wisdom causes us to be no longer affected by things which would naturally disturb the mind. Use insulting language to one who possesses this gift, he is careless about it, he does not even give it a thought : as those who are fools from natural imbecility are insensible to insults, and such things as most affect other people, because they are deprived of reason and judgment ; in like manner, they who are wise with a supernatural wisdom are insensible to the ill treatment they meet with, and undisturbed by any human thing, not out of stupidity, but from a higher order of reason, which, owing to the habit they have acquired of relishing nothing but the sovereign good, causes them to have no longer any taste for temporal goods, or any sense of temporal evils.

The fruit of the Holy Spirit which answers to the gift of wisdom is that of faith ; because the soul relishing divine things cleaves more firmly to the belief of them, and the sort of experimental knowledge which it thus obtains serves it as a kind of evidence of their reality.

ARTICLE II.

Of the gift of understanding.

Understanding is the intimate knowledge of an object: *intelligere est intus legere.*

The gift of understanding is a light which the Holy Spirit bestows, in order to penetrate intimately those obscure truths which faith proposes; and this penetration, says St. Thomas, must cause the mind to conceive a true idea and a right judgment of the last end and of every thing which has reference thereto, otherwise it would not be a gift of the Holy Spirit.

Faith contemplates three kinds of objects. 1st, God and His mysteries; 2dly, creatures in their relations to God; 3dly, our own actions to direct them to the service of God. We are naturally very obtuse with regard to all these things, and know nothing rightly about them, except as we are illuminated by the Holy Spirit through faith, and through the other lights which He communicates to us.

That which faith makes us simply believe, the gift of understanding enables us to penetrate more clearly, and in such a manner as, although the obscurity of faith still remains, appears to render evident what faith teaches; so that he who possesses it marvels that some refuse to believe the articles of our belief, or that they can doubt of them.

They whose office it is to instruct others, preachers and directors, ought to be filled with this gift. It has been conspicuous in fathers and doctors, and it is especially necessary for rightly comprehending the sense of Holy Scripture, its allegorical figures and the ceremonies of divine worship.

Holy Scripture is difficult to understand, because God therein speaks His own thoughts, which are infinitely removed from ours; but He tempers them in such wise that by purity of heart we are able to understand them. St. John, for example, says in his first epistle, "It is the last hour;" this is repugnant to our ideas, and we cannot comprehend how the holy Apostle could say, speaking of his own time, that it was at its last hour. It is true, however, in the mind of God.

All other spiritual books speak the language partly of grace and partly of nature. The frequent reading of Holy Scripture is a means of receiving the Holy Spirit and of being guided by His direction.

It is a great mistake to read spiritual books so much and Holy Scripture so little. St. Gregory Nazianzen, who is the only one among the Fathers whose works are free from errors which have been condemned by the Church, and St. Basil, whose doctrine is remarkable for its solidity, for eleven or twelve years read nothing but Scripture. We ought to read it even in preference to the Fathers, and so much the more, because by purity of heart we enter gradually into the various meanings which it contains; and although we may have read it through a hundred times, yet if we still make progress in purity of heart and persevere in the study of it, we shall penetrate its mysteries continually more and more.

Scripture, besides the four senses which the Holy Spirit directly intended, viz. the *literal*, which is the sense of the words taken in their proper signification; the *tropological*, or moral, which has respect to morals; the *allegorical*, which regards Jesus Christ and the Church militant; the *anagogica* which regards the Church triumphant and the state o the blessed,—Holy Scripture, I say, besides these four senses, will bear also a fifth, which is called the *accommodated* sense, in which use is made of some sentence or some words of

Scripture to express a meaning which it is plain that it was not the Holy Spirit's object to convey by the words of the sacred text. St. Bernard often takes Scripture in this sense; and they who find much sweetness in the Word of God are extremely fond of expressions of this sort. St. Jerome possessed the gift of understanding particularly for the literal sense; St. Gregory for the moral; St. Ambrose and St. Augustine for the allegorical.

This gift is of use also in political matters for discovering the designs of God therein, as, for example, perceiving that the crown of France remained in the house of St. Louis in reward for his zeal in quitting his kingdom to extend that of Jesus Christ in the East.

It was told St. Louis that it was not for his interest to make peace between the princes his neighbours as he was doing; but he, endued with that penetration which the gift of understanding bestows, knew clearly that God, who governs all things by His providence, would give peace to his own realm, if he succeeded in securing it in those of other princes. And in fact France enjoyed peace as by miracle during the time of the imprisonment of the holy king in Egypt and his death before Tunis.

When Louis XIII. undertook the war of Bearn against the heretics, politicians declared that it was a dangerous enterprise in the cause of foreigners. But persons who were enlightened by the gift of understanding discerned in the designs of the king the counsel of God, who would subdue the pride of heresy, and reduce rebels to lawful obedience.

People commonly speak with much inconsideration on affairs of state. It would be well to speak neither for nor against without supernatural light. We may be guilty of two faults in this: one, of approving and commending certain things from passion; the other, of condemning and blaming them rashly.

As, for example, when Catholic princes form alliances with heretics, either we favour too much the side of these heretical allies, and speak too advantageously of their successes, which gives occasion to many scruples and sins; or we disapprove in our governors certain actions which are done in the interest of these same allies; which is the result of false zeal, instead of considering that God may draw hence great and good results which are hidden from us. It is better not to censure such conduct on the part of princes and their ministers in any way; but rather to leave it to God to act, and await with patience and in silence the issue of things which His providence will know how to turn to His own glory.

The vice which is opposed to the gift of understanding is dulness in respect to spiritual things. This vice is natural; and we increase it still more by our sins, our passions, and irregular affections. It is palpably perceptible in such persons as are in mortal sin. David was possessed of a heart excellently framed for loving God. He had imbibed an admirable knowledge and lofty ideas of God. Nevertheless, after his adultery, after his having procured the death of Urias, he was nine months without coming to his senses, and perhaps his eyes would never have been opened, had not God sent to him the prophet Nathan to represent to him his evil state.

The beatitude which answers to this gift is the sixth: " Blessed are the clean of heart." This purity, says St. Thomas, extends to all the powers of the soul, banishing thence every thing that can excite the passions and the disorderly movements of the appetite, the vicious affections of the will, the errors and false maxims of the intellect. It even regulates the imagination, in such a way that no thought comes into the mind except at its proper time and place, and lasts only so long as is necessary for the action to be performed. Thus St. Bernard, when about to pray, dismissed all thoughts of other occupations, and resumed them afterwards when his prayer was concluded. This is the case with souls that are truly pure. They have acquired by their purity this perfect dominion over themselves.

The fruit of the Holy Spirit which corresponds with this gift, as well as with the others which enlighten the mind, is the fruit of faith. Faith precedes gifts, and is their foundation; but gifts, in turn, perfect faith. We must first believe, says St. Augustine, and establish ourselves firmly in that pious affection which is so necessary to faith. Then the gifts of the Holy Spirit come, and render faith more penetrating, more lively, and more perfect.

ARTICLE III.

Of the gift of science.

Science is defined to be an assured knowledge acquired by reasoning; but in God it is without reasoning, and by a simple view of objects.

The gift of science, which is a participation in the knowledge of God, is a light of the Holy Spirit which illuminates the soul to understand human things, and to form a true judgment of them in reference to God and so far as they are the objects of faith.

The gift of science assists that of understanding in discovering and comprehending obscure truths, and that of wisdom in possessing them.

Wisdom and science have something in common; both bestow the knowledge of God and of creatures. But when we know God by means of creatures, and rise from the knowledge of second causes to the First Universal Cause, it is an act of science; when we know human things through the experience we have of God, and judge of created beings by the knowledge we possess of the Supreme Being, it is an act of wisdom.

The discerning of spirits belongs to both one and the other; but wisdom possesses it by the way of taste and experience, which is a more exalted mode of information; science possesses it by simple knowledge alone. The gift of science enables us to see readily and clearly every thing that regards our own conduct and that of others.

First, what we ought to believe or not believe; what we ought to do or not do; the mean we ought to observe between the two extremes into which it is possible for us to fall in the exercise of virtues; the order we ought to follow in our study of them; how much time we must give to each in particular: but all this in the general, for as regards details, it belongs to the gift of counsel to prescribe what we ought to do under the circumstances in which we find ourselves, and on occasions when we have to determine how to act.

Secondly, the state of our soul, our interior acts, the secret movements of our heart, their qualities, their goodness, their malice, their principles, their motives, their ends and their intentions, their effects and their consequences, their merit and demerit.

Thirdly, the judgment we ought to form of creatures, and the use we ought to make of them in the interior and supernatural life; how frail they are and vain, how short-lived, how little capable of making us happy, how injurious and dangerous to salvation.

Fourthly, the mode of conversing and dealing with our neighbour, as respects the supernatural end of our creation. By this gift a preacher knows what he ought to say to his hearers, and what he ought to urge upon them. A director knows the state of the souls he has under his guidance, their spiritual needs, the remedies for their faults, the obstacles they put in the way of their perfection, the shortest and the surest road by which to conduct them safely; how he must console or mortify them, what God is working in them, and what they ought to do on their part in order to co-operate with God and fulfil His designs. A superior knows in what way he ought to govern his inferiors.

They who have the largest share of the gift of science are the most enlightened in all knowledge of this kind. Wonderful things are disclosed to them with respect to the practice of virtues. They discover therein degrees of perfection unknown to others. They perceive at a glance whether actions are inspired by God and conformable to His designs; let them deviate ever so little from the ways of God, they discern it at once. They remark imperfections where others cannot see them; they are not liable to be deceived in their opinions, neither are they apt to allow themselves to be surprised by illusions with which the whole world is filled. If a scrupulous soul applies to them, they know what to say to remove its scruples. If they have to make an exhortation, whether to monks or to nuns, thoughts will occur to them suited both to the spiritual needs of the religious themselves, and to the spirit of their order. If difficulties of conscience are proposed to them, they will give an admirable solution. Ask them for the reason of their reply, they cannot tell you, because they know it without reasoning, by a light superior to all reason.

By this gift it was that St. Vincent Ferrer preached with that wonderful success which we read of in his life. He abandoned himself to the Holy Spirit as well in preparing his sermons as in delivering them, and every body went away deeply affected. It was easy to see that the Holy Spirit animated him, and spoke by his mouth. One day that he had to preach before a prince, he thought he must use more study and more human diligence in the preparation of his sermon. He applied himself thereto with extraordinary pains; but neither the prince nor the audience generally were as satisfied with this studied discourse as they were with that of the next day, which he composed in his ordinary way, according to the movement of the Spirit of God. His attention was called to the difference between the two sermons. "Yesterday," said he, "it was brother Vincent that preached; to-day it was the Holy Spirit."

Every preacher must keep himself in entire dependence on the Spirit of God. The chief preparation for the pulpit is prayer and purity of heart. Sometimes God keeps you in expectation a while in order to try you; but grow not weary of waiting for Him. Use all due diligence on your part, and for the rest put your trust in God; He will come in the end, and will not fail to shed His light upon you. You will perceive its effects, and will sometimes see that by a single suggestion He will make you say things admirably calculated to benefit your hearers.

A religious is troubled with scruples or temptations against his vocation. The cause of his uneasiness is some secret sin of which he is neglecting to correct himself, and although God is urgent with him and offers him His grace, he continues in his evil habit, and his temptation as well as his uneasiness never ceases. By the gift of science the cause of this is discovered.

It is by the light of this gift that we know what creatures are in themselves, and what they have from God. By this light it was that St. Paul "counted all earthly things but as dung." Men do not commonly thus judge of them, because they consider in them only that which flatters the senses. Thus it is that almost all the world lets itself be beguiled by their deceitful appearance, and every one is eager to enjoy the satisfaction which they promise. Every one wishes to taste them, and few are they who perceive their error before they die. Most of the Saints even have at one time been deceived by them.

We are so full of illusions and so little on our guard against the fascinations of creatures, that we deceive ourselves continually. The devil deceives us also very frequently. His device for entrapping the more advanced is to make them fall into error in their choice of the means of perfection; and he deceives the least perfect and the tepid, by presenting difficulties to their minds in an exaggerated shape, and by displaying before their eyes the attractions of pleasure and the false brilliancy of vain honours. The science of the Holy Spirit teaches us how to preserve ourselves from these seductions.

Happy they whom God favours with this rare gift, like Jacob, of whom the wise man says: "God imparted to him the science of the Saints." We ourselves, above all, have need of it, who, by the duty of our vocation are obliged to mix in the world. This gift of science is much more necessary to us than to solitaries and other religious, whose life is more retired and purely contemplative.

In order that intercourse with men may not be hurtful to us, in the functions which we exercise in their regard to gain them to God, we must observe that our life ought to be a mixture of action and contemplation, in such wise that the former may be animated, directed, and ordered by the latter; that among the exterior works of the active life, we may always enjoy the interior repose of the contemplative; and that our employment may not hinder our union with God, but rather serve to bind us more closely and more lovingly to Him; making us embrace them in Him by contemplation, and in our neighbour by action.

We shall enjoy this advantage, if we possess the gifts of the Holy Spirit, to such a degree as to be, to use a familiar expression, more than half filled with them. But meanwhile the best thing for us to do, after satisfying the requirements of obedience and charity, is to give ourselves to recollection and prayer, as also to reading and the exercises of the contemplative life.

Let us take as our model, Jesus Christ, who devoted thirty years to the contemplative life, and three or four only to that which is called *mixed;* and God Himself, whose life, before time began, was purely contemplative, His sole occupation being the knowing and loving of Himself. In time, indeed, He acts externally, but after such a manner, that action bears scarcely any proportion to contemplation; and in eternity, when time is ended, He will give Himself still less to action, seeing that then He will no longer create new creatures.

To make much progress in perfection two things are necessary, one on the part of the master, the other on the part of the disciple. In the master, that he should be greatly enlightened with the gift of science, as was St. Ignatius; in the disciple, that he should have a will perfectly subject to grace, and a great courage, like St. Francis Xavier.

It is a great misfortune to a soul towards which God has great designs, to fall into the hands of a director who is guided only by human prudence, and has more policy than unction.

An excellent means of acquiring the gift of science is to study greatly purity of heart; to watch carefully over our own interior, to mark all its irregularities, and note its principal faults.

Such strictness will draw down the blessing of God, who will not fail in time to pour His lights into the soul, and will give it little by little the knowledge of itself, which is the most useful He can impart to us next to that of His own divine majesty.

This is the first study in the school of perfection. When we have applied ourselves to it constantly for some time, we begin to see clearly into our interior; and this we may do without difficulty, by means of the sudden lights which God communicates to the soul according to its state and present dispositions. At this point it is not far from contemplation, and enjoys, as it were, some pledges of the great gifts which God is about to confer upon it, provided it be faithful in corresponding with His designs. For God lays firm the foundation before He builds the edifice; and this foundation is the knowledge of ourselves and our own wretchedness, lest we should come afterwards to pride ourselves in the gifts of God. Now it is little to believe and know that of ourselves we are nothing and can do nothing. The most vicious believe and know this well enough. God would have us obtain an experimental and sensible knowledge of ourselves; and to this end He makes us keenly feel our wretchedness.

You will sometimes see persons who say they practise prayer of simple regard,* or take the divine perfections for the subject of their meditations, and yet are

* It is difficult to render into English, and, so to say, naturalise the terms of mystical theology. This will serve to account for any expressions in this as well as in subsequent volumes of the series, which may have an un-English sound: but in the absence of any authority as to the rendering of the terms in question, an endeavour has been made to employ such terminology as seemed most appropriate, and best calculated to convey the

full of the grossest errors and imperfections, because they have attempted too high a flight before they have purified their heart. But tell them what you think of this, and they get angry, believing themselves already highly spiritual, and consider you but little enlightened in mystical theology; so that, after all, they must be sent back to the first elements of the spiritual life, that is to say, to keeping watch over their hearts, as at the very beginning, if they are to make any progress.

In vain do we practise so much spiritual reading, and consult so many books, in order to acquire the science of the interior life: the unction and the light which teaches come from above. A pure soul will learn more in one month by the infusion of grace, than others in several years by the labour of study.

More beyond all comparison is learnt by the practice of virtues, than by all the spiritual books and all the speculations in the world. It was to convince us of this truth that our Lord gave to mankind examples of virtue, before giving lessons in them and laying down precepts; "*Cœpit Jesus facere et docere:*" and David said to God, "I have had understanding above ancients,

sense of the original. The following description of *oraison de simple vue*, here translated " prayer of simple regard," is taken from the *Spiritual Conferences* of Father Guilloré, S. J. C. :—
" 1. It regards some one single truth, or holy object, by a simple contemplation of that which is before the mind, unaccompanied by any chain of reasoning. 2. The mind consequently does not, as thus engaged, perform any distinct act which *multiplies* it, or marks a diversity in its operations. 3. It is not to be denied, nevertheless, that certain indistinct and imperceptible acts are formed by the mind, not easily to be discerned on account of their delicate nature. 4. Generally speaking, the mind while occupied with this simple regard is not cognisant of its own acts by any conscious reflection on them ; for this would be to come out of its state of simplicity, and to destroy by this self-retrospection what we described as essentially constituting it."

because I have sought Thy commandments." In this book it was that St. Anthony studied, in order to learn the science of the Saints, and soar above the proud teaching of the philosophers. In this book it is that so many simple souls, without the study of letters, have acquired knowledge hidden from the learned of this world.

All our life long we ought to lay open our conscience to our Superior and our spiritual Father with great candour and simplicity, hiding from them none of the movements of our heart; so as to be willing, were it possible, to put our whole interior in their hands for their inspection. By the merit of this humility we shall obtain from God the gift of discernment of spirits, for the guidance of our own conduct and for the direction of others.

The vice which is opposed to the gift of science is ignorance, or the want of that knowledge which we might and ought to have for our own guidance and that of others.

Our life is commonly spent in the three kinds of ignorance to which, as St. Lawrence Justinian observes, persons who profess the spiritual life are subject. They have been described above, in Chapter IV., 'On purity of heart.'

The beatitude which answers to this gift is the third: "Blessed are they that mourn;" for the knowledge we receive from the Holy Spirit teaches us to know our faults and the vanity of earthly things, and shews us that we ought to expect from creatures only wretchedness and mourning.

The fruit of the Holy Spirit which corresponds therewith is that of faith, inasmuch as this gift perfects the knowledge we have gained of human actions and of creatures from the light of faith.

ARTICLE IV.

Of the gift of counsel.

Counsel is an act of prudence prescribing the means to be chosen for attaining an end.

Thus the gift of counsel regards the direction of particular actions. It is a light by which the Holy Spirit shews what we ought to do in the time, place, and circumstances in which we find ourselves. What faith, wisdom, and science teach in general, the gift of counsel applies to particular cases. And it is easy to perceive its necessity, since it is not enough to know that a thing is good in itself; we have also to judge whether it is good under actual circumstances, whether it is better than something else, and more suited to the object we are aiming at: and this knowledge we acquire by the gift of counsel.

It will sometimes happen that when we are deliberating what we ought to do, one thing will appear to us, even in a supernatural light, the best and the most perfect, and perhaps it really may be so in itself. And yet if we do it, great inconveniences will ensue; either dangers or faults, which would not have happened had we chosen something else, which, although less perfect in itself, would have been better in our particular case, because it would not have had the evil consequences involved in the other which appeared the best.

Thus the safest guidance is that which the Holy Spirit gives us through the gift of counsel, and we ought not to follow any other. First, because in following it we are certain to be walking in the way of God and His divine providence; secondly, because it is the means of never going astray, the Holy Spirit being the infallible rule as well of our actions as of our knowledge; thirdly, because this dependence on the guidance of the Holy Spirit makes us live in great peace, free from disquietude and care, like the children of a prince, who have no anxiety about their table, or their retinue, or any thing else that concerns their maintenance, trusting for all this to the care of the prince their father.

The Holy Spirit communicates this gift more or less, according as we are faithful in corresponding therewith. He who has but little of it, if only he makes good use of the little that he has, may be sure of receiving more, until he is replenished therewith according to the measure of his capacity; that is to say, until he has as much as he needs in order to fulfil the designs of God and to discharge worthily the duties of his office and his vocation. For it is rightly held, that a person is full of the Spirit of God when He so dwells in him as to enable him to perform all the duties of his state.

For ourselves, who are called to an Apostolical order, wherein we ought to combine together action and contemplation, we may without presumption aspire to the highest degree of excellence in both the contemplative and the active life. For it is no presumption to aspire to the perfection of one's state and to the accomplishment of the designs of God to the full extent of one's vocation.

To this end we have need of the gift of counsel in an excellent degree, because we are so much engaged in action: and if this gift of the Holy Spirit be wanting to us, we shall do nothing without committing many faults, and our whole conduct will be purely human. We shall act only from a principle of natural sagacity, or an acquired prudence. We shall but follow the devices of our own mind, which are for the most part greatly opposed to the Spirit of God.

In the morning we ought to beg the assistance of the Holy Spirit for all the actions of the day, humbly acknowledging our ignorance and weakness, and protesting that we will follow His guidance with a full and entire submission of mind and heart.

Then at the beginning of every action we ought again to ask the light of the Holy Spirit to perform it well, and when concluded, beg pardon for the faults we may have committed while engaged in it. By this means we keep ourselves all the day long in a state of dependence upon God, who alone knows the particular circumstances in which we are to be placed, and therefore can guide us more surely on all occasions by His counsel than by all other lights, whether of faith or the other gifts, which are not so applicable to individual cases.

Purity of heart is an excellent means of obtaining the gift of counsel, as well as the other gifts already treated of.

A person of good sound judgment, who should study constantly purity of heart, would acquire a supernatural prudence and a divine skill in conducting all sorts of affairs, would receive an abundance of infused light and knowledge for the guidance of souls, and discover a thousand holy contrivances for the execution of enterprises which concern the glory of God. In these things, human prudence, with all its foresight and address, commits many blunders, and is often altogether unsuccessful. It was by purity of heart, and by a faithful reliance on the guidance of the Holy Spirit, that St. Ignatius and St. Francis Xavier acquired that rare gift of prudence for which they have been admired.

It is in prayer especially that directors of souls and superiors ought to seek that light which is to guide them in the duties of their office. It is an error to suppose that the most learned are the best fitted for offices and the direction of souls, and that they are the most successful therein.

Natural talents, human science, and prudence profit but little in the matter of spiritual direction, in comparison with the supernatural lights communicated by the Holy Spirit, whose gifts are above reason.

The persons best fitted to guide others, and to give counsel in what concerns the things of God, are those who, possessed of a pure conscience and a soul free from passion and detached from every interest, and sufficiently provided with science and natural talents, although they may not possess them in any eminent degree, are closely united to God by prayer, and yield a humble submission to the movements of the Holy Spirit. This was the opinion of St. Ignatius; and it was on this account that he appointed to the rectorship of the Roman College Father Sebastian Romano, who, though not one of those who were most remarkable in the Company for human talents, was a man filled with the Spirit of God.

Superiors in subordinate situations have great need of the gift of counsel on particular occasions when the practice of obedience is concerned; for an inferior who has no subjects to govern has not the same difficulties in the exercise of obedience, as an inferior who is also superior over others, like a rector, a provincial, or an assistant. The latter, for example, finds himself sometimes embarrassed and in danger of being too compliant, even to the violation of the duties of his office, unless he is enlightened by the guidance of the Holy Spirit; for he may fall into different extremes, as letting the provinces have all their own way, or yielding to the wishes of individuals, who have prejudiced the Father General, and gained him over to their views. Thus being bound on the one side to obey, and on the other to discharge the duties of his office, he is in danger either of being too submissive for or against his office, or, again, of falling into the other extreme of not being obedient enough. In such circumstances they who govern themselves by the gifts of the Holy Spirit cannot go astray; but our misfortune is, that we have so little practical knowledge of those excellent gifts, which are the guiding principles of the Saints, because we do not apply ourselves in earnest to the study of perfection.

They who are learned must be on their special guard against a certain spirit of self-sufficiency and confidence in their own lights, and attachment to their own views.

They who would govern either a state or any other body, ecclesiastical, religious, or civil, by the light of the Holy Spirit, will not always succeed to the mind of those who are guided only by human prudence.

The latter will often condemn them, because their own view does not extend beyond the limits of reason and good sense, which are the sole principles by which they are guided; they discern nothing at all in the direction of the Holy Spirit, which is infinitely exalted above all human reasonings and all mere views of policy.

The government of superiors, or rather the government of God by superiors, being supernatural, it is not possible but that the faults that are committed therein must be great, and attended with grievous consequences.

Superiors must not only be endued with zeal to punish the faults of which inferiors are guilty, they must also be possessed of charity, to prevent, by salutary warnings, the faults they might commit; it is even fitting sometimes that they should content themselves with a secret and paternal reprimand, without any other punishment, so as by kindness to oblige one who has fallen into some error to correct himself, and thus prevent those other faults which the asperity of punishment might lead him to commit.

Good superiors consider themselves possessed of power and authority only to do good to their subjects and lighten their burdens, not to injure and inflict mortifications upon them.

A maxim of great importance to good government, and one that is strongly recommended to us in our last general congregation, is to avoid a multiplicity of useless regulations, which serve only to burden inferiors, and make the yoke of religion heavier, when we should strive to render it easier. Let it be sufficient to enforce the strict observance of the rules and ordinances already existing.

The failings of Saints consist in neglecting to follow certain lights of the Holy Spirit, or in omitting certain points of perfection; as, for example, if on occasion of having several supernatural lights on the same matter, out of weariness of mind or from want of consideration, they should follow the least exalted.

When we see that there is nothing wrong in doing or saying this or that; that we are not led to it by any natural inclination or affection, by any motive of complaisance, by the example of others, or by any habit or custom; and moreover that we are disposed to follow any other course the Holy Spirit might inspire, that we are equally ready to determine for or against, according as the Holy Spirit moves us,—wherever these three circumstances concur, we may generally act with safety, and there is no danger in going forward.

We may notice in several places of Scripture admirable instances of the gift of counsel; as in the silence of our Lord before Herod, and in the answers He made to save the woman taken in adultery, and to confound those who demanded of Him if it were lawful to pay tribute to Cæsar; in the judgment of Solomon; in the enterprise of Judith to deliver the people of God from the army of Holofernes; in the conduct of Daniel to justify Susanna from the calumny of the two elders; in that of St. Paul when he set the Pharisees against the Sadducees, and when he appealed from the tribunal of Festus to that of Cæsar.

The vice that is opposed to the gift of counsel is precipitation, when we act with too much haste, and without having considered every thing well beforehand; when we follow the impulse of our natural activity, and do not give ourselves time to consult the Holy Spirit.

This defect, as well as the others which are opposed to the gifts of which we have already spoken, viz. folly, dulness, ignorance, are sins when they proceed from our neglecting to dispose ourselves to receive the lights of the Holy Spirit; when we do not take sufficient time to ask His counsel before acting, and in acting hurry forward in such a way as to incapacitate ourselves for receiving His assistance, or when we let ourselves be carried away and blinded by the impetuosity of some passion.

Eagerness is greatly opposed to the gift of counsel. The saintly Bishop of Geneva often combats this defect in his writings. We ought to avoid it most carefully, because it fills the mind with darkness, introducing trouble, vexation, and impatience into the heart, nourishing self-love, and making us lean upon ourselves; instead of which, the gift of counsel, by enlightening the mind, pours into the heart an unction and a peace wholly opposed to eagerness and its effects.

Rashness, again, is very adverse to this gift. It is a want of attention to the lights and counsels of reason and grace, because we trust too much in ourselves. We are very subject to this vice, especially if we are defective in prudence and maturity of spirit, if we accustom ourselves to childish conduct, and entertain too good an opinion of ourselves.

Slowness is a fault which is also opposed to the gift of counsel. We ought to employ mature deliberation; but when once our resolution is taken in accordance with the light of the Holy Spirit, we ought to proceed promptly to its execution by the movement of the same Spirit, because if we delay, circumstances change, and opportunities are lost.

The beatitude which answers to the gift of counsel is the fifth: " Blessed are the merciful; for they shall obtain mercy." And the reason St. Augustine gives for this is, that God does not fail to aid with His light those who charitably assist others in their need. "*Est autem justum consilium, ut qui se a potentiori adjuvari vult, adjuvet infirmiorem in quo est potentior. Itaque beati misericordes, quia ipsorum miserabitur Deus.* It is a sound recommendation to one who is desirous of being assisted by another more powerful than himself, to assist his weaker brother in that wherein he is stronger than he. Therefore blessed are the merciful, because God will have mercy on them."

We cannot specify any fruit of the Holy Spirit which answers immediately to the gift of counsel, because it is a practical knowledge, which has no other fruit, properly speaking, than the operation which it directs and in which it terminates. However, as this gift specially directs works of mercy, we may say that the fruits of goodness and benignity answer in a manner thereto.

ARTICLE V.

Of the gift of piety.

Piety is that tender and loving disposition of the heart which leads us to honour and serve our relations and friends.

The gift of piety is an habitual disposition which

the Holy Spirit communicates to the soul to excite it to a filial affection towards God.

Religion and piety both lead us to the worship and service of God; but religion considers Him as Creator, and piety as a Father : and in this the latter is more excellent than the former.

Piety has a wide scope in the exercise of Christian justice; it reaches not only to God, but also to every thing relating to Him : as Holy Scripture, which contains His word; the blessed, who possess Him in glory; the suffering souls in purgatory, and those still living on the earth.

The gift of piety, says St. Augustine, communicates to those who possess it a loving reverence for Holy Scripture, whether they are able to enter into its meaning or not.

It gives us the spirit of a child towards our superiors, the spirit of a father towards our inferiors, the spirit of a brother towards our equals, bowels of compassion for those who are in necessity and trouble, and a tender disposition to succour them.

This gift is found in the superior part of the soul, and also in the inferior : in the superior, communicating to it an unction and a spiritual suavity, whose source is in the gifts of wisdom and understanding; in the inferior, exciting therein emotions of sensible sweetness and devotion. From this fountain flow the tears of Saints and devout persons. This is the principle of that sweet attraction which draws them to God, and of that alacrity which makes them run in the way of His service. It is this that makes them afflict themselves with the afflicted, weep with them that weep, rejoice with them that are glad of heart, bear without irritation the weaknesses of the infirm and the faults of the imperfect, and make themselves all to all.

It should be well understood that to make ourselves all things to all men, as did the Apostle, is not, for example, to break silence with those who break it, for we must always adhere to the practice of virtue and the observance of rules. But it is to be grave and collected with those who are so; quick and fervent with those who are of a quick and fervent spirit; lively with those who are of a lively humour, without overstepping, however, the bounds of propriety: for instance, when acting with alacrity, doing so after the manner of those perfect persons whose disposition is naturally quick and ardent, and practising virtue with discretion and condescension, according to the humour and taste of those with whom we have to do, as far as virtue itself will allow.

Some disapprove of certain devotions grounded on theological opinions which they do not themselves hold, although others do. They are wrong; for in the matter of devotion every probable opinion is sufficient to form a principle and foundation for it: consequently such criticism is unjust.

Of all the gifts of the Holy Spirit, that of piety seems to be the portion of the French. They possess it more strikingly than any other nation. Cardinal Bellarmine, when he came into France, was charmed with the devotion which he every where observed; and he said afterwards that Italians scarcely seemed to him like Catholics when he compared them in piety with the French.

The vice that is opposed to the gift of piety is hardness of heart, which springs out of an ill-regulated love of ourselves; for this love makes us naturally sensible only to our own interests, so that nothing affects us except in reference to ourselves. We behold the offences done against God without tears, and the miseries of our neighbour without compassion; we are unwilling to incommode ourselves to oblige others; we cannot put up with their faults; we inveigh against them on the slightest ground, and harbour in our hearts feelings of bitterness and resentment, hatred and antipathy, against them.

On the other hand, the more charity or love of God a soul possesses, the more sensitive it is to the interests of God and those of its neighbour.

This hardness is worst in the great ones of the world, in rich misers and voluptuaries, and in those who never soften their hearts by exercises of piety and familiarity with spiritual things.

It is also often to be found amongst men of learning who do not join devotion to knowledge, and who, to disguise this fault from themselves, call it strength of mind; but the truly learned have been the most pious, as a St. Augustine, a St. Bonaventure, a St. Bernard; and of the Company, a Laynez, a Suarez, a Bellarmine, and a Lessius.

A soul which cannot weep for its sins, at least with tears of the heart, is full either of impiety or of impurity, one or the other, as is generally the case with those whose heart is hardened.

It is a great misfortune when natural and acquired talents are more esteemed in religion than piety. You will sometimes see religious, and perhaps superiors, who will loudly declare that they attach much more value to a practical active mind than to all those pretty devotions, which, say they, are all very well for women, but are unbecoming in a strong mind, meaning by strength of mind that hardness of heart which is so opposed to the spirit of piety. They ought to bear in mind that devotion is an act of religion, or a fruit of religion and of charity, and consequently that it is to be preferred to all moral virtues, religion following immediately in order of dignity the theological virtues.

When a grave Father, respectable both for his age and the offices he has filled in religion, declares in the presence of the younger brothers that he sets high value on great talents and situations of distinction, or prefers such as excel in ability and knowledge to such as are inferior therein, although they possess greater virtue and piety, grievous injury is done to these poor young people. It is to infuse a poison into their hearts, from the effects of which they will perhaps never recover. A single such word said in confidence to another is enough to destroy him.

The harm that has been done to religious orders by those who have been the first to introduce a high esteem for talents and employments of distinction is incalculable. It is a draught of poisoned milk presented to young children; such language to youths just coming out from their noviciate, staining their souls with a hue which nothing ever effaces.

The beatitude which answers to the gift of piety is the second: "Blessed are the meek;" and the reason is, that meekness, clearing away all obstacles to acts of piety, assists it in its exercise.

The fruits of the Holy Spirit which answer to this gift are those of goodness and benignity.

ARTICLE VI.

Of the gift of fortitude.

Fortitude is a virtue which strengthens us against fear and dread of the difficulties, dangers, and toils which present themselves in the execution of our undertakings.

This the gift of fortitude admirably effects; for it is

an habitual disposition which the Holy Spirit communicates to the soul and to the body both to do and to suffer extraordinary things; to undertake the most arduous actions; to expose themselves to the most formidable dangers; to undergo the most toilsome labours; to endure the most grievous pains, and that with constancy and heroism.

This gift is exceedingly necessary on certain occasions, when we feel ourselves assailed with pressing temptations, to resist which we must resolve to lose our goods, our honour, or our life. It is then that the Holy Spirit powerfully assists with His counsel and strength a faithful soul, which, distrusting itself and convinced of its own weakness and nothingness, implores His succour and places all its confidence in Him.

On such occasions ordinary graces are not sufficient, —there is need of extraordinary lights and aids; and therefore it is that the prophet joins together the gift of counsel and that of fortitude; the one to enlighten the mind, and the other to fortify the heart.

We have much need of this gift in the Company, on account of the difficulty of certain employments which obedience may oblige us to undertake; as when we are sent on foreign missions; when we are left very long in the arduous duties of the classes, or are detained in a place which we feel to disagree with our health; and when some calumny or persecution is excited against us in discharging our functions of zeal and charity.

The opportunity of making a noble death is so precious, that no wise man ought to lose it when it offers.

We ought to be convinced that by this single act of Christian generosity, we may gain as much merit in the sight of God as we should during the remainder of our life, were it further prolonged; just as when any one, on entering religion, bestows at once all his goods upon the poor, his merit is as great as if, remaining in the world, he gave them away in abundant alms at different times. And how know we what our life would be afterwards, and in what state we should die another time? What would Origen and Tertullian be now, if, before their fall, they had had an opportunity of dying for Jesus Christ, and had faithfully embraced it?

Now there are three ways of dying nobly: first, to die in the service of those who are stricken with a pestilential disease; secondly, to die on a foreign mission, whether by the hand of unbelievers, or through excessive labour, or some accident incurred in the exercise of zeal; thirdly, to give our life for our flock, as prelates, pastors, and superiors may do.

It is impossible to say what graces the virtue of those amongst us who thus expose their lives draws down upon all the other members of the Company.

The gift of fortitude as respects the body renders those on whom God bestows it capable of performing deeds requiring miraculous strength, as David, Samson, and certain others of the Old Testament. We find in the lives of the Saints that some, like St. Dominic Loricatus, St. Catherine of Sienna, Father Gonzalez Silveira, have had this gift to enable them to practise prodigious mortifications beyond their natural strength.

But the gift of fortitude is chiefly bestowed to strengthen the mind, from which it banishes all human fears, imparting to the will and to the appetite a divine firmness which renders the soul intrepid.

It was by this spirit of fortitude that our Lord, in His Agony in the garden, overcame the dread of His Passion and death, and rising from prayer all on fire with zeal, said to His disciples, "Arise, let us go: behold, he is at hand that will betray Me."

It is this spirit that has made Saints fear no danger

when it was question of executing the designs of God and promoting His glory. A St. John Chrysostom feared nothing but sin. The Empress Eudoxia sent persons to sound him, in order to discover what it was that he most dreaded, intending afterwards to avail herself of this discovery to bring him by intimidation to the point she desired. But they found that the holy Bishop dreaded neither chains nor exile nor death; all that he feared was to offend God.

St. Francis Xavier, animated with this spirit, braved whole armies of unbelieving foes, tempests, shipwrecks, death, as was wonderfully displayed in his voyage to Japan, which he made in a wretched little vessel belonging to a pirate, an idolater and a worshipper of the devil, who appeared to him more than once to terrify him, threatening him that he should feel the effects of his vengeance; but the Saint laughed his threats to scorn, all his confidence being fixed on God. In one of his letters he writes that "the surest remedy in such circumstances is to fear nothing, putting our trust in God;" and that "the greatest evil that can befal us is to be afraid of the enemies of God when we are maintaining His cause."

We must be courageous, then, and fearless in the service of God, that we may advance in perfection and become capable of doing great things. Without the gift of fortitude no notable progress can be made in the spiritual life. Mortification and prayer, which are its principal exercises, demand a generous determination to overcome all the difficulties to be encountered in the way of the Spirit, which is so opposed to our natural inclinations. St. Theresa said that "a soul which has entered upon the practice of prayer with a firm resolution never to abandon it, has already performed half the journey."

The Martyrs hold the first rank amongst the heroes of Christianity, because fortitude is much more conspicuous in suffering than in action. In action nature finds relief, and has, as it were, the dominion; but suffering is entirely opposed to nature, and is therefore more difficult and more heroic.

It is to the holy Martyrs that the Church owes its propagation through the whole world, and the subjection of the Roman empire to the faith. We place the palm-branch in their hand to mark their fortitude and their victory.

Some attribute to this gift the power with which God sometimes endues the words of Saints in persuading minds and touching hearts; but they are mistaken: this is another special gift, which is called *gratia sermonis*, the 'grace of speech;' a free gift which is bestowed not for the advantage of those who receive it, but for the good of others. The evangelical labourers who have this grace, although they at times deliver very simple and rude discourses, do not fail to produce marvellous impressions on souls, as was the case with the Apostles, St. Vincent Ferrer, St. Ignatius, and St. Francis Xavier.

The vice opposed to the gift of fortitude is timidity or human fear, and a certain natural cowardice which proceeds from the love of our own superiority and a fondness for our own comforts, which hamper us in our undertakings, and make us fly the sight of abjection and suffering.

Nothing is more prejudicial in the spiritual life than the fears which the devil excites by a thousand human respects, which ought to be generously resisted. It is this which has caused the downfall of many great persons, and which cast down, if we may so express ourselves, even pillars of the Church, as the famous Osius,

Bishop of Cordova, who, after presiding as Papal legate at the Council of Nice, after defending the faith so long and with so much zeal against the Arians, after winning so many glorious victories over these heretics, the sworn enemies of the Son of God, in the end overcome by fear, consented to sign the condemnation of St. Athanasius. Words cannot tell the harm which human respect does us.

A religious is resolved to speak of spiritual things, to observe the rule of silence, or some other rule, to practise some act of mortification; and yet if he falls in with such and such persons, he has not the courage to perform his good resolution, although he well knows he will afterwards keenly regret having failed therein. On the one side is our rule and the cause of God, and on the other the gratification of this or that person and the fear of displeasing him. We weigh these two considerations, and the latter prevails. What infidelity! what cowardice! And this is what we do every day. Nothing more surely marks our want of virtue, and the dominion that human respect exercises over us. This is why God leaves us to ourselves and withdraws His graces, and we then fall insensibly into miserable faults.

As the gift of counsel accompanies that of fortitude and directs it, leading us to undertake great things, so also human prudence and timidity keep each other company, mutually supporting one another, and suggesting reasons in self-justification.

They who are guided only by human prudence are timid beyond measure. This fault is very common in superiors, and makes them, through fear of committing mistakes, fail of doing half the good they might do.

A thousand apprehensions hinder us every moment, and prevent our advancing in the way of God, and doing a vast amount of good, which we should do, if we followed the light of the gift of counsel, and possessed the courage which springs from the gift of fortitude : but there is too much in us of human views, and every thing alarms us. We fear lest an employment which obedience would impose upon us should not succeed, and this fear makes us refuse it. We are apprehensive of ruining our health, and this apprehension makes us limit ourselves to some little easy office, without the possibility of zeal or obedience stirring us up to undertake any thing more. We are afraid of incommoding ourselves, and this makes us shrink from corporal penances, or leads us to spare ourselves too much in the practice of them. It is impossible to say how many omissions fear makes us be guilty of. There are but very few who do for God and their neighbour all that they might do. We ought to imitate the Saints in fearing nothing but sin, like St. John Chrysostom; in braving risks, like St. Francis Xavier; in desiring insults and persecutions, like St. Ignatius.

The beatitude which answers to the gift of fortitude is the fourth : " Blessed are they that hunger and thirst after justice ;" because one who is animated by the strength of the Holy Spirit has an insatiable desire of doing and suffering great things.

The fruits which answer to this gift are longanimity and patience : the first enabling us not to grow tired or weary in undertaking or doing good; the second, not to grow tired or weary in suffering evil.

ARTICLE VII.

Of the gift of the fear of God.

The gift of the fear of God is an habitual disposition which the Holy Spirit communicates to the soul to maintain it in a state of reverence before the majesty of God, and of dependence upon and submission to His will, causing it to fly from every thing that can displease Him.

This gift is the foundation and basis of all others, because the first step in the way of God is the avoidance of evil, which appertains to this gift. It is through fear that we attain to the sublime gift of wisdom. We begin to *taste* God when we begin to fear Him, and wisdom in its turn perfects fear. It is the taste of God which renders the fear of God loving, pure, and detached from all self-interest.

The effects of this gift are to impart to the soul, first, a continual reserve, a holy trembling, a profound self-annihilation before God ; secondly, an extreme horror of the least offences against Him, and a constant resolution to avoid all occasions of displeasing Him ; thirdly, a humble confession when we have fallen into any fault ; fourthly, a watchful care in binding the irregular inclinations of the appetite, and frequent self-observation, in order to investigate the state of our interior, and see what is passing within contrary to perfect fidelity in the service of God.

It is a great delusion to think, as some do, that after making a general confession it is not necessary to be as scrupulous for the future to avoid the slightest sins, the smallest imperfections, the least irregularities of the heart, its incipient movements. They who act thus in their own case, through a secret despair of attaining a higher perfection, generally inspire others with similar sentiments, and use the same latitude in regard to the souls under their guidance ; which is a great error. We ought to cultivate such delicacy of conscience, and to be so strict with ourselves, as not to pass over the slightest fault, but combat and suppress the least disorders of the heart. God is worthy of being served with this perfect fidelity; to this end He offers us His grace, and we ought to co-operate therewith.

Never shall we attain to perfect inward purity until we so watch over all the movements of our heart and all our thoughts, that scarcely any thing escapes us of which we may not be able to render account to God, and which does not tend to His glory; so that in the space of eight days, for example, we should perform very few exterior actions or interior acts of which grace is not the principle; and if any exceptions occur, they should be owing simply to surprise, and last but for a few moments, our will being so closely united to God that it represses them the instant it perceives them.

It is seldom that we achieve a complete victory over our disorderly movements; scarcely ever do we so perfectly overcome any single one but there escapes something, or there remains something, either through want of attention, or for lack of a sufficiently vigorous resistance. Thus one of the greatest graces which God bestows upon us in this life, and which we ought most to beg of Him, is to be so watchful over our heart as that the least irregular movement shall not secretly arise in it without our perceiving it and immediately correcting it; for every day we are betrayed into a multitude of such which escape our observation.

As soon as we perceive we have committed a sin, we ought instantly to repent of it and make an act of contrition, for fear such sin should hinder subsequent graces; and this assuredly will be the result, if we fail in doing penance for it.

Some have no need of making a particular examination, because they no sooner commit the least fault than they are immediately reproved for it and made aware of it; for they walk always in the light of the Holy Spirit, who is their guide. Such persons are rare, and they make a particular examination, so to say, out of every thing.

The spirit of fear may be carried to excess, and then it is prejudicial to the soul, and hinders those communications and effects which divine love would operate in it, if it were not thus shut up and chilled with fear.

The vice opposed to the gift of fear is a spirit of pride, independence, and license, which makes men unwilling to do any thing but follow their own inclinations, and unable to endure any subjection, so that they sin without scruple, and make no account of slight faults, appear before God with little awe, commit many irreverences in His presence, despise His inspirations, neglect the occasions that offer themselves of practising virtue, and live in a state of laxity and tepidity.

It is said that an idle thought, a careless word, an action performed without direct intention, is a small matter. This would be true, were we in a state purely natural; but supposing that we are raised, as indeed we are, to a supernatural state, which has been purchased for us by the precious blood of the Son of God; supposing that on each moment of our life an eternity depends, and that the least of our actions merits the possession or the deprivation of a glory which, being eternal in its duration, is, in a manner, infinite,—it must needs be confessed that every day, by our negligence and by our cowardice, we incur losses inconceivable for want of an abiding conversion of the heart to God. Let us be convinced, once for all, that the exterior actions to which we devote all our attention are nothing but the body, and that the intention and the interior constitute the soul.

The path of tepidity is dangerous beyond measure:

we hardly know what takes place in it. Let us remember all our life long, that God endures for a time the sins we commit without scruple. But if we persist in them, it comes to pass, through the deserved chastisement of Divine justice, either that we fall into manifest mortal sin, or become involved in some distressing affair, or find our character aspersed by some calumny for which we have given no occasion, but which God permits, in order to correct some other fault which we have allowed to pass unheeded.

St. Ephrem,* in his youth, being cast into prison for some supposed crime, made complaint to God, and representing to Him his innocence, seemed to reproach Providence for having neglected him. An angel appeared to him, and thus addressed him: "Do you remember the wrong you did on such a day to a poor peasant by pelting his cow to death with stones? What penance have you done, or what satisfaction have you made? God will deliver you from prison, but it will not be till after fifteen days. And besides, you are not the only one thus dealt with by God. Such and such persons, who are confined here with you, are innocent of the crimes laid to their charge; but they have committed others of which human justice is ignorant, but which Divine justice would punish. The judges will condemn them for crimes of which they have been falsely accused; and God will permit them to be executed, in punishment for secret transgressions known but to Him alone."

The judgments of God are terrible: having called us to a higher perfection, and having long waited for us, when He sees that we continue to resist Him, He

---

* The Life of St. Ephrem deserves to be read at length, and as he himself relates it. Raderus also gives the narrative in his book entitled *Viridarium Sanctorum*.

withholds from us the graces He had prepared for us, He deprives us of those He had given us, and sometimes He takes us out of this life by a premature death, lest we should end by falling into still greater evil. This it is that often happens to religious who live in tepidity and negligence.

The beatitude which answers to the gift of fear is the first : " Blessed are the poor in spirit ;" for that nudity of spirit which includes the putting off all affection for temporal goods and honours is a necessary consequence of the perfect fear of God, the very spirit which leads us to submit ourselves entirely to God, and to esteem nothing great but Him alone, causing us to despise every thing else, and permitting no self-exaltation, either in ourselves by seeking to assert our own superiority, or above others, by seeking temporal riches and comforts.

The fruits of the Holy Spirit appertaining to this gift are those of modesty, temperance, and chastity. The first, because nothing more conduces to modesty than that loving reverence towards God which the spirit of filial fear inspires ; the other two, because in retrenching or moderating the use of the comforts of life and the pleasures of the senses, they contribute together with the gift of fear to restrain concupiscence.

CHAPTER V.

OF THE FRUITS OF THE HOLY SPIRIT.

ARTICLE I.

Of the nature of the fruits of the Holy Spirit.

WHEN we have long exercised ourselves with fervour in the practice of virtues, we acquire a facility in producing acts of them. We no longer feel the repugnances we experienced at first. We have no longer to combat and do violence to ourselves. We do with pleasure what before we did only with difficulty. The same thing happens to virtues as to trees. As the latter bear fruits which, when they are ripe, lose their sharpness, and are sweet and pleasant to the taste; so when acts of virtue have attained a certain maturity, we perform them with pleasure, and find in them a delicious flavour. At this stage, these acts of virtue inspired by the Holy Spirit are called *fruits of the Holy Spirit;* and certain virtues produce them in such perfection and sweetness, that they are called beatitudes, because they cause the soul to be wholly filled with God. Now the more God possesses a soul, the more He sanctifies it; and the more holy it is, the nearer it approaches to that happy state in which nature being healed of its corruption, virtues become as it were natural.

They who strive after perfection by the way of systematic practices and acts, without abandoning themselves completely to the guidance of the Holy Spirit, never have this sweetness and as it were ripeness of virtue; they always feel difficulty and repugnances, they have always to combat, and are often vanquished, and commit faults: instead of which, they who proceed under the direction of the Holy Spirit, in the way of simple recollection, practise what is good with a fervour and a joy worthy of the Holy Spirit, and win glorious victories without a struggle, or if they have to combat, they do so with pleasure.

Whence it follows, that tepid souls have twice as much trouble in the practice of virtue as the fervent, who devote themselves to it in earnest and without reserve; because the latter possess the joy of the Holy Spirit, which renders every thing easy to them; whereas the former have their passions to fight against, and experience the weaknesses and infirmities of nature, which counteract the sweetness of virtue, and render its acts difficult and imperfect.

Frequent communion is an excellent means of perfecting virtues in us, and acquiring the fruits of the Holy Spirit; for our Lord, uniting His Body to our body and His Soul to our soul, burns and consumes within us the seeds of our vices, and communicates to us by degrees His own divine temperament and perfections, according as we are disposed and suffer Him to operate in us. He finds in us, for example, the remembrance of some displeasure, which, though passed away, has made on our mind and heart an impression that remains as a seed of vexation, the effects of which we feel on occasions. What does our Lord do? He effaces the remembrance and image of this discontent; He obliterates the impression which had been left on all our powers, and entirely destroys that seed of sins, putting in its place the fruits of charity, joy, peace, and patience. He tears up in like manner the roots of anger, intemperance, and our other faults, and communicates to us virtues and their fruits.

ARTICLE II.

Of the fruits of charity, joy, and peace.

The first three fruits of the Holy Spirit are charity, joy, and peace, which appertain to the Holy Spirit in a special manner; charity, because He is the love of the Father and the Son, and the love of that which is good; joy, because He is most present to the Father and the Son, and is, as it were, the consummation of their beatitude; peace, because He is the bond and the tie that unites together the Father and the Son.

These three fruits are joined together, and follow

naturally one after the other. Charity, or fervent love, makes us to possess God; joy springs from the possession of God, being no other than the repose or contentment which is found in the enjoyment of the good we possess. Peace, which, according to St. Augustine, is the tranquillity of order, maintains the soul in the possession of joy against every thing opposed thereto. Charity excludes every other joy, and peace every kind of trouble and fear.

Charity is first in order of the fruits of the Holy Spirit, because it most resembles the Holy Spirit, who is Himself love, and consequently it brings us nearest to true and everlasting happiness, and bestows upon us a joy most solid, a peace most profound.

Give a man the dominion of the world, with an authority the most absolute possible; let him possess all the riches, all the honours, all the pleasures that could be desired; impart to him the most perfect wisdom you can imagine; let him be another Solomon and more than Solomon, and be ignorant of nothing that the mind can know; add thereto the power of working miracles; let him stay the sun in its course, divide seas, raise the dead; let him be endued with divine power in as high a degree as you please, and let him, moreover, have the gift of prophecy, the discernment of spirits, the knowledge of the secrets of hearts,—I say that the least degree of holiness this man may possess, the least act of charity he may perform, is worth more than all; it brings him nearer to the Sovereign Good, and invests him with a being more excellent than all these other advantages would bestow upon him, if he had them. And this for two reasons.

First, because to partake of the holiness of God is to partake of that which is, so to say, most essential in Him. The other attributes of God, as knowledge, power, may be communicated in such wise as to be natural to men; holiness alone can never be natural to them.

Secondly, because holiness and happiness are, as it were, two inseparable sisters, and God communicates Himself and unites Himself only to holy souls, and not to such as, without holiness, have knowledge, power, and all other perfections imaginable.

Thus the smallest measure of holiness, the least action that increases holiness, is to be preferred before sceptres and crowns. Whence it follows, that by losing every day opportunities of doing so many supernatural actions, we incur losses of happiness inconceivable in extent and all but irreparable. We cannot find in creatures joy and peace, which are the fruits of the Holy Spirit, for two reasons.

First, because it is the possession of God alone that can strengthen us against troubles and fears; instead whereof, the possession of creatures causes a thousand apprehensions and a thousand disquietudes. He who possesses God is troubled by nothing, for God is all to him, and every thing else is nothing to him.

Secondly, because no created goods can fully satisfy or content us. Empty the bed of the ocean, and then let fall therein a single drop of water; will you refil that immense void? Were God to produce unto infinity creatures more perfect and more perfect still, not all together would be able to fill our soul; there is a void within that cannot be filled but by God.

It is peace that causes God to reign in the soul, and gives Him the entire sovereignty of it. This it is that keeps the soul in that perfect dependence which it ought to have on God.

By sanctifying grace God forms to Himself, as it were, a citadel in the soul, wherein He entrenches Himself. By peace He makes a kind of sally and takes possession of all the faculties, fortifying them so strongly that creatures can no longer enter there to disturb them. God occupies all the interior: thus Saints are as united to God in action as in prayer, and events the most distressing never cause them any trouble.

ARTICLE III.

Of the fruits of patience and meekness.

The preceding fruits dispose the soul to those of patience and meekness, or moderation.

The property of the virtue of patience is to moderate excess of sadness; and the virtue of meekness allays the gusts of anger which rise impetuously to repel any present evil.

These two virtues combat and win the victory only by violent efforts, and that not without difficulty; but patience and meekness, which are the fruits of the Holy Spirit, reduce their enemies to obedience without combating, or if they combat, it is without labour, nay with pleasure. Patience beholds with joy objects calculated to produce sadness: thus martyrs rejoice at the threat of persecutions and the sight of tortures. When once peace is firmly established in the heart, meekness has no longer any trouble in regulating the movements of anger. The soul retains its equilibrium and never loses its tranquillity. And this is the effect of the Holy Spirit, who, residing in it and possessing it in all its powers, banishes all objects of sadness, or prevents them from making any impression; so that the devil even stands in awe of such a soul, and does not venture to approach it.

ARTICLE IV.

Of the fruits of goodness and benignity.

These two fruits respect the good we do to our neighbour. Goodness is the inclination which leads us to oblige others, and communicate to them of what we possess. We have no term in our language which exactly expresses *benignitas;* for the word *benignity* is not in general use, except perhaps to denote kindness, and this sort of kindness consists in our obliging others willingly, cordially, joyfully, without feeling the difficulty which is experienced by one who possesses benignity only in the quality of a virtue, and not also in the quality of a fruit of the Holy Spirit.

ARTICLE V.

Of the fruit of longanimity.

Longanimity, or perseverance, prevents the weariness and fatigue which are especially caused by the expectation of some hoped-for good, or the length and duration of some good we are doing, or of some evil we are suffering, and not by the greatness of the thing itself, or other circumstances connected with it. Longanimity, for example, has the effect of making us more fervent at the end of our third year's noviciate than we were at the beginning.

ARTICLE VI.

Of the fruit of faith.

Faith, so far as it is a fruit of the Holy Spirit, is a certain facility in believing every thing that appertains to the belief of the faithful, a constancy in adhering thereto, and an assurance of the truth of what we believe, without feeling those repugnances and doubts, that darkness and dulness of mind, which we naturally experience in regard to matters of faith.

In order to this there must be in the will a pious affection inclining the understanding to believe, without hesitation, the things proposed to it.

For want of this pious affection, the Jews, although convinced by the miracles of our Lord, did not believe in Him, having their understanding darkened and blinded by the malice of their will. Now that which happened to the Jews in regard to the substance of the faith happens often to us in what concerns the perfection of the faith.; that is to say, in things which may perfect it, and which are the consequence of truths which it makes us believe. For example, we are taught that our Lord is both God and man, and we believe it. If thence the conclusion be drawn, that we ought therefore to love Him above all things, to visit Him often in the Holy Eucharist, to prepare ourselves to receive Him, and to make all this our first duty and business, then we hesitate, and our will in practice resists the belief of the understanding. If it did but yield thereto, our faith in the mysteries of our Lord would daily increase. But we stifle by our vices this pious affection, so necessary for arriving at the perfection of faith. Did we possess a good will truly devoted to God, we should have a penetrating and perfect faith.

Some understand by the word *faith*, fidelity, constancy in keeping the promises we make; others, a facility of believing in what regards human things, without allowing ourselves to harbour groundless distrusts, suspicions, and rash judgments.

ARTICLE VII.

Of the fruits of modesty, temperance, and chastity.

Modesty, in so far as it is a virtue, is well known. It regulates all the movements of the body, the gestures, and the words. In so far as it is a fruit of the Holy Spirit, it does this easily and naturally; and, moreover, it composes all the interior movements of the soul, as in the presence of God.

Our mind is light and restless, always in action, fluttering on all sides, fastening on all sorts of objects, prattling unceasingly. Modesty checks it, moderates it, and settles the soul in a profound peace, which disposes it to become the habitation and the kingdom of God; thus the gift of the presence of God follows speedily on the fruit of modesty. The latter is to the former what the dew was to the manna; and the presence of God is a transcendent light, in which the soul beholds itself before God, and observes all its interior movements, every thing that passes within it, more clearly than we see colours at noon-day.

Modesty is absolutely necessary to us; because immodesty, although in itself it seems to be a small thing, is notwithstanding of great importance on account of its consequences, and is no slight mark of a mind but little religious.

The virtues of temperance and chastity regard the pleasures of the body, repressing such as are illicit, and moderating those that are lawful. The former restrains a disorderly affection for eating and drinking, and prevents excesses we might commit therein. The latter regulates or retrenches altogether the use of carnal pleasures.

But the fruits of temperance and chastity so detach the soul from the love of its body, that it scarcely feels its rebellions any more, keeping it in subjection without difficulty.

CHAPTER VI.

THE OBSTACLES WHICH THE DEVIL PUTS IN OUR WAY IN THE PRACTICE OF DOCILITY TO THE GUIDANCE OF THE HOLY SPIRIT.

ARTICLE I.

How the devil prevents our spiritual advancement.

How greatly the devil prevents our spiritual advancement is past all conception. Since the commencement of this year of retreat he has deceived not a few by means of some trouble, some vexation, some scruple, or other evil disposition. When he sees the first assaults have succeeded, he proceeds to others, always occupying us with some new design or desire or hope, in order to amuse us, and turn us aside from the ways of God and the care of our perfection.

For this purpose he makes use of such opportunities as offer, the remembrance of past occurrences, the news we hear, objects that strike the senses, our humour and our passions, setting these different springs in motion, sometimes one, sometimes another, in order that our mind and heart may be continually occupied with some trifle which keeps us engaged, either with useless thoughts and reflections, or with vain desires and fears, or with some other movement of an unmortified passion.

When this retreat is over, and we return to college occupations, there again he will put equal or stronger attachments in our way, and obstacles as great or more dangerous; so that, unless we take care, he will keep us all our life long thus miserably attached to something out of God.

And thus death will surprise us ; we shall die as we have lived, imperfect ; and the enemy will have gained his purpose, which is to confound us before the tribunal of Jesus Christ. This is the end, alas, but too often.

To prevent such misfortune, let us examine ourselves carefully, and observe on what object our thoughts are most fixed, what most engages our heart, what passions most disturb our interior peace. And when we have discovered what it is, let us immediately root it out, as a manifest device of the enemy, who wishes to destroy us. Let us consider, also, whether our most ardent desire and our most anxious care is to advance in the perfection of our state ; and if not, let us bend all our efforts to attain this holy disposition.

ARTICLE II.

Different artifices of the devil to deceive us.

§ I.

The way in which the devil deals with beginners is either to prevent the good they do, or to diminish it, or to change it into some less good, or such as is only apparent, or into something prejudicial, or above their strength, or too elevated for the present disposition of their soul.

His artifice with perfect souls is to keep them in a state of disturbance, never leaving them any repose ; to the end that, having tired and wearied them, he may at last turn them away, if possible, from their close application to God, fill their heart with sadness and discouragement, enfeeble them in the practice of good, and lead them to relaxation and tepidity.

§ II.

There are persons whom the devil does not prevent

from doing much good, because the good they do serves to deceive them. His first attacks are directed to casting souls into mortal sin; but if he sees he cannot succeed in his design, he changes his mode of assault, and leads them to commit many venial sins in the good they do. Having weakened them by this means, he has little difficulty, in the end, in making them fall into some mortal offence.

§ III.

In our good designs the devil behaves as Pharaoh did in the case of the Israelites when they wished to go to offer sacrifice to God in the wilderness. That prince not being able absolutely to refuse them permission, limited it as much as he could. It was with the condition one while that they should leave their wives and their children in Egypt, at another that they should not take with them their cattle.

The devil uses nearly the same kind of artifice. When we have formed some holy resolution, if he cannot prevent all the good we wish to do, he prevents as much as he can; provided he can always subtract something from the service of God, so that it may not be full and entire, he is content.

§ IV.

Sometimes we have determined upon doing some good action in a certain time; but the devil interferes with its performance, and frustrates it, either by representing difficulties, exciting opposition on the part of others, or creating repugnances in ourselves; or he endeavours to make us give up some part of our undertaking, or to quit altogether our first design, for want of resolution and constancy.

If he sees he cannot represent the things he sets before our imagination to scare us as absolutely imminent, he represents them to us as at least doubtful or uncertain; and he shews us how much they are to be feared, in order to discourage us by the dread of dangers and difficulties.

To this end he makes use of our evil dispositions; and so long as we are in a state of imperfect subjection to grace, we give him much hold upon us to turn us aside from good, and herein incur incalculable losses of grace and merit.

§ V.

It often happens that when the Holy Spirit puts some thought into our mind, the devil steals it away, playing off a cheat upon us, and suggesting in its stead another, which, although perhaps it be not in itself bad, nevertheless does us much harm, since it deprives us of that good impulse, and that peace resulting from the first thought, which came from God; so that we ought to be upon our guard, in order to confirm ourselves in the one and reject the other; and it is of the utmost importance that we should watch attentively over our thoughts, and test them thoroughly at their commencement, in their progress, and in their conclusion.

ARTICLE III.

Of distinguishing between the operations of God and those of the devil.

§ I.

Every thing that destroys the peace and tranquillity of the interior proceeds from the devil. God has joined together happiness and holiness in such wise that His graces not only sanctify the soul, but also console it, and fill it with peace and sweetness. The suggestions of the devil have the very contrary effect, either at once, or at least in the end; the serpent is known by his tail, that is to say, by the effects he produces, and the conclusion to which he leads.

§ II.

All hypothetical or conditional propositions, calculated only to cause trouble, come from the devil; as, for example, Were God to abandon me on such an occasion, what should I do? and the like. We should make no reply to such propositions, nor allow the mind to rest on such thoughts, which the enemy suggests to take from us our confidence in God, and to cast us into disquietude and despondency. Let us trust in God, for He is faithful, and will never fail those who, having wholly given themselves up to Him, seek only to please Him in all things.

ARTICLE IV.

Secret illusions.

§ I.

It happens very often that when we feel some irregular movement excited in our heart, we are unwilling to consent to the sin, but are unwilling also resolutely to drive away the evil feeling. We reject the sin which would be manifest in the eyes of men, and we allow the interior irregularity which God sees, and which is displeasing to Him. For example, we have a feeling of bitterness against some one; we are unwilling to consent to display this feeling towards him, but we allow our heart to be filled with it, instead of ridding ourselves of it at once. This is one of our most secret and most dangerous illusions.

§ II.

When we have a desire for any thing, a thousand reasons occur to us to give a colour to our passion. We deceive ourselves when, having formed some design from natural inclination, we seek for some reason on the side of grace to lend it support. "I am going to see Mr. So-and-so; I will also exhort him to make a retreat." Generally speaking, this also comes from a bad principle; it is an invention of self-love, which is ingenious in discovering such reasons.

§ III.

It sometimes happens that when God gives us the light and the inspiration of His grace to correct us of certain faults to which we are subject, we turn our thoughts another way; we apply ourselves to some other action of virtue, and practise a deception upon God, in order to avoid the stings and reproaches of our conscience, escape the shame which the sight of our fault would cause us, and delude ourselves agreeably with the persuasion of our own virtue. But we shall never attain to this holy liberty, this largeness of heart, which we are seeking, unless we correct ourselves of the faults which God makes known to us.

§ IV.

Sometimes we do not sufficiently observe, that while meditating on the highest subjects or engaged in the holiest occupations, our mind is not so completely engrossed therewith but that we are thinking at the same time of other idle things; and this is so much of our life that is lost, when it ought to be given to God.

ARTICLE V.

Marks of a deluded soul.

§ I.

To be continually speaking of extraordinary graces, visions, and revelations; to think of nothing else; to take but little pains to observe and regulate the movements of the heart; to be deficient in simplicity and openness with superiors and directors ; to choose to meditate only on the Divinity, and not at all on the sacred Humanity of our Lord ; to adopt conduct and opinions repugnant to the doctrine and practice of holy Church,—these are marks of a deluded soul.

§ II.

The devil sometimes raises souls to sublime thoughts of God, in order to turn them away from a close application to Jesus Christ, who is the source of all good, and the great object of hatred to devils.

ARTICLE VI.

What we ought to observe in the movements leading us to good.

All the movements that lead us to good are worthy of being noted.

We must examine :

1. With what readiness we have followed them, whether it has been with our whole strength both of mind and body.

2. By what motive we have been led in so doing, and for what end.

3. Whether in the progress of the action we have maintained the fervour and purity of intention with which we set out.

For it happens but too often that we undertake some good work for a truly holy end, but scarcely have we begun when we lose sight of that end, or keep our eyes only half fixed upon it. Vanity, interest, and self-seeking glide insensibly into the heart. We relax little by little, we get tired, we allow ourselves to yield to the impulse of a natural inconstancy ; so that it is rarely that we finish with the same ardour and the same purity of intention with which we had begun.

FIFTH PRINCIPLE.

RECOLLECTION AND THE INTERIOR LIFE.

CHAPTER I.

OF THE NATURE AND CAUSES OF THE INTERIOR LIFE.

ARTICLE I.

In what the interior life consists.

§ I.

THE interior life consists in two sorts of acts, viz. in thoughts and in affections. It is in this only that perfect souls differ from imperfect, and the blessed from those who are still living on earth. Our thoughts, says St. Bernard, ought to be "ever following after truth, and our affections ever abiding in the fervour of charity." In this manner, our mind and heart being closely applied to God, being fully possessed by God, in the very midst of exterior occupations we never lose sight of Him, and are always engaged in the exercise of His love.

§ II.

Good and bad religious differ from each other only in the nature of their thoughts, their judgments, and their affections. In this also consists the difference between angels and devils, and it is this that makes the former holy and blessed, and the latter wicked and miserable. Accordingly we ought to watch with extreme care over our interior, and pay continual attention to regulate our judgments according to truth, and to keep our affections in subordination to charity.

§ III.

The essence of the spiritual and interior life consists

in two things: on the one hand, in the operations of God in the soul, in the lights that illumine the understanding, and the inspirations that affect the will; on the other, in the co-operation of the soul with the lights and movements of grace. So that to hold communion with God, and to dispose ourselves to receive from Him larger and more frequent communications, we must possess great purity of heart, great strength of mind, and observe a constant and inviolable fidelity in co-operating with God, and following the movement of His Spirit in whatever direction it may impel us.

§ IV.

One of the occupations of the interior life is the examining and ascertaining particularly three sorts of things in our interior. First, what comes from our own nature — our sins, our evil habits, our passions, our inclinations, our affections, our desires, our thoughts, our judgments, our sentiments; secondly, what comes from the devil — his temptations, his suggestions, his artifices, the illusions by which he tries to seduce us unless we are on our guard; thirdly, what comes from God — His lights, His inspirations, the movements of His grace, His designs in our regard, and the ways along which He desires to guide us. In all this we must examine and see how we conduct ourselves, and regulate our behaviour by the Spirit of God.

We must carefully observe what it is that the Holy Spirit most leads us to, and in what we most resist Him; at the beginning of our actions ask grace to perform them well, and mark even the slightest movements of our heart.

We ought not to devote all our time of recollection to prayer and reading, but employ a portion in examining the disposition of our heart, in ascertaining what passes there, and discovering what is of God, what is of nature, and what is of the devil; in conforming ourselves to the guidance of the Holy Spirit, and strengthening ourselves in the determination of doing every thing and suffering every thing for God.

ARTICLE II.
How we ought to imitate the interior life of God.

We ought to imitate the interior life of God in this, that He possesses within Himself an infinite life, as well by the operation of the understanding, by which He is the principle of the Person of the Word, as by that of the will, by which He is the principle of the Person of the Holy Spirit. Moreover, He acts externally to Himself, according to His good pleasure, by the production and government of the universe, without this exterior action causing any diminution or any change in His interior life; in such wise that in respect thereto He acts externally, as though He were not acting at all.

This is our model: in the first place, we ought to have within ourselves and for ourselves a most perfect life by a constant application of our understanding and will to God. Then we shall be able to go out of ourselves for the service of our neighbour without prejudice to our interior life, not giving ourselves up wholly to others, nor applying ourselves to exterior occupations, except by way of diversion, so to say; and thus our principal business will ever be the interior life. *Tuus esto ubique,* says St. Bernard to Pope Eugenius; *concha esto, non canalis.* Do not give thyself up to thy neighbour, so as to be no longer thine own; possess thyself always; fill thyself with grace as a reservoir; then thou wilt be of use in communicating thereof to others. Be not like a canal, through which the water passes without staying therein.

This advice of St. Bernard ought to be the rule of evangelical labourers. But often they do the very reverse. They pour themselves forth entirely; they exhaust themselves for others, and remain themselves dry. All the marrow of their soul, if one may use the expression, all the vigour of their mind, spends itself in their exterior actions. There remains scarcely any thing for the interior.

Hence it follows, that unless they take care, they have just ground to fear that, instead of being raised to heaven, according to the excellence of their vocation, they will be of the number of those who will be detained the longest time in purgatory and placed in the lowest ranks in glory.

ARTICLE III.

How it is that we make so little progress in the interior life.

This proceeds from two causes:

1. Exterior objects attract us to them by the appearance of some good which flatters our pride or our sensuality. This happens especially to those whose feelings are warm and who easily take fire.

2. The devil, exciting the phantoms of the imagination, awakening the recollection and the image of past things, corrupting and inflaming the humours of the body as occasions offer, produces in us disquietudes, scruples, and a variety of passions. This he effects chiefly in those who not having their heart as yet thoroughly purged, give him more hold upon them and are more in his power.

3. Our soul does not enter into itself except with pain, seeing there nothing but sins, miseries, and confusion. So that to avoid this distressing and humiliating sight, it hurries instantly out again, and goes to seek

its consolation in creatures, unless we keep it carefully to its duty.

CHAPTER II.

OF THE MOTIVES THAT LEAD US TO THE INTERIOR LIFE.

ARTICLE I.

We make no progress in the ways of perfection unless we give ourselves to the interior life.

THE exterior life of religious employed in the service of their neighbour is most imperfect, and even perilous, unless it be accompanied with the interior life; and they who are engaged in these kinds of offices of charity and zeal, unless they join thereto exercises of interior recollection, will never make any notable progress in perfection.

And first, they will never arrive at the perfection of the purgative life. It is true they will have at times some of its sentiments. They will do things that appear great in the eyes of the world. They will preach; they will labour in missions; they will traverse seas, and expose themselves to danger of death, and to the fatigues attendant on the longest journeys, for the salvation of their neighbour. But with all this they will never make much progress in the purgative life. The acts of virtue they perform will proceed partly from grace and partly from nature. They will never do such as are purely supernatural, and under specious pretexts self-love will always make them follow their own inclinations and do their own will. They will fall continually into their ordinary faults and imperfections, and will be in great danger of being lost; for as they are occupied in any thing but discovering the irregularities of their hearts, they never think of purging it; so that it is continually filling with sins and miseries, which gradually enfeeble the strength of the soul, and end at last in entirely stifling devotion and the Spirit of God.

Secondly, they will never attain to the perfection of the illuminative life, which consists in discovering in all things the will of God ; for it is only interior men who can discern it in every thing. My superiors, my rules, the duties of my state, may indeed direct me in regard to the exterior, and indicate to me what God desires me to do at such a time and in such a place ; but they cannot teach me the way in which God wills that I should do it. I know, for instance, that it is God's will that I should pray when I hear the clock strike which calls me to prayer according to my rule ; but the rule does not tell me what my comportment ought to be during my prayer. My superior will tell me what God wills that I should apply myself to ; but he cannot teach me how I ought to apply myself.

In order to do the will of God well, it is not sufficient to know that it is God's will; for example, that I should forthwith sweep my room ; I must also know with what thought He would have me occupy myself while performing this exterior act of humility which my rule prescribes, for God desires to regulate the interior of my actions as well as the exterior. I must fulfil God's will as well in the manner as in the substance of the action. He desires to govern it even in the smallest details, and His providence extends to the direction of all my powers and all the movements of my heart ; without this there will be a void in my actions ; they will not be full of the will of God ; I shall do what He demands of me only in part and by halves ; the best will be wanting, which is the interior. Thus I shall incur great losses of grace and glory, losses that are irreparable ; and I shall be the cause of others, whose salvation and perfection I am bound to promote, incurring the same.

Where, then, shall I be able to learn the will of God in regard to the manner of performing well those things which He desires me to do? It must be in my own interior and in the depth of my own heart, where God gives the light of His grace, in order to enlighten me inwardly, that I may listen attentively to Him, and converse familiarly with Him. I will walk in His light, which will enable me to see what He desires of me, and the means of performing it, and the interior perfection which it is His will I should practise therein.

Thirdly, it is clear they will never attain to the perfection of the unitive life, since it consists in the interior union of the soul with God.

For the rest, whoever is resolved to lead an interior life, and to be really spiritual and a man of prayer, must expect that when he has reached a certain point, people will cry out against him; he will have adversaries, and other contradictions; but in the end God will give him peace, and will make every thing turn out to his profit and the advancement of his soul.

ARTICLE II.

Without prayer we cannot acquit ourselves of the duties of our vocation, nor gather fruit from our ministrations.

§ I.

Without a solid devotion and a close familiarity with God, we cannot carry on our functions nor discharge them properly. The Prophets, Apostles, and other Saints have wrought wonders, because they were inspired by God, and conversed familiarly with Him.

Saints succeed in every thing, because by their prayers they obtain a benediction and a virtue which render their labours efficacious. Although they be infirm and suffering from constant ill health, like St. Gregory and St. Bernard, they effect wonders.

In vain we toil and form great projects for the glory of God and the service of souls, without prayer nothing can be hoped from our labours and undertakings; but with the gift of prayer, we may do great things, even in matters of prudence and the management of affairs.

Let us season our exertions in behalf of our neighbour with recollection, prayer, and humility; God will make use of us for great ends, although we may not possess great talents.

We ought to undertake nothing, whatever the matter be, without having disposed ourselves thereto by prayer.

§ II.

It is to God we ought to look for every success in our employments. We are His instruments, and we work under Him as under a master-architect, who, directing singly the whole design, allots to each one his task, according to the end he proposes, and the idea he has conceived. Thus we shall produce the more fruit the more united we are to God, and the more we yield ourselves to His guidance, always supposing we possess the talents and the capacity requisite for the active service of our neighbour. Now it is prayer that unites us to God. It is by this holy exercise that we dispose ourselves to receive the impression and movement of grace, as instruments to work out His designs.

§ III.

St. Gregory Thaumaturgus, explaining that saying of the wise man, "All is vanity," says, that the devil displays before the eyes of men of the world honours, pleasures, riches, and all the creatures of the universe, like puppets which he sets in motion, shifting them, turning them, shewing them in different aspects and different colours, decking them out with various ornaments and a false brilliancy; but in reality it is but a child's game, a vain amusement; there is nothing solid in it; it is but a pleasing illusion.

The devil employs the same artifice with those who compose the little world among religious: for in religion there is a little world, the elements of which are, the esteem of human talents; preference for employments, offices, and stations of importance; the love and the seeking for distinction and applause, or repose and an easy life. These are the things of which the devil makes, as it were, a puppet-show to amuse and deceive us. He sets it all moving before our eyes in such a way that we stop to gaze, and allow ourselves to be seduced by it, preferring vain appearances to true and solid goods.

§ IV.

Prayer alone can secure us from this delusion. Prayer teaches us to judge soundly of things by looking at them in the light of truth, which dissipates their false splendour and false charms.

Therefore it is that St. Ignatius desires that the professed and those who have taken their last vows should give to prayer all the time they have remaining, after fulfilling the duties of obedience. This ought to be the employment of those who in the colleges are not occupied with the office of regent, but only with hearing confessions, or some other duty which leaves them a good deal of leisure. They ought to be men of prayer, who by the help of their prayers sustain the whole house, the whole Company, nay, the whole Church; and this it is to be a Jesuit, this it is to be a child of those great Saints who desired more worlds to convert.

Behold how we may spend our days sweetly in the

beauty of peace, in the security of a pure conscience and repose, rich with holy treasures: instead of wasting our time in trifles unworthy of an evangelical labourer, we ought to visit often the Blessed Sacrament, then apply ourselves to reading, then again return to our devotions, say the Rosary of the Blessed Virgin, and refer every thing to prayer.

§ V.

The Company does much good; nevertheless it might do much more. There are souls whom God has determined to assist only by us and our ministrations. If we fail them, or if we do not discharge our ministry well, these souls will remain unaided, and the Church will mourn. They who are not as interior nor as united to God as they should be, ought to ponder well these things; but we think very little of faults of this sort, and yet they are fearful; God knows what account we must one day render to Him for them.

§ VI.

As there are certain humours which cause the death of the body when they gain too much strength and are too abundant, so in the religious life, when action is carried to excess and is not moderated by prayer and recollection, it infallibly quenches the spirit.

And yet there will sometimes be found persons who, being occupied whole days and years in study and in the turmoil of exterior employments, will feel it difficult to devote a quarter of an hour a day to spiritual reading; and then how is it possible they should become interior men? Hence it is that we gain no fruit, because our ministrations are not animated by the Spirit of God, without which, with all our talents, we cannot attain the end we are aiming at, and are but "as sounding brass and a tinkling cymbal."

An interior man will make more impression on hearts by a single word animated by the Spirit of God, than another by a whole discourse which has cost him much labour, and in which he has exhausted all his power of reasoning.

ARTICLE III.

Peace is not found except in the interior life, and our dissatisfactions spring only from our not being interior men.

§ I.

Never shall we have peace until we are interior men and united to God. Repose of mind, joy, solid contentment, are found only in the interior world, in the kingdom of God which we possess within ourselves. The more deeply we enter therein, the more happy shall we be. Without this we shall always be in trouble and difficulty, always discontented, complaining, and murmuring; and if any temptation, any rough trial come upon us, we shall not overcome it.

§ II.

St. Augustine says, that they who have an ill-regulated interior are like married men with peevish and ill-tempered wives. They leave home early in the morning and return as late as they can, because they dread a domestic persecution; in like manner, the former, having no peace in their interior, and finding there only remorse and the reproaches of their conscience, avoid as much as possible entering into themselves.

§ III.

The greatest misfortune to a man of our profession is to be wholly absorbed, both in action and in affection, in the exterior life, being scarcely acquainted with any other; for this life being limited, the office that one man desires and obtains cannot fall to the lot of another who equally wishes for it: and this is what causes his dissatisfaction. Instead of which, if he did not attach himself to a little miserable portion of the exterior life, and would but devote himself heartily to the interior, which has no limit, he would find, as it were, boundless regions of graces, virtues, and perfection, where his soul would be abundantly satisfied. But no one will ever give himself to the interior life in his old age who has not done so in his youth; so that unless we carry away from our third year's noviciate a will absolutely resolved to cultivate the interior life at whatever cost, we shall relapse into our first state, *et fient novissima pejora prioribus.*

§ IV.

If in our employments we practise the exterior of virtue without the interior, we are miserable, bearing the weight of exterior labour, but never tasting interior unction and sweetness: and this makes us fall often into notable faults; whereas by means of recollection and prayer, we should effect more in our ministrations with less difficulty, weariness, and danger, and with more perfection to ourselves, more advantage to our neighbour, and more glory to God. "This," adds Father Rigoleu in his collection, "is what our father director represented to us with much force, and it is one of the points he most urged upon us."

CHAPTER III

THE OCCUPATIONS OF THE INTERIOR LIFE.

ARTICLE I.

Of watchfulness over our interior.

§ I.

OUR principal study ought to be to watch over our interior, in order to ascertain its state and correct its disorders. To this the following considerations powerfully excite us :

1. We remain immersed and as it were buried in a mass of faults and imperfections, which we never see, and never shall see till the hour of death, unless we exercise ourselves in observing the movements of our interior, wherein the devil and nature play strange parts, while we are wholly absorbed in the hurry and excitement of exterior occupations.

2. The ruin of souls in the path of perfection proceeds from the multiplication of venial sins, whence follows a diminution of divine lights and inspirations, spiritual consolations, and other succours of grace ; next, a great weakness in resisting the attacks of the enemy ; and finally, a fall into some grievous fault, which makes us open our eyes and perceive that, whilst we were thinking of any thing else, our heart was betraying us for want of watchfulness in guarding it, and from not entering often into it to ascertain what was passing.

3. It is this living out of ourselves, and this carelessness in ordering our interior, which is the reason that the gifts of the Holy Spirit are almost without effect in us, and that the sacramental graces which are given us by virtue of the sacraments we have received, or are frequenting, remain without profit.

By sacramental grace is meant the right which each sacrament gives us before God, of receiving from Him certain succours which preserve within us the effect that sacrament has wrought in our soul. Thus the sacramental grace of baptism is a right which baptism gives us to receive lights and inspirations to lead a supernatural life, as members of Jesus Christ, animated by His Spirit. The sacramental grace of confirmation is a right to receive strength and constancy to combat against our enemies, as soldiers of Jesus Christ, and to win glorious victories over them. The sacramental grace of confession is a right to receive an increase of purity of heart. That of communion is a right to receive more abundant and efficacious succours to unite us to God by the fervour of His love. Each time we confess and communicate in a good state, these sacramental graces and the gifts of the Holy Spirit increase in us; and yet we do not perceive their effects in our daily life. Whence comes this? From our unmortified passions, our attachments and disorderly affections, and our habitual faults. We allow these vicious principles to have more dominion over us than sacramental graces and the gifts of the Holy Spirit, so that the former keep the latter, as it were, bound and captive, without the power of producing their proper effects. And why do we let sin and the vicious principles of corrupt nature usurp this despotic empire over the divine principles of grace and the Spirit of God? It is for want of entering often into ourselves. If we did so, we should discover the state of our interior and correct its disorders.

§ II.

1. By watching over our interior we gradually acquire a great knowledge of ourselves, and attain at last to the direction of the Holy Spirit; and at times God brings before us in an instant the state of our past life, just as we shall see it at the Judgment. He makes us see all our sins, all our past youth; at other times He discloses to us the whole economy of the government of the universe: and this produces in the soul a perfect subjection to God.

2. They who have applied themselves for three or four years to watch over their interior, and have made some progress in this holy exercise, know already how to treat a multitude of cases with address and absence of all rash judgment; they penetrate, as it were natu-

y, the heart of others, and discover almost all its movements by the knowledge they possess of their own interior, and of the natural movements of their own heart.

3. Without performing extraordinary mortifications, or any of those exterior actions which might be the occasion of vanity to us, by simple attention in watching our own interior, we perform excellent acts of virtue and make prodigious advances in perfection; whereas, on the contrary, by neglecting our interior we incur incalculable losses.

4. This exercise may be practised at every age, at all times, and in all places, in the midst of our exterior functions and in time of illness; and there is no business so embarrassing, which does not allow us to enter into ourselves from time to time, to observe the movements of our heart.

5. What exterior actions did St. Paul the Hermit perform, and so many other Saints, and so many holy Virgins? It is the merit of their interior life which raised them to the highest ranks of the blessed.

But, alas, we are so little enlightened, or so bewitched with all the brilliancy of exterior employments, that we understand not the excellence, nor the necessity, nor the merit of that life which is hidden from the eyes of men and known to God alone.

§ III.

Nothing is so dangerous as to neglect the care of our interior, and to take no pains to know what is passing therein. This negligence and this ignorance give occasion to a multitude of venial sins, which dispose us insensibly to some mortal sin or great temptations, whence ensue fatal falls.

Such is often the end of the purely exterior life of those amongst us who are continually engaged in the tumult of action, abandoning the care of their interior under pretext of zeal and charity, because they labour for the service of their neighbour. But even should they not proceed to this extremity, it is still certain that by wasting themselves exteriorly, and giving scarcely any attention to the regulation of their interior in the exercise of their functions, they suffer incalculable losses of grace and merit. Their labours produce but very little fruit, not being animated by that strength and that vigour which come from the interior spirit, nor accompanied with the benedictions which God bestows on men of prayer and recollection. They do nothing purely for God, they seek themselves in every thing, and always secretly mix up their own interest with the glory of God in their best undertakings.

Thus they pass their lives in this mixture of nature and grace, without once taking a single step forward towards perfection for ten or twenty years, the mind as distracted, the heart as hard, amidst all the exercises of Christian piety and the religious life, as if they had never enjoyed all these aids.

At last death comes; and then they open their eyes, they perceive their illusion and blindness, and tremble at approaching the dread tribunal of God.

The means of avoiding all these woes is to regulate our interior so well, and to keep watch over our heart so carefully, as to have ground for desiring, rather than fearing, to appear before our Sovereign Judge. This watchfulness it is that our Lord so much recommends to us in the Gospel, when He says so often, *Vigilate*, "Watch." "Our father director," says Father Rigoleu, "requires nothing else from us but this constant attention to our interior."

ARTICLE II.

How important it is that we should join the interior life with our exterior occupations.

§ I.

Our occupations are often indifferent in themselves, and yet may be most glorious to God, and more to His glory than others which in themselves are supernatural. Thus our studies and our office of regent conduce to the salvation of souls, and promote the glory of God, more than would the assisting in choir and chanting the Divine Office, were such the practice of the Company, as of the other orders. But unless in this occupation of the classes and of study we act from the principle of the interior spirit, we are just like seculars, and often merit only chastisements in the next life.

§ II.

We ought to join together action and contemplation in such a way, as not to give ourselves more to the former than to the latter, endeavouring to excel as much in one as in the other. Otherwise, if we throw ourselves altogether into the exterior life, and give ourselves wholly to action, we shall undoubtedly remain at the lowest degrees of contemplation; that is to say, we shall practise only ordinary prayer, and perform the other exercises of piety in a low and imperfect manner.

§ III.

We ought so to unite action and the exterior life with contemplation and the interior life, as to give ourselves to the former in the same proportion as we practise the latter. If we make much mental prayer, we ought to give ourselves much to action; if we have made but moderate progress in the interior life, we ought to employ ourselves only moderately in the occupations of the exterior life; and if we are but little advanced in the ways of the interior, we ought to abstain altogether from what is exterior, unless obedience prescribes the contrary; otherwise we shall do no good to others and ruin ourselves.

§ IV.

We must be like the eagle, who soars into the air as soon as he has seized his prey. Thus we ought to retire for prayer after any active employment for our neighbour, and never intrude ourselves into such, unless obedience enjoins it.

§ V.

A labourer of the Company must say like our Lord, "I am not come to be ministered unto, but to minister, and to give my life a redemption for many." He must serve God and his neighbour, occupy himself with God in his interior, and devote his labours and his life, even to the last breath, to promoting the salvation and perfection of his neighbour.

Let us be thoroughly convinced that we shall gain fruit in our ministrations only in proportion to our union with God and detachment from all self-interest. A preacher when he is much followed; a missionary when he produces a great sensation; a confessor when he sees his confessional surrounded by a crowd of penitents; a director when he is the fashion; a person who devotes himself entirely to good works,—one and all flatter themselves they are gaining much fruit, and to judge from appearances we might believe it. The world praises them; applause confirms them in the good opinion they have of their success. But are they united to God by prayer? Are they perfectly detached from themselves? Do they act only from divine motives? Do not human views mix themselves up with their designs? Let them beware of deceiving themselves.

Men are easily deceived in this matter. They seek God, it is true; but do they not also seek themselves? They intend the good of God and the good of souls; but do they forget their own glory and their own petty interests? They employ themselves in works of zeal and charity; but is it out of a pure motive of zeal and charity? Is it not because they find their own satisfaction in it, and love neither prayer nor study, and cannot live retired in their own room or endure recollection.

If we examine ourselves well, perhaps we shall find in our soul so little union with God, and in the services we render our neighbour so much self-seeking, that we shall have just ground for doubting whether we do all the good to others we imagine, and do not inflict more evil upon ourselves than we are aware.

To labour profitably for the salvation of others, we must have made great progress in our own perfection. Until we have acquired perfect virtue, we ought to practise very little exterior action. But if superiors lay too much upon us, we may trust that Providence will so dispose things that the burden will soon be diminished, and all will turn out to the greater good of inferiors, if they are good men.

§ VI.

We must first acquire virtues in a solid degree, and after that labour to promote the salvation of souls; then exterior action will aid us in the interior life. But until we have acquired solid virtues and are closely united to God, exterior occupation will certainly be injurious to us.

ARTICLE III.

We ought not to engage in exterior occupations of our own accord.

It is not for us to choose our own employments. Of our own free will, we ought to give our whole attention to ourselves, unless obedience imposes on us functions for the service of our neighbour. From obedience must come the movement which leads us to external action for the good of others. So long as it leaves us at rest, let us willingly remain so. God will know very well how to find us when He wishes to make use of us to His glory. It is great rashness to intrude ourselves into the government of souls, an office which the most perfect Saints, the Ambroses and the Gregories, fled from with fear. The blessed Louis Gonzaga had a scruple in having speculated for a moment as to what employment superiors would allot to him.

CHAPTER IV.

ADVICE FOR THE INTERIOR LIFE.

ARTICLE I.

We ought to cultivate the will more than the understanding.

APPLICATION to study is befitting a religious, especially if he is called by his vocation to apostolical labours; but there are some who devote themselves thereto with more of passion and curiosity than zeal. We are sometimes bent only on filling the mind with such knowledge as serves rather to harden and chill it, than to soften it by devotion, and inflame it with fervour. It is the will we ought principally to cultivate. We have generally sufficient knowledge, but we are not sufficiently united to God. We ought to make it our chief study to acquire the spirit of prayer, and to become filled with a great love of God.

Cardinal du Perron, when dying, testified his repentance for having during life applied himself more to perfecting his understanding by the sciences than his will by the exercises of the interior life. Some of us will perhaps feel the same regret in that last passage. Woe to that knowledge which makes us neither humbler nor better men!

ARTICLE II.

The path of faith is a safer way to perfection than that of sensible graces.

God leads souls by two sorts of ways; some He guides by interior lights, consolations, and sentiments of devotion. And this way is the most dangerous; because it gives occasion to self-love to luxuriate in favours of this kind, on account of the relish we find in them, and the high esteem we hence conceive of ourselves. Along this road lies the precipice of the bad angels, whose sin was pride, which puffed them up by the consideration of the spiritual goods they had received from God.

Others are led by reason and faith, assisted by the ordinary aids of actual graces, but without sensible consolations, except on rare occasions. And this road is the safest, and leads most directly to perfection, because therein we walk more in spiritual poverty and humility.

ARTICLE III.

The best mode of practising the virtues.

§ I.

We ought to tend continually towards God, without stopping short at His gifts and graces. Some are too much engrossed with the formal objects of virtues, which are merely natural. It would be far better to act on a principle which would raise us straight to God, as does divine love. It is true that all the virtues lead us to Him by their own proper motives, but it is with greater slowness and with less perfection.

§ II.

There are some whose minds are intent upon discovering several motives of virtue with a view of performing their actions thereby, thinking by such means to render them more agreeable to God. We ought merely to try to ascertain what virtue God desires we should practise in each action, and then simply perform that action in the presence of God, according to the intention with which He inspires us, and with the motive and purpose of imitating our Lord.

It is to this end that the love of our Lord is so strongly urged upon us, the motive of which is easy, suited to all the world, and full of sweetness. And the good that is done by the principle of this love,—an act of temperance, for example, performed with the view of imitating our Lord and pleasing Him,—is far more excellent than when it is done simply to observe such moderation as temperance prescribes.

SIXTH PRINCIPLE.

UNION WITH OUR LORD.

The soul is united to our Lord in three ways: by knowledge, by love, and by imitation.

FIRST SECTION.

OF THE KNOWLEDGE OF OUR LORD.

CHAPTER I.

OF THE MYSTERY OF THE MAN-GOD.

ARTICLE I.

Of the excellence of the Incarnation.

§ I.

God has been pleased to honour human nature as much as He could honour it by communicating to a man the Divine Person of His Word, and to a woman the Divine maternity. God can produce nothing greater than a Man-God and a Mother of God. These two great works limit the omnipotence of God each in its own kind. They are the pinnacle of that height to which God can exalt His creatures.

Grace and glory ennoble us, and the sacred Humanity of Jesus Christ deifies grace and glory.

§ II.

It is in the incarnation that God operates the rarest marvels of His power.

The first is the union of the Divinity with the Humanity. A *substantial* union, and in one and the same Person; hence it is called the hypostatic union, because by it two substantial natures, the Divinity and the Humanity, remain always distinct, and are united one with the other in the Personality of the Word, so as to form but one Person. A union the strictest and the closest of all possible unions; a union by which God is man and a man is God.

The second is the abasement of the Being of beings to nothingness. It is no marvel, says St. Gregory of Nyssa, that God should have drawn the whole universe from nothing; that He should have " stretched out the heaven, and walked upon the wings of the winds:" but it is a wonder past all understanding that He should have reduced Himself to a state in which it may be said that He has annihilated Himself.

The third is the exaltation of man even to the throne of God. It is no matter of astonishment that man should be feeble, subject to error, sin, miseries, and death; but that he should be almighty, infinitely wise, infinitely holy, impeccable, immortal,— this is a wonder of the omnipotence of God.

Our Lord also shews forth His almighty power in the Holy Eucharist, doing what He pleases with His Body, putting it in this sacramental state, uniting it to the species miraculously separated from their subject, and then to the faithful, who receive it to the sanctification of their souls.

§ III.

After the incarnation, there is nothing more to be admired. It is dangerous to bestow our admiration on creatures. An incarnate God alone deserves it. To admire any thing in the order of nature is to shew how little virtue we possess.

§ IV.

We have difficulty in believing certain extraordinary graces that we read of in the lives of the Saints. But he who believes the favour which God conferred on men by making Himself man ought to find no other incredible or surprising. All the communications which God can make after this are as nothing. God having given Himself in such wise to men, can now refuse them nothing. It was to give them all else, that He gave Himself in the incarnation. We have only to dispose ourselves by purity of heart, as did the Blessed Virgin.

§ V.

Every thing in our Lord Jesus Christ belongs to us in a most especial manner. His holy Soul was created only out of love to us; His sacred Body was formed only for our sakes; His Humanity was united to the Divine Person of the Word only for the sake of men.

ARTICLE II.

Of the Person of the Word.

§ I.

In the Man-God three personal properties are to be considered, which are as it were the source and foundation of all His greatness: He is the Son of God; He is the Image of His Father; He is His Word.

1. He is the Son of God properly and truly, because He proceeds from God the Father by way of generation, and is of the same nature as His principle. He is the Son of God in the most perfect manner possible. He is so necessarily, being necessarily begotten; and He has not only a portion of the substance of His Father, as the children of men, but the whole substance of God the Father, and the whole plenitude of the Divinity.

2. He is the Image of God the Father, because He represents Him, and is His perfect image; because He is like unto Him in every thing, and bears in all things the nature and the substance of His original, which cannot belong to any created image.

3. He is the Word of God. He is called the Word, the idea or spiritual portraiture which the understanding forms to itself of an object when it applies itself to the knowledge thereof. Thus God knowing Himself and all possible creatures, the term of this knowledge is His Word; His image is His Son. And as the understanding is of all the faculties the purest and the most detached from matter, it is not possible to conceive a purity more perfect than that of the generation of the Word, who is produced by the understanding of God the Father; thus by uniting Himself to our nature He joins uncreated purity to flesh; a prodigy which will be the admiration of the angels for all eternity.

§ II.

We participate in these three qualities of Jesus Christ, and it is this that forms our true greatness. This is the foundation of the perfection after which we ought to strive.

1. Jesus Christ is the Son of God; we are also His children. He is His Son by nature, we are His children by adoption. We ought to live, as He lives, of the life of God, seeing that for this end He rendered us, like Him, partakers of the divine nature.

2. Jesus Christ is the image of God the Father. We ought to be the copies of that image. It is our model. We ought to express in ourselves the features of His resemblance, His virtues, His mind, His interior life, and His exterior life.

3. Jesus Christ is the Word of God. We ought to be His echoes, and respond faithfully to all His graces. We must be the echoes of His doctrine, His sentiments, and His whole conduct.

ARTICLE III.

Why the Son of God was to become incarnate, and not the Father or the Holy Spirit.

From the three preceding properties of the Son we may conclude, that it was He who was to become incarnate, and not the other two Persons of the Holy Trinity.

1. God was pleased to be made man that He might make men children of God. It was the Son, therefore, who was to take human nature, in order to associate it with His own divine Sonship, and make it partaker in His heritage.

2. God was pleased to be made man that He might give to men in a Man-God a visible model of a holy and divine life. It was the Second Person, therefore, who was to clothe Himself with a human body, in order to serve as a model of perfection to men, since it is this Person who is properly the image of God the Father.

3. God was pleased to be made man that He might teach men the truths of salvation. It was to the *Logos*, therefore, that is to say, the Word of God, that it belonged to come into the world to teach mankind.

ARTICLE IV.

Why the Son of God became incarnate by way of generation.

God might have become man without being born of a woman; He might have formed for Himself a body as He had formed that of Adam. But it was fitting, not only that it should be the Son of God who became incarnate, but that it should be by way of generation.

1. Because, so far as He is God, He is produced by

way of generation ; thus also it was necessary that His temporal generation according to the humanity should correspond with His eternal generation according to the divinity.

2. In order to the creation of a Mother of God,— a dignity the highest of all that can be communicated to a pure creature.

3. Because the incarnation tends principally to deliver us from the original sin which we contract by being engendered of the race of Adam, and to make us children of God by the spiritual generation of Baptism.

4. In order that the holy and perfectly pure generation of Jesus Christ might sanctify that of men. For all that He took of us, He took that He might sanctify it in us : a soul, that He might sanctify our souls ; a body, that He might sanctify our bodies ; senses, exterior and interior, that He might sanctify ours ; our labours, our pains, our sorrows, sin excepted, that He might sanctify all these in His adorable Person.

CHAPTER II.

THE PROPERTIES OF THE MAN-GOD.

ARTICLE I.

The self-annihilations of the Man-God.

§ I.

The Word annihilated Himself.

It may be said that the Divinity in some wise annihilated itself in this mystery of the incarnation, by uniting itself personally to a nature drawn from nothingness.

We see in the Incarnate Word three kinds of self-annihilation.

The first, in that He made Himself man. It would seem as if He could not have descended lower, supposing He could unite Himself hypostatically only to the angelic nature or to human nature, because those being the only reasonable natures, they alone are capable of being united to a Divine Person. Had the Word taken the nature of the highest seraph, or of any possible creature, the most excellent that could be, He would still have infinitely abased Himself. What, then, was it to become man?

The second, in that He made Himself the child and son of a daughter of Adam, the head of sinners. Who among men, having the use of reason, would consent to return to the state in which he was while his mother bore him in her womb? The Son of God might have created a body of a matured age, and united Himself thereto; but He chose to remain nine months in the womb of His Mother.

The third, in that He divested His Body of the qualities of glorious bodies, and numberless admirable effects which would rightly have belonged to it in virtue of its union with the Person of the Word and its state of glory; as brightness, subtlety, impassibility, immortality, and the exercise of the power inherent in it of performing continual miracles. Who amongst the blessed would consent to return to this mortal life? Jesus Christ did more; He wrought a miracle to render His Body passible and mortal. It seems as if He took it only that He might immolate it for us on the cross, and then leave it to us in the Holy Eucharist for the sanctification of our souls, which He operates by the application of His merits to us.

The holy Soul of the Incarnate Word, beholding this self-annihilation of the Divinity, desired on its part to annihilate itself as much as it could, and abased itself to the manger and the cross; to an infant state; to a life poor, laborious, obscure; to persecutions and to death, rendering, in a manner, all these divine. We ought also to annihilate ourselves after His example.

§ II.

Jesus Christ, by virtue of the hypostatic union, ought to have had a body exempt from the humiliations of infancy, and endowed with the advantages of a matured age, and the qualities of a state of glory. He deprived Himself of them for love of us; and what is it we do for the love of Him?

We love Him only for our own interest. We seek to acquire devotion only for the satisfaction of our taste. We desire perfection only with a view to our own excellence; just as every one seeks to excel in his profession,—a soldier in the use of arms, an artisan in his trade. There are very few souls that love and serve God purely, without reference to themselves. Our works are full of self-interest, and a multitude of deceits, by which we disguise ourselves from ourselves, and delude our own souls. Scarcely in the course of a whole year do we perform one single action from the pure love of God.

We must quit this wretched slavery to our own interests, and serve our Lord purely for the love of Him. Seeing that He has given Himself to us, for the sake of the glory of His Father, and the love which He bore us, we ought to give ourselves to Him purely for His love, and pay Him a disinterested service from the sole desire of pleasing Him.

ARTICLE II.

The alliances of the sacred Humanity of Jesus Christ with the three Persons of the Holy Trinity.

In the mystery of the incarnation the sacred Humanity contracts admirable alliances with the three Persons of the Trinity.

1. With the Son: it is impossible to conceive a closer union than this. Nothing participates so truly in another as the Humanity participates in the Person of the Son, and as the Person of the Son reciprocally participates in the sacred Humanity. The connexion of soul and body, and the intercommunion that subsists between these two parts of man, is not so close. Human nature is as much the nature of the Word as my nature is mine, although the two natures, the divine and the human, remain always distinct.

2. With the Father: because this divine union of the Word and the sacred Humanity is the Son of God by nature; and sonship is the first degree of relationship. The son is the heir of the father; he has a right to every thing that the father possesses. Thus Jesus Christ, inasmuch as He is man, is heir of all the possessions of God. He is King. He is sovereign Judge. Our adorations are due to His Person, His Soul, His Body, and His Blood.

3. With the Holy Spirit: because this divine Spirit, proceeding from the Son as well as from the Father, bears as close a relation to the Son as the Son bears to the Father, although the relation is diffcrent. We may say that Jesus Christ is the principle of the Holy Spirit: and it is for this reason that the fulness of this divine Spirit was not given to the Church till after the coming of Jesus Christ into the world.

ARTICLE III.

Of the three crowns which Jesus Christ received from His holy Mother in His Incarnation.

"Go forth, ye daughters of Sion, and see King Solomon in the diadem wherewith his mother crowned him in the day of his espousals, and in the day of the joy of his heart."

This day is that of the incarnation. On this day the holy Virgin gave three admirable crowns to her Son.

The first is that of the life divinely human, which on this account is called *theandric*, and which consists in the union of the Divine Essence and the Person of the Word with human nature; because, according to St. John of Damascus and certain other doctors, the Blessed Virgin co-operated even actively with the Holy Spirit in the incarnation of the Word.

The second is that of the life of glory, which consists in the beatific vision, which the sacred Humanity of Jesus Christ began to enjoy from the first moment of His conception. For this life being a necessary consequence of the preceding, since the Son of God received the first from the Blessed Virgin, it cannot be denied that He received the second also, according to that maxim of philosophers, that "he who gives being is accounted as giving all that must follow being."

The third is that of the life of influence in His mystical members, by which He communicates to them grace, as their head; and it is by the incarnation that He is made head of men and the source of all sanctity to them, having merited as many graces as God can create, and as much sanctity as there is in God, and together with this the power of communicating it.

ARTICLE IV.

Of the royalty of Jesus Christ.

[The royalty of Jesus Christ is described in Psalm lxxi.]

1. He is King by all sorts of titles: by right of nature and of heritage; by right of excellence and of merit; by right of conquest; by right of election.

Never was any one king in such wise. Seldom do the kings of the earth possess even one just title to reign.

2. He is King of the whole world and of all beings. His kingdom has no limits upon earth. It extends beneath the earth, to purgatory and hell, which are the prisons of justice; and above the earth, into heaven, which is the citadel of His empire and the theatre of His glory. The greatest monarchs of this world have but a portion of His earthly kingdom, whatever be the extent of their territories.

3. He is "the King of ages," the "immortal" King, whose kingdom shall never end. Other kings are mortal; they reign only for a few years, then their power is lost in nothingness. But Jesus Christ reigns for ever and ever: *regni ejus non erit finis*. St. Theresa could not hear these words of the Nicene Creed without being ravished with joy; and we should share the feelings of this great Saint, if we had the same love that she had for our Lord.

4. He is "the King of kings and the Lord of lords." "All the kings of the earth shall adore Him, and all nations shall serve Him." One day He shall see the pride of monarchs annihilated at His feet, and all nations, whether by love or by force, shall do homage to His glory.

5. He is the King of all hearts and of the interior life itself. Other kings have power only over the goods and the bodies of their subjects; they cannot govern the interior save by the exterior. Their empire extends not over hearts. That domain God has reserved to Himself alone; and He is so jealous of it that He will not have creatures divide it with Him. All our affections must be subjected to His laws, and to Him we owe the tribute of all the movements of our heart.

6. He never ceases from the actual exercise of His

royalty. The kings of the earth cannot give an unceasing application to the government of their states. Their capacity is too limited, and their personal wants do not allow them to devote an uninterrupted attention to their subjects. But Jesus Christ, at every moment and throughout the whole universe, exercises all the functions of His royalty, and He will exercise them eternally both in heaven and in hell.

7. It is not from His subjects that He receives His riches and power, like other kings, who in themselves possess nothing beyond the rest of men. In themselves they are poor and weak; and therefore it is that their subjects must pay tribute and take up arms to defend them and maintain their interests. But Jesus Christ has all His greatness, power, and riches from Himself, without our being able to add any thing thereto, except a little accidental glory.

8. His subjects are happy under His empire, because He is infinitely rich and infinitely bountiful, and the goods that He bestows are the only true and solid goods. The subjects of other kings are often miserable, and burdened with taxes and subsidies. If their princes are themselves poor, they cannot afford to be very liberal; and however rich they may be, if they are liberal, their largesses exhaust their finances. After all, the goods they possess are but dust compared with those of Jesus Christ. His merits, His satisfactions, His graces, which are the riches of His royal treasure, are inexhaustible. He is so lavish of them, that He offers them unceasingly to all the world, more ready to give than we are to receive. "Come," says He, "and buy, without money and without price." These are the only goods, spiritual and eternal, which fully satisfy hearts, and the possession of which can make us perfectly happy.

9. What the kings of the earth give to some, they

have taken away from others; and it is often with the spoils of the poor that they enrich their favourites. But what Jesus Christ gives to some does not diminish the share of others; rather it augments it, and each of His subjects may profit by the abundance of his neighbour.

10. The favour of the kings of the earth is inconstant and of short duration. It is subject to a thousand casualties, and followed often with some sad disgrace or tragical catastrophe. But that of Jesus Christ is sure and as lasting as His kingdom, provided we do not render ourselves unworthy of it. Whoever is in favour with Him may, if he will, secure his good fortune for an eternity. His faithful subjects become so many kings; and the greater their subjection to Him, the more are they exalted.

What tribute shall we pay to this sovereign monarch, who loads us with good things? Let us render Him the homage of a faithful heart, a heart pure and burning with charity, full of zeal for His glory, and an ardent desire to sacrifice a thousand lives, if we had them, to His love and service.

ARTICLE V.

Of the three principles of the actions of Jesus Christ.

§ I.

The actions of Jesus Christ had three principles.

The first, the powers of His soul, enriched with all the fulness of grace, and the senses and members of His body, adorned with all qualities befitting the majesty of a Man-God. Thus His actions were free from all imperfection and infinitely holy, as proceeding from an infinite holiness, and consequently infinitely noble and infinitely precious.

The second is the Person of the Word, which rendered the actions of the sacred Humanity divine, in the same way as those of angels are angelical, and those of men human. Thus the actions of Jesus Christ are adorable on account of their principle and of the subject in which they reside, that is to say, a nature, as it were, deified. Whence we may judge what man is worth, and what he has cost God; that the price he has cost is infinite; and that his value is incalculable since his redemption by the Blood of a Man-God; and that for the same reason we are under infinite obligation to Him.

For although the grace and glory Jesus Christ has merited for us are not infinite, yet the actions by which He has merited grace and glory for us are infinite. It is as if a person who was infinitely rich had given all his riches to redeem a captive; the latter would be under an infinite obligation to him, though the liberty he had restored him was not an infinite good.

The third is the Holy Spirit, who governed the whole order and economy of the actions of Jesus Christ in general, and each action in particular. It was by this principle that the sacred Humanity wrought the same things that it saw wrought by the Divinity. The same effects of mercy, for example, justice, sweetness, severity, love, and hatred; so that it was, as it were, the seal of the Divinity, whereon the features of its original are stamped, so far as the Humanity was capable thereof. This was done by the direction of the Holy Spirit, who wished to trace out for us in the life and actions of Jesus Christ a way to conduct us safely to the glory and sovereign bliss of eternity.

§ II.

Our Lord having been conceived by the Holy Spirit in the womb of the Blessed Virgin, willed to be guided in all His actions, not only by the Person of the Word, but also by that of the Holy Spirit, in order to teach us that, as this Divine Spirit is the principle of our spiritual regeneration in baptism, He must also be the principle of our conduct; that He must govern us in all things, and that we must depend absolutely on His direction, since the members must be animated with the same spirit as the head.

It is not, then, from the senses, the passions, or from the mere reason, that we must take our direction, but solely from the Holy Spirit. Let us consider whether we allow ourselves to be governed by Him, and whether it is not the spirit of the flesh or of the world that governs us. If it be the Holy Spirit, we shall rejoice in the liberty of the children of God. If it be another spirit, we shall be the very slaves of that spirit, following its movements and its directions.

CHAPTER III.

THE DIFFERENT STATES OF THE LIFE OF JESUS CHRIST.

In the mortal life of the Incarnate Word we remark six states, which ought to form the ordinary subject of our meditations.

The first is His abode for nine months in the womb of the Blessed Virgin.

The second, His infancy to the age of twelve years.

The third, from the age of twelve years to thirty, which was a hidden life.

The fourth, from the age of thirty to His Passion, which was a life of zeal, of labours, and of persecution.

The fifth, from the Last Supper to the Cross, which was a purely suffering life.

The sixth, the time He hung upon the Cross, which was a languishing and dying life.

To these states may be added that of His glorious life, and that of His abode in the most Holy Sacrament.

ARTICLE I.
Of the infancy of Jesus Christ.

§ I.

Few persons have a devotion to the holy Infancy of our Lord. They are touched in some little degree by the pains and ignominy of His Passion, but they scarcely ever think of the other mysteries of His life: this is from want of a true and living faith.

The Infancy of Jesus Christ is a state infinitely adorable and amiable, demanding the close application of our minds to honour and imitate it.

We may consider therein the virtues He exercised: His humility in supporting the abjection of such a state, His patience in suffering persecutions and exile, His poverty, His contempt of the world. We may, indeed, humble ourselves for the love of Him, love poverty, despise the world, endure contradictions; but we cannot become children like Him, except it be spiritually, by expressing in ourselves the peculiar qualities of childhood, —purity, innocence, simplicity, meekness, docility, obedience.

The love of purity is the first virtue of which He gave us the example at His coming into the world, leaving the pure womb of His Blessed Mother, without injury to her virginity, as He had been conceived in like manner: nourished with her virginal milk, being Himself alone a virgin by extraction, making it manifest that the first and the proximate disposition for His incarnation was purity; for thirty years working no other miracle by His sacred Humanity than that of being born of a virgin Mother, making Himself like to other children in all beside.

§ II.

Innocence is of all things the most essential, and that which most constrains God to love us. Nothing brings us nearer to God. He gave no other commandment to Adam than to preserve the innocence in which he had been created. On this one thing alone hung the salvation of men.

Innocence and purity form the grand disposition for receiving the graces of God.

ARTICLE II.

Of the hidden life of Jesus Christ.

It is impossible to conceive how our Lord loves the hidden life. He hides Himself in all His states.

He is hidden in the bosom of His Father, in the womb of His Mother, in His birth, in His childhood, in His exile into Egypt, in His abode at Nazareth, in the course of His ordinary life, in the ignominy of His death, in the world after His resurrection, in heaven after His ascension, in the Holy Eucharist, which may be called the great mystery of the hidden life. When we love Jesus Christ, we love to abide with Him. " Your life is hid with Christ in God."

Our Lord gave thirty years to the contemplative life, and three or four only to that which is called *mixed*, because it is composed of action and contemplation. Two reasons for this conduct may be alleged.

1. He did not wish to teach before the time prescribed by the law.

2. He wished by His example to instruct the Blessed Virgin and St. Joseph, who alone were more important in His eyes than all other creatures.

ARTICLE III.

Of the glorious life of Jesus Christ.

§ I.

The glorious life of our Lord is divided into three parts.

The first, from the Resurrection to the Ascension.

The second, from the Ascension to the day of Judgment.

The third, from the general Judgment through all eternity.

§ II.

In this state of glory we must consider Jesus Christ as the prince of liberty.

During this life we suffer three sorts of slavery on the part of creatures.

The first is that of the dominion which creatures exercise over our faculties, over the imagination and the appetite, over the understanding and the will, making impressions on them which we cannot prevent. If a noise is made, it distracts my mind from its attention. The remembrance of something past disturbs me; the thought of some future evil causes me alarm; all objects affect me in spite of myself, and set my passions all at play like puppets. The devil even has the power of exciting the humours and irritating the temper of unmortified persons, and of those who have not as yet attained to perfect purity.

The second is that of our dependence on creatures for daily sustenance: as on bread and other food to nourish us, on sun and light to enable us to see, on air to enable us to breathe.

The third is that of the power which creatures possess of making us suffer. Cold, heat, wind, rain, and a thousand other things, incommode and trouble us.

Our Lord never suffered the first kind of subjection to creatures, because it is a mark of imperfection. Creatures made only such impression on His soul as He permitted them to make. Noise did not distract Him. None of the objects that were in His imagination and His mind moved Him more than He chose. Insults did not affect Him. Nothing prevented Him from doing whatever He pleased.

As the second subjection does not involve any thing of moral imperfection, our Lord was pleased to undergo it for love of us: thus He submitted to eat and drink.

As for the third, He was exempt from it in part, creatures having made Him suffer only as the instruments of the malice of men. Thus it was that the scourges lacerated His body, that the thorns pierced His head, that the nails fastened Him to the Cross. But in His glorious state He entirely freed Himself from these two servitudes. After His Resurrection He no longer needed the sun to give Him light, or food to nourish Him. He was impassible, and beyond the reach of all creatures.

We ought to aspire after this blessed state of the Prince of holy liberty, endeavouring to free ourselves as much as possible from the slavery of creatures, so that they may no longer excite in us irregular movements, nor disturb any longer the peace of our soul. But if we must depend upon them for daily sustenance, at least let us not increase this dependence by our self-indulgence and sensuality, but rather diminish it by mortification and holy poverty.

If we are obliged to suffer the pain and molestation which creatures cause us, let us endure them with joy, in a spirit of penance and for the love of God, who for our sakes has borne so much greater; but let us rise as much as we can above our sufferings, and occupy ourselves with them only as little as possible.

§ III.

Our Lord during His mortal life was not subject to the illusions of the senses, which often deceive us in the case of a number of objects: the sun, for example, which seems to us much smaller than it is.

Jesus Christ beheld the sun and all creatures in their just proportions.

Now that He is in glory He beholds even with His bodily eyes all that passes in heaven, on the earth, throughout the whole universe, whether He sees it by a single species which He is able to create, or without species, as Suarez, that doctor of the Church, supposes.

Oh, if we beheld the things of this life such as they really are, mean, transient, delusive! But we see them under a false appearance, as when the clouds appear to us to touch the sky, in which case reason corrects the error of the senses. But in respect to the moral judgment we pass upon things, as we have but very little supernatural light to correct the error of our senses and our reason, we let ourselves be easily deceived on every occasion.

§ IV.

The glorious Body of Jesus Christ possesses as extensive and as subtle a power of hearing as of sight. As He sees every thing, so does He hear every thing, not only with the mind, but also with the bodily ears; He hears our vocal prayers, He hears our jestings, our murmurs, our slanders, all the bad or idle words we are constantly saying. Ah, how careful in speaking ought this consideration to make us! with what reserve, with what modesty, ought we to regulate all our movements, weigh all our words, before our Lord! what reverence ought we to pay to the Presence of that Adorable Humanity before whose eyes we live, and whose observation we cannot escape!

§ v.

The brilliancy and the beauty of the glorified body surpasses not only every thing we see, but also every thing we can imagine of beauty and splendour. Were this body placed in the vicinity of the sun, it would so eclipse the lustre of that bright orb, that it would give no more light than a candle at noon-day.

This body is transparent; and it is a beautiful sight, says St. Anselm, to behold the marvellous symmetry of all its parts, even the most interior. Its eyes have no need of any other light than their own to see every variety of object. It sheds light and withholds it as it pleases. If the least among glorious bodies has so much brilliancy and so much beauty, what must we think of the Body of Jesus Christ, which has infinitely more than all glorious bodies united? St. Theresa, having beheld only for a moment one of the hands of the King of glory, was so enraptured at the sight, that ever after she could see nothing beautiful on earth, nor love any thing therein. Could we but behold the Son of God in the splendour and majesty of His glorious state, we should feel only contempt and horror for all perishable grandeur and beauty.

ARTICLE IV.

Of the state of Jesus Christ at the last Judgment.

The Father hath given all judgment to the Son.

The exercise of the justice of God belongs to the Man-God, because He has paid an infinite satisfaction to the justice of God. This sovereign justice has communicated to Him the right of judging men and angels.

The Apostles, and those among religious who have

excelled in the virtue of poverty and in the perfection of their state, will be the assessors of this sovereign judge.

Now men are in two sorts of ignorance regarding our Lord. One which is called *ignorantia facti*, ignorance of fact: this is the ignorance of idolators and pagans, who do not know Jesus Christ. The other, which is called *ignorantia pravæ dispositionis*, ignorance of evil disposition: this is the ignorance of Jews, Turks, Arians, who refuse Him adoration, and will not acknowledge Him as God.

These two sorts of ignorance will cease on the great day of judgment. Angels, devils, all mankind will know the Man-God, the Son of God equal to the Father, true God as the Father. They will behold visibly the majesty of God in the countenance of a man, and their eyes will be dazzled by it. They will behold uncreated justice gloriously displayed in the throne of that sacred Humanity to which God has given the sovereign power of judging the living and the dead, in the solemnity of that judgment, the destruction of the elements, and the terror of all nature.

The blessed will behold Him in a new state, in which He had never before been seen by them, terrible and appalling. The reprobate will be confounded thereat, and will be unable to endure His brightness. They will wish to hide themselves in the depths of the earth, and will call upon the mountains to cover them. And what will be the horror of the devils, whom of old His word alone drove from the bodies they possessed, and who trembled at His very Name when invoked by the faithful? How shall they endure the presence of His Adorable Person? the lightnings that shall flash from His eyes, the flames of His wrath that shall dart from His countenance?

Then shall all creatures pay Him homage, and shall annihilate themselves before Him in profoundest reverence. His very enemies shall be compelled to adore Him. "Every knee shall bend before Me, and every tongue confess that I am God."

What will the Jews say then who put Him to death? the tyrants who persecuted His Name, that Adorable Name by which alone we are to be saved? the apostates who deserted His faith? the heretics who assaulted it? the atheists who made a mock of His mysteries and His religion? the impious who outraged Him? the bad Catholics who dishonoured Him?

After being thus adored, or rather in the very act of being thus adored, Jesus Christ will "bring to nought all principality and power and virtue." Now all is governed by the powers established by God. St. Thomas and other theologians, following St. Paul, acknowledge a subordination among the angels for the government of the Church, and even among the devils in regard to the war they wage against men. But then the exercise of all these powers, human, angelical, and diabolical, will cease. There will be no more popes, no more emperors, kings, or princes: all will be vassals of one only sovereign Lord; and the song with which the Church addresses Jesus Christ will be perfectly fulfilled: *Tu solus sanctus: Tu solus Dominus: Tu solus altissimus, Jesu Christe, cum Sancto Spiritu, in gloria Dei Patris.* Men will no longer have the power of remitting the sins of men, and of offering to God the sacrifice of a Man-God. Satan will no longer have the power of tempting souls; he will only suffer his own torments.

At the same time will take place the general manifestation of consciences, which will be so complete that nothing will remain unknown to any one, either of his own conscience or of that of others. Then will be seen the graces which every one has received, and their value, as well as the use or abuse he has made of them; the temptations he has had, their strength and duration, together with the manner in which he sustained them; the sins he committed, their gravity, their circumstances and number, all his actions, thoughts, affections, desires, even to the slightest movements of the heart. Now we are masters of the secret of our own heart, we can keep it concealed, and no one can know it, unless we choose to divulge it; but then nothing will be hidden any longer. The deepest folds of the heart will be laid open before Him who is the light of the world.

All will be ended by the sentence which the sovereign Judge will openly pronounce by the mouth of His sacred Humanity. An irrevocable sentence, and one which will make the separation between the elect and the reprobate. A sentence of life everlasting to the former, and of death to the latter.

After this sentence, all creatures taking the part of God will arm themselves to execute His vengeance; and all His designs being accomplished, the course of ages will be finished; time will be swallowed up in the bosom of eternity. The temporal reign of Jesus Christ will give place to His eternal kingdom; and all things being absolutely submitted to His power, He will give up His kingdom to God His Father, and become Himself "subject unto Him that put all things under Him, that God may be all in all."

CHAPTER IV.

OF THE BLESSED VIRGIN.

ARTICLE I.

The dignity of the Most Holy Virgin.

THE dignity of the Mother of God is something so great, that the Blessed Virgin cannot herself fully comprehend it. We may form some idea of it from the following considerations.

1. What preparation the Blessed Virgin brought to this august dignity! It was in prescience of the divine maternity that God exempted her, not only from original sin, but also from the obligation of contracting it, and from the first instant of her being bestowed upon her more graces than on all angels and men together. Indeed, her graces and her merits being multiplied every moment twofold, threefold, and on certain occasions, as at her presentation, fourfold, it is scarcely possible to conceive how she increased in grace and merit in a single day. To what a height, then, had she attained at fourteen years? and what purity, what charity, what virtues did she acquire by so faithful and so admirable a correspondence with grace? All this was but a preparation for the divine maternity, which she was to merit by a *merit of congruity*.

2. This dignity is in a manner infinite, differing in this respect from the light of glory, since the latter is more or less excellent, according to the different degrees of merit. But there cannot be more or less in the hypostatic union, or in the divine maternity. As both one and the other are unique in their kind, and incommunicable to any beside Jesus Christ and Mary, there cannot be others of like dignity more perfect. It is impossible to conceive another mother more excellent

than the Mother of God, or another Mother of God beside Mary.

3. Dignities, graces, prerogatives of every sort, are due to this Virgin Mother; her Son, who is God, being bound, even by natural duty, to love her. Now what is it to be naturally the object of God's love! Hence theologians conclude that all favours that have been communicated to any creature whatsoever have been bestowed upon the Blessed Virgin, with the exception of those which would not have been suitable to her sex or condition, as the priesthood, the apostolical ministry, the government of the Church. Accordingly some suppose that at the moment of the incarnation she had a clear vision of Him she conceived, and of God His Father, and of their mutual love, which is the Holy Spirit.

4. It is on the divine maternity that those high titles of queen, lady, mediatrix, advocate, are grounded, which mark either the sovereign authority which she exercises over creatures, or the power of her intercession with God.

5. This dignity of Mother of God merits a peculiar worship, which is called *hyperdulia*, and which is due to the Blessed Virgin alone, seeing that it could not be rendered even to one who, not being the Mother of God, should possess as much grace and holiness as she possesses, if that were possible.

ARTICLE II.

The Blessed Virgin stands alone in each of her alliances with the three Persons of the Holy Trinity.

My dove is but one.

1. She stands alone in her quality of Mother of the Son, since she is truly and properly His Mother, and there can be but one Mother of God.

2. She stands alone in her quality of Daughter of the Father, since her adoption is altogether singular, and she alone of the children of God was adopted at the instant of her conception.

3. She stands alone in her quality of Spouse of the Holy Spirit, since she alone contracted with Him, in the name of all human nature, a holy marriage, that she might be Mother of a Man-God without ceasing to be a virgin.

The solemnisation of these holy espousals took place publicly in the Temple, when the Blessed Virgin was presented there.

How high is this dignity, and what great advantages it carries with it! What participation in the possessions of this Divine Spouse! what plenitude of His gifts! what sanctity! Never did this holy bride resist the movements of the Holy Spirit! Never did she perform a single action of which the Holy Spirit was not the principle! Alas, how far removed are we from such fidelity! We are continually resisting the Spirit of God. We follow only our own inclinations. Daily do we reject, every one of us, a thousand graces, and hold the gifts of the Holy Spirit in a disgraceful bondage.

ARTICLE III.

The glory of the Blessed Virgin in the Incarnation.

§ I.

It is in the chaste bosom of Mary that the greatest marvels of time and eternity are beheld: a God man; a God adoring God; a God the servant of God; a God an infant; a God clothed with a mortal body, and with all the infirmities of men; a God a victim; a man the Son of the living God; a child the offspring of a virgin mother.

§ II.

The Incarnate Word continued to retain the substance of the body which the Holy Spirit had formed for Him from the most pure blood of the Holy Virgin at the moment of the incarnation. That which the food wherewith He was nourished, like other men, added afterward thereto, was consumed as in the rest of men. This is the opinion of Suarez; and the Blessed Virgin, appearing one day to St. Ignatius when he was at the altar, told him that a portion of her substance was in the Most Holy Sacrament.

§ III.

How glorious is the Incarnation of the Son of God to His holy Mother, and how full of profit to her was the union she enjoyed with Him during the nine months that He abode within her womb! He was united to her as the fruit to the tree that bears it. He lived only by dependence on her, and on the substance He derived from her.

But what communications did He not make her in return! What mutual converse passed between the soul of the Son and the soul of the Mother! Jesus Christ disposing her by a profusion of graces to be the mother of His mystical body, as she was mother of His natural body; for He willed that we should receive through her the life of the Spirit, as He had received through her the life of the body; that we should depend on her for the support and increase of our spiritual life, as He depended upon her for the support and increase of His corporal life.

Let us enter into the sentiments of our Lord towards His Mother, who is our Mother also. Let us willingly accept the dependence He wishes us to have on her, and by this humble and loving subjection honour that in which He was pleased to place Himself.

SECOND SECTION.

THE LOVE OF OUR LORD.

CHAPTER I.

MOTIVES FOR LOVING OUR LORD IN HIMSELF.

§ I.

ALL imaginable reasons induce us to love and honour the sacred Humanity of Jesus Christ as much as in us lies. The principal ones are as follow:

1. This Man, who is united to the Person of the Word, is the Son of God, and is "made so much better than the Angels, as He hath inherited a more excellent name than they. For to which of the Angels hath God said at any time, Thou art My Son, to-day have I begotten Thee. . . . Sit Thou on My right hand." He must, then, be honoured with the same honour as is given to God. The worship of God and that of the Man-God are not two different worships; they are one and the same: accordingly, since the incarnation of the Son of God, the Church every where joins to the worship of God that of the Man-God. St. Paul almost always joins together in his Epistles "God and Jesus Christ," "God the Father and the Lord Jesus;" and St. Ignatius, in our constitutions, says continually, "God and our Lord."

2. He Himself prayed God His Father that He might be honoured: "Father, the hour is come; glorify Thy Son, that Thy Son may glorify Thee." His prayer was heard; God promised Him the homage and adoration of the nations. To us it belongs to fulfil this promise of God the Father; on us its execution depends.

3. God the Father was Himself the first to honour Him: before His coming into the world, by the ceremonies of the old law, which were instituted to represent

the mysteries of the Man-God; during His mortal life, by the splendour of His miracles, and by the incontestable proofs of His divinity; after His death, by the manifestation of His glory throughout the world, by the preaching of His Gospel, and by the foundation of His Church, by the blood of the martyrs shed for the confession of His faith, by the greatest and the most holy personages of the new law, who are all images of the greatness and holiness of the Son of God, as those of the old law were figures thereof.

4. It is God's will that we should honour Him: and to this end it is that He has placed in His hands all His power and all His rights; that He has established Him to be the Head of Angels, Mediator and Saviour of men, Judge of the living and the dead; that He has made our salvation to depend upon Him, and constituted Him the arbiter of our destiny for eternity. When God created the Angels, He made known to them the plan of the incarnation, and set before them the Man-God to be adored by them, having willed that their eternal happiness should be dependent on Him. The glory of the good Angels is their reward for the homage they rendered to the Incarnate Word. The damnation of the bad Angels is their chastisement for refusing to adore a God made man.

"All things are yours," said St. Paul to the Corinthians, "and you are Christ's, and Christ is God's." Such is the order of the service and glory which God desires to draw from creatures, that He may be worthily served and glorified. He desires that His Son should serve Him and honour Him; that men should serve and honour His Son; that the whole world should be employed in the service of men. The Son of God renders to His Father an eternal and infinite honour. All the creatures of the world render us continually an infinity of services, and are consumed for our use. Such is the model and the measure of what we ought to do for our Lord; we ought, in our degree, to honour Him as He honours God. We ought to serve Him as all creatures serve us; and we ought to be consumed in His service as they are consumed in ours.

5. God loves us only in Jesus Christ; and if He looks at us out of His Son, seeing in us nothing but sins, He prepares for us nothing but punishment.

6. Jesus Christ is the gate and the way to go to God. The more we attach ourselves to Him, the more we advance in perfection. The first of the martyrs, " seeing the heavens opened, and Jesus standing on the right hand of God," addressed himself to the Son of God, and not to the Father, because the Son is the way, and the only way, to go to the Father.

Thus we shall never arrive at a great perfection without a great devotion to our Lord, because God has determined by an eternal decree that no one should enter into His glories save by Jesus Christ, who is the gate thereof. But when a soul has exercised itself well in the love and imitation of the Incarnate Word, God draws it on to the highest degrees of virtue and divine communications; and when He has once taken possession of the interior, and has established His abode therein, He governs from thence the whole man, interior and exterior, the mind, the heart, the imagination, the appetite, the eyes, the tongue, all the senses. The more Jesus Christ resides within, the more He reveals Himself without, the exterior clothing itself with the perfections of the interior, or rather, the interior grace diffusing itself over the body; in the same way, after its kind, as in the mystery of the transfiguration the glory of the blessed Soul diffused itself over the Body in a sensible and wonderful manner.

7. All the good we do, Jesus Christ does in us. We may say that He has done, in a manner, all the good works of the Saints, seeing that He communicated to them the thought thereof, which He had himself first conceived, and conceived for them; seeing that they undertook them only through the movement of His Spirit, and executed them only by the help of His grace. Thus, when we keep the feast of some Saint, we keep the feast of Jesus Christ, who is the author of all the sanctity of Saints.

In fine, we are Christians, and our profession is to adore Jesus Christ, and to devote to Him our homage, our love, and our obedience. "If any man, then, love not our Lord Jesus Christ, let him be anathema."

§ II.

We ought to consult our Lord in all things which come before us for our choice, and consider what value His Heart sets upon them; for we must banish from our heart every thing we find has no place in the Heart of Jesus.

§ III.

The Holy Spirit spoke by the prophets and apostles; but as it is in His power to go on speaking for ever, still more admirably and more clearly, He has through the organ of the Incarnate Word spoken in the most perfect and the clearest manner. We ought, then, to have a most peculiar esteem and affection for the words of our Lord as related in the Gospel.

CHAPTER II.

MOTIVES FOR LOVING OUR LORD IN THE HOLY SACRAMENT OF THE ALTAR.

ARTICLE I.

The wonders of the Holy Eucharist, and especially the sacramental species.

§ I.

OUR Lord has left us His Body in the Holy Eucharist, to be therein the memorial of His Passion, the sacrifice of our altars, and the nourishment of our souls. In this mystery of faith Jesus Christ, while giving Himself to us, hides from our eyes and from our senses the boon He bestows upon us, that splendour of beauty, majesty, and glory which is the delight of the blessed; those treasures, those riches, and those infinite perfections which are the admiration of the Angels; that perfume of His glorious Body which regales all Paradise; but faith, supplying the defect of our senses, ought to make us remain as rapt with astonishment, as transported with love and joy at the sight of this divine mystery, as if what He conceals were manifested to us.

We ought to desire neither to see nor to admire any thing else on earth save the Holy Sacrament. Were God Himself capable of admiring, He would admire nothing but this mystery and that of the Incarnation. As for us, what is it we admire? honour, human talents, other vile and despicable trifles, which one day will fill us with confusion, when at the hour of death we shall see how we have treated our Lord in the Holy Eucharist. To priests, above all, this Adorable Sacrament, whose ministers they are, ought to be as the breath they draw; as much as possible, they ought to think of nothing else.

§ II.

This miracle of the species separated from their subject in the Holy Eucharist is an unheard-of wonder. The like was never under the ancient law. Such a miracle ought to produce a similar one in us, viz. the separation of our evil inclinations and vicious habits from our soul, to which we may say they are, in a manner, as much attached as the accidents to their substance. The Word of God works daily on our altars in the Holy Sacrament the first miracle; and it would also work in us the second, which is the end of the first, if we were obedient to it, and co-operated with grace, the fulness of which we possess in the Holy Sacrament.

This miraculous effect has been wrought in many Saints, who by means of communion have wonderfully divested themselves of their defects and the corruption of the old man. Our falls and our miseries ought not to prevent us from hoping that it will be wrought also in us.

God sometimes lets us sink under the weight of our own weakness, and experience the most dangerous wounds of sin, in order to make us know what we are in ourselves; that seeing ourselves afterwards delivered from our miseries, we may be convinced that it is to the grace and the pure mercy of our Lord we are indebted for our escape, and not to our own endeavours. Never, then, ought we to despair of attaining to perfection, or put bounds to God's designs, contenting ourselves with a certain degree, and not aspiring higher.

ARTICLE II.

The excellence of the Body of our Lord.

The love that our Lord displays towards us in the Holy Sacrament constrains us to meditate frequently with delight on the marvellous excellences of this sacred

Body, which He has given us to be the nourishment of our souls.

The first is founded on the hypostatic union, in virtue of which It is to be adored; and all that can adorn a body in the order both of nature and of grace, in time and in eternity, is due unto It.

The second is drawn from the greatness and dignity of the Soul, which being full of all the graces and perfections which result from the hypostatic union, must endue the Body with a corresponding nobility.

The third proceeds from the acts of the Soul, of which this sacred Body was the organ, even making abstraction of the hypostatic union. For if the bodies and relics of Saints are worthy of veneration, because they subserved their holy actions, what shall we say of that divine Body which was the instrument of an infinity of acts, the least among which rendered to God an infinite honour?

The fourth is taken from the purely miraculous manner in which this Body was formed by the Holy Spirit in the chaste womb of the Blessed Virgin, and from the mode in which It is produced upon our altars by the omnipotence of God.

The fifth, from Its having been animated with a divine life, and with a life glorious and beatific.

The sixth, from the great mysteries of our redemption being accomplished in It, and that by Its death God saved the world.

The seventh, from Its being now, properly speaking, the only sacrifice of the new law; and that all the sacrifices of the old law were pleasing to God only through the relation they bore to this, as being Its figures.

The eighth, from Its being the chief instrument of the sanctification of souls, whether as being the victim offered to God in perpetual sacrifice for all mankind, or as being the sacrament instituted to maintain in us the life of grace and to conduct us to that of glory. "He that eateth My Flesh and drinketh My Blood hath everlasting life ; and I will raise him up in the last day. For My Flesh is meat indeed, and My Blood is drink indeed." Admirable words, the meaning of which will never be perfectly understood but in heaven !

ARTICLE III.

The Eucharistic Presence of our Lord is more profitable to us than His sensible Presence was to the Jews.

True it is that the corporal and sensible Presence of our Lord whilst He abode in the world was an inestimable grace. To behold a God conversing visibly with men, to hear Him speak, to see Him work miracles, to behold resplendent in His countenance the features of divine majesty, its benignity and sweetness ; to receive Him under one's roof, to give Him food to eat, to talk familiarly with Him,—this was a happiness which methinks might excite the jealousy of Angels. But I am bold to say that it is far more profitable to us to have Him with us as we possess Him invisibly present in the Holy Eucharist ; and it is in this sense that certain of the Fathers explain those words of St. John : "Having loved His own who were in the world, He loved them unto the end." That is to say, the love He shewed His disciples in instituting the Holy Sacrament on the evening before His death, surpassed the love He had shewn them in keeping them near Him during His life.

For 1st, in the mystery of the Eucharist He seems to extend that of the Incarnation to each of the faithful to whom He unites Himself, and restores to us that same nature which He vouchsafed to take of us ; but with this advantage, that having taken it in its abasement and miseries, He restores it to us wonderfully elevated and united to God, in order to unite us also to Him, and to exalt us to the highest degree of greatness and glory to which we are able to rise.

2. Here He abides day and night as a living victim before the eyes of His Father, appeasing His anger and satisfying His justice, communicating the life of grace and the seed of the life of glory to those who approach Him worthily. So that we ought to picture Him to ourselves upon our altars, continually offering to God the sacrifice of His death, for the very same ends for which He offered it on Calvary, the Sacrifice of the Altar being the figure of that upon the Cross, but a figure which is itself that which it represents. Is not this an advantage to us far more considerable than was the visible Presence of Jesus Christ to the Jews, from which, through their evil disposition, they derived so little fruit?

3. They possessed Him only in one place. If He was at Jerusalem, He was not at Nazareth; and even at Jerusalem, if He was to be seen in the Temple, He was not to be seen in any other quarter of the city. Here we possess Him every where at the same time in all our churches.

4. They possessed Him only at certain times for a few days, for a few hours. The whole time He was with them did not make thirty-four complete years; and, what is more, for thirty whole years He was unknown to almost all the world. Here we possess Him every hour, day and night; and for how many centuries! Add to those that are past the centuries yet to come.

5. They beheld Him only outwardly with the bodily eyes, and generally without advantage to themselves.

Here we behold with the eyes of the spirit, His Body, His Blood, His Soul, His Divinity, and never without the merit of acts of faith, adoration, and other virtues with which His Presence inspires us.

6. To them He did not appear except in a natural state. We have Him present here in a state of pure grace, and to the end that He may operate in us all the effects of grace, which it is as little possible to reckon up as it is to count the stars of heaven, the leaves on the trees, or the grains of sand on the sea-shore.

7. They possessed Him only by means of the senses; we possess Him here in a manner much more intimate, which is above sense. He comes into us, He unites His Body and His Soul to our body and our soul. The union formed between Him and us, says one of the Fathers, is like that of two pieces of melted wax which blend and commingle together. But if our senses have no part in this possession, far from losing any thing thereby, it is this that constitutes the merit of our faith; and besides, neither God His Father, nor the Angels, nor beatified souls, enjoy His Presence through the senses.

8. Of all those who beheld Him and who listened to Him while He conversed visibly with men, how many were there who joined themselves to Him? A very small number. There were not more than five hundred disciples when He ascended into heaven. Compare this little troop with the countless multitudes who adore Him in the Holy Sacrament through all the earth, and who, by faith in this mystery, instead of His corporal and sensible Presence, find His Body and Blood really present under the species of bread and wine, and by concomitance, as theologians say, His Soul and His Divinity, together with the treasure of all the possessions of grace and glory.

What did the Jews, who beheld Him heal the sick and raise the dead, possess like unto this? The very Apostles and disciples, before the institution of this divine Sacrament, did not enjoy so great a privilege.

Who can say what our Lord operates by means of communion in a pure soul? God only knows. The very soul in which these marvels are wrought is not conscious of them. A soul well disposed receives in a single communion a fervour greater beyond comparison than all that flows from all the visions and revelations which all the Saints united have ever had.

After this, how does it come to pass that we are so little affected by this admirable Sacrament? How can we love aught else but it on earth? How can we think of any thing more frequently than it? By faith we behold the marvels it contains, the Body and the Blood of Jesus Christ, the majesty of a God, and the most astonishing excess of His love for men. And yet we have scarcely any other feelings at His presence than those which the senses and the imagination give us. We are destitute of devotion, tepid and dull in His regard, so that at times He scarcely produces more effect by His presence in the souls of a whole religious community than on the walls of the church in which He abides, because He does not find in us any dispositions for the effects of His grace. And whence comes this? What is it in us that hinders the operations of this mystery of love? trifles, nonentities that occupy us; and yet we fill our mind with them, we attach our heart to them, and place our happiness in them. A wretched little attachment will deprive us of the marvellous effects which the Holy Sacrament would operate in us, were we well disposed.

ARTICLE IV.

Of our union with our Lord in the Holy Sacrament.

"He that eateth My Flesh and drinketh My Blood abideth in Me and I in him."

These words denote the admirable union that we have with our Lord in the Holy Sacrament. It is of faith that therein we are really united with His Body. But what is this union? in what does it consist? Four kinds are specified.

The first is only a local presence of the sacred Humanity of Jesus Christ in him who communicates. This union is the least, and is found even in those that communicate unworthily and in a state of mortal sin.

The second, which presupposes the first, is a moral union, and is formed by the mutual love which binds Jesus Christ to us and us to Him in communion. Such is the union of two friends, whose hearts are joined together by the affection which they bear each other. This is more perfect than the first, and belongs only to souls in a state of grace; but it does not suffice to satisfy the force of the words of our Lord, and the mode in which He communicates Himself to us, as food to nourish our souls.

The third, which is of a far higher order, consists in the extraordinary effects which the Holy Sacrament produces in the soul and body; so that it is as if we touched the sacred Flesh and tasted the precious Blood of Jesus Christ with sweetnesses and transports of joy, ravishing the soul, as happened to St. Philip Neri. This union, again, does not adequately fulfil the words of our Lord, which extend to all who communicate, whereas this union belongs only to a small number of perfect souls; besides that this mode of explaining the words of the Saviour regards rather the effects of the union than the union itself.

The fourth is an union, not indeed substantial or essential, but accidental, the most perfect that can possibly be in this kind. By it we are united immediately to the Body and the Blood of Jesus Christ, and by means of His Body and Blood to His Soul and His Divinity. His Body becomes blended with our body, His Blood with our blood, His Soul is joined to our soul; whence there results in us an accidental change which makes us like unto our Lord, our body participating in the divine qualities of His Body, and our soul in the graces of His Soul, according as He is pleased to communicate Himself to us, and according to the disposition we bring to the reception of Him. Thus His imagination stays and regulates our imagination; His understanding enlightens our understanding; His will invigorates and fortifies our will; His appetite moderates our appetite, and extinguishes therein the fire of concupiscence; His senses purify our senses; He roots up our evil dispositions; He destroys the seeds of sin; He mortifies our humours, and disposes every thing in such wise that the practice of virtue becomes easy to us. This it is that was represented to a certain devout person, who, as Platus relates, once beheld in one of his communions the Body of our Lord in the act of uniting Itself to his; Its eyes, Its arms, and each of Its sacred members mingling with his own, as one piece of melted wax mixes with another.

If we do not experience the effects of this admirable union, this proceeds only from our want of disposition.

"If after communion," says St. Bonaventure, "you do not feel any effects of the spiritual food you have eaten, it is a sign that your soul is either sick or dead.

You have put fire into your bosom and you do not feel its heat, honey into your mouth and do not taste its sweetness."

We are full of passions and vices, which, like so many malignant humours, take from us our relish for Holy Communion, and prevent our finding therein the delights we should experience if we approached the holy table with the disposition it demands, having our soul thoroughly purged from all its disorders.

This disposition consists chiefly in purity of heart, peace and tranquillity of soul, in noting and repressing the rebellions of our mind against grace, in discovering our illusions, our errors, our blindness, the depth of our malice, and in correcting all these disorders. When we have done this, we shall experience a hunger and a thirst for that divine nourishment, we shall taste its sweetness, and it will produce in us from day to day fresh increase of spiritual life.

ARTICLE V.

Some thoughts on Communion.

§ I.

Souls are wonderfully changed and perfected in Holy Communion, our Lord removing all their weaknesses, clearing away their stains, tearing away their evil habits, rooting up their passions, and quenching in them the fire of concupiscence, in proportion to the dispositions they bring to the holy table. It is in the participation of this divine mystery that we may say, "our youth is renewed like the eagle's." Then our Lord enters into the powers of our soul according as we are disposed to receive Him ; He unites really His Flesh to our flesh, and His Spirit to our spirit, albeit we know not how this union is brought about. Thus our whole life should be but one continued preparation for communion and unceasing converse with our Lord.

§ II.

When we are united to Jesus Christ in communion, ah! what union of His Heart with our heart, His power, His senses, His sacred members with ours! And what a difference between Him and us! Every thing in Him is a principle of eternal life for Himself and for men; every thing in us is a principle of corruption and of death for ourselves and for others.

§ III.

The Spirit of God, when we are faithful in following His guidance, shews us little by little the infinite goods we possess in Holy Communion. Often the most learned and the wisest of this world are blind to all this; and as they lean too much to their own opinion and judgment, and guide themselves only by their own individual lights, without caring to rise above human reason, for want of humility and devotion they remain grovelling all their life long amidst the littleness of their own ideas and sentiments; a littleness incredible in all that regards the mysteries of the faith and the spiritual direction of souls.

§ IV.

We suffer incalculable losses from want of knowing the treasures we possess in Holy Communion, and preparing ourselves for their reception. Our stupidity in this respect is most deplorable. Generally speaking, we find ourselves after communion as we were before; and after so many communions we continue just the same, just as tepid, as little mortified, as imperfect, as at the beginning. We, who have the happiness of approaching the altar daily, ought to prepare ourselves each day for to-morrow's communion. Our life ought to be one continual preparation for saying Mass and communicating. Every hour we ought to be in a fitting disposition to approach the holy altar.

§ V.

To what holiness does not communion oblige us! How can we forget the honour we have enjoyed in being united to Jesus Christ in communion? How is it He is not always present to our mind, seeing that He assures us, that "they who eat His Flesh and drink His Blood abide in Him and He in them?" How can we sully our imagination with those impure images we fill it with, after it has been sanctified by its union with that of Jesus Christ? How can we occupy our senses, exterior and interior, with so many profane objects, after our Lord has consecrated them by uniting them to His own?

§ VI.

We would wish to enjoy a facility in conversing familiarly with our Lord after communion, all imperfect as we are, and we are vexed at not feeling devotion. What we ought to do is to abandon ourselves to the operation of His hand, and let Him blot out our sins and pluck them up by their roots. When this is done, and our soul made pure, then He will speak to us, and we shall be able to treat familiarly with Him.

§ VII.

Were the Blessed Virgin to pay us a visit every day and converse with us familiarly for the space of half an hour, what a favour would it be! And yet it would be but an union of familiar intercourse with a creature, the holiest and the highest of all pure creatures; but in communion we are united to a Man-God, and this union is wholly interior, and infinitely more perfect than all the favours that angels and saints, and the Mother of God herself, can ever shew us.

Communion may be called the beatitude of this life. A single communion, did we but bring to it the necessary dispositions, would fill us with more delight and cause us greater transports of joy, than to see and converse with all angels and saints together.

THIRD SECTION.

ON THE IMITATION OF OUR LORD.

CHAPTER I.

MOTIVES FOR IMITATING OUR LORD.

§ I.

JESUS CHRIST desires that we should be His images, as He is the image of God His Father, not only as He is God, but also as He is man. And as the perfections of God shine forth in His sacred Humanity, He desires that we should manifest His spirit and His graces in our conduct, and by a perfect expression of His virtues make ourselves like unto Him. The acts of virtue produced by this motive of imitating our Lord and resembling Him are far more noble and more pleasing to God than such as are formed by the motives proper to the virtues themselves.

§ II.

Jesus Christ is the model of Saints, and His life bears all the features of the virtues and the perfection which He has communicated to the Saints; so that His life is, as it were, a mirror of the whole life of the Church in general, and that of each of the faithful in particular, even to the end of time. Every one beholds therein the very pattern of his own state.

§ III.

The Apostles and first Christians were all full of

Jesus Christ; the love and imitation of Him were the idea of perfection they set before themselves; as we may observe in the Epistles of St. Paul. He who had this idea fixed deeply in his heart would exercise virtues from no other motive; for, remembering that Jesus Christ did this or that, and acted thus on such and such occasion, he would immediately desire to do the same, and would be led thereto far more readily, effectually, and meritoriously, than by proposing to himself all the motives of each virtue. We may indeed love virtues for their own beauty and excellence; but when we consider them as they are displayed in the adorable Person of the Son of God, we find them to be incomparably more worthy of love and esteem, such consideration clothing them with a divine lustre. In Jesus Christ they are not only consecrated as in the Saints, they are also, in a manner, deified.

Add to which, that we can enjoy no greater or more glorious distinction in this life than to wear the badge and livery of our Lord; nor have the greatest Saints practised, or taught others to practise, virtues, except from the motive of imitating Him. St. Paul laboured only to form Jesus Christ in the faithful. "My little children," he says to the Galatians, "of whom I am in labour again, until Christ be formed in you." And St. Ignatius, exhorting us to that which is most difficult in the spiritual life, viz. the love and desire of contempt and ignominy, adduces no other reason to urge us on to this point of perfection, than that in so doing we shall shew in an excellent manner our love and gratitude towards our Lord, and shall attain the honour of resembling Him.

Father Balthazar Alvarez used to say, that he considered himself to have made no way in the spiritual life until he had formed in his heart Jesus crucified.

CHAPTER II.

ON IMITATING OUR LORD IN SEPARATION FROM ALL CREATURES.

SINCE creatures serve only to increase our misery, and all our happiness is in God, our sole endeavour ought to be to detach ourselves from creatures, and to be united to God. This it is to which the example of our Lord so powerfully excites us.

1. Jesus Christ, in His mortal life, received on the part of creatures only pain and sorrow. Mankind, whom He had come to save, calumniated and persecuted Him. His disciples betrayed or deserted Him. Even His relations according to the flesh were opposed to Him. There were but His holy Mother, St. Joseph, St. John Baptist, and a very few others, who did not cause Him grief.

What hope of finding in creatures what the Son of God found not? Would we have them treat us better than they treated Him? Have we any right over them He had not, that we should expect them to afford us nothing but satisfaction? We ought to make up our minds to accept that which was the lot and the choice of our Lord; that is to say, detach ourselves from creatures by a general abnegation, expecting from them nothing but suffering unmingled with pleasure.

2. As the sacred Humanity of Jesus Christ, during His mortal life, received only evil on the part of creatures, so was it replenished with all blessedness on the part of God, by reason of its union with the Person of the Word, and the beatific vision which His soul enjoyed in the same manner as it now enjoys it. Hence we learn that it is from God alone, and not from any creature, that our happiness comes; that it is only our union and familiar converse with God that can render us happy in this world; and that if we attach ourselves

to Him by recollection, prayer, and the other exercises of the spiritual life, He will pour down upon us in profusion His heavenly benedictions, which are a paradise on earth.

3. From these two considerations we must conclude that it is a lamentable misfortune if, after having left the world to unite ourselves to God, after having renounced the riches, the honours, and the pleasures of earth, yea, and ourselves also, by vows of religion, with the view of being wholly God's, and God being wholly ours,—we should nevertheless remain attached in affection to the things we have left, and should not attain the end we aimed at in embracing religious perfection, viz. union with God, wherein that very perfection, and consequently our happiness, consist.

CHAPTER III.

ON IMITATING OUR LORD IN HIS POVERTY.

" The foxes have holes, and the birds of the air nests ; but the Son of Man hath not where to lay His head."

ONE of the first virtues that present themselves to us for imitation in our Lord is poverty; on which we may make three points of meditation.

First point. If we consider poverty in itself naturally, we shall find nothing in it but what is repulsive; but if we look at it with the eyes of faith in that supernatural state to which the Son of God has exalted it, it will appear most attractive, and we shall see that it is the foundation of the Apostolic life.

Its merit was unknown before the coming of Jesus Christ; the world shrunk from it in horror. But the Incarnate Word, having espoused it with human nature, consecrated it in His adorable Person. He ennobled and, in a manner, deified it; He communicated to it so many graces and spiritual treasures, that it is become the delight of Saints, and the object of their love. St. Francis honours it as his queen, and cherishes it as his spouse. St. Ignatius would have us love it as our mother, and regard it as the rampart of religion, protecting us from the assaults of our enemies.

Second point. Let us consider to what a degree the Son of God loved it, and how He practised it. When He was pleased to become man, He chose a poor woman for His mother. He was born in the bosom of poverty. The cave of Bethlehem and the manger are proofs of this. Poverty was His constant companion during the whole course of His life. He lived for thirty years by His own labour, and that of the Blessed Virgin and St. Joseph. From the time He began to converse with men He lived only on alms, and never possessed any thing of His own. "The foxes," said He, "have holes, and the birds of the air nests; but the Son of Man hath not where to lay His head." He chose for His first disciples only poor fishermen. He suffered every abjection and all the discomforts that commonly attend on poverty; and, in fine, He died naked on the Cross, having lost all—friends, honour, reputation, credit; stripped of his raiment and all his temporal goods; deprived even of the divine consolations which belong to His state of glory; with nothing remaining to Him that earth could give but shame and suffering.

Third point. Let us consider how we imitate our Lord in the practice of this virtue. In what esteem do we hold poverty? What love do we entertain for it? Are we glad to experience its effects? Do we not rather dread them? Do we trust entirely to God for the support of life, and for all our temporal wants? Do we not prize riches, and seek them with eagerness? Do we not cause useless expenses to be incurred in furnishing our apartments? Are we content that what is meanest and poorest should be assigned to our use? Do we not display more esteem and affection for rich people just because they enjoy the advantages of fortune?

Nothing is so injurious to Christianity as when religious are seen to be as much attached to their own interest as seculars. This it is that fills the world with scandals, especially when they are religious of a reformed order, or are believed to be still in their first fervour. It would not be so scandalous in the members of such orders as have already fallen into laxity.

The poverty and humility of our first fathers won more esteem to the Company than their science, their great talents, and the favour of the princes of the earth.

If we abandon the practice of these two virtues, we shall lose our reputation, and shall bear no more fruit.

CHAPTER IV.

ON IMITATING OUR LORD IN HIS CHASTITY.

§ I.

"Oh, how beautiful is the chaste generation with glory!"

THESE words apply admirably to our Lord. It is in the bosom of God the Father, where He was begotten without mother, and in the bosom of the Blessed Virgin, where He was conceived without father, that we seek for the origin as well as the model of perfect chastity, on which we will make four points of meditation.

First point. Jesus Christ is infinitely pure in His eternal generation, because He proceeds from the Father by way of understanding and knowledge, as the Holy

Spirit proceeds from the Father and the Son by way of will and love. Now, the understanding is of all the faculties the purest in its operation; and nothing is more completely separated from matter than the word it produces. Hence it follows, that as the Holy Spirit, in virtue of procession, is the principle of grace and charity, so the Son, in virtue of generation, is the principle and the source of all purity. This incomprehensible purity of the Incarnate Word is, and will eternally be, the object of the adoration of Angels and Saints.

Second point. Jesus Christ is also infinitely pure in His temporal generation, because of the personal union of the Word with our nature, to which He so communicates the formal effect of His uncreated sanctity, that the Humanity is holy with the holiness of God Himself. The other divine perfections are not communicated to it in the same manner. Omnipotence does not constitute the Humanity formally almighty, nor immensity immense; but holiness does constitute it formally holy; so that in virtue of the hypostatic union, the man in Jesus Christ is infinitely holy, infinitely pure, infinitely removed from all sin.

Third point. Moreover, in this same temporal generation He derives another kind of purity from the manner in which He is conceived, His conception being wrought by the Holy Spirit in a virgin. Unheard-of miracle! which also is a new source of purity,—a purity which, though, strictly speaking, it be not infinite like the former, nevertheless surpasses all imagination.

Thus the sacred Humanity of Jesus Christ is pure in every possible way; and His mind, His body, His blood, His senses, are not only pure, but so many sources of purity, above all in the souls He chooses to be His spouses, and in which He is pleased to be spiritually conceived.

Fourth point. This mystical generation of Jesus Christ in souls must imitate that which the Holy Spirit wrought in Mary. An immaculate purity disposed the Blessed Virgin to co-operate with the Holy Spirit in the incarnation of the Son of God; and we may say, in a manner, that it was by her incomparable purity she conceived Him in her chaste womb. And thus it is, in its measure, that the soul which has given itself to our Lord, and has taken Him for her spouse, must be disposed to conceive Him spiritually; and having formed Him in her heart, must have Him always present as the centre of all her thoughts and all her affections, "running after the odour of His ointments."

§ II.

The different kinds of purification practised under the old law were figures of the pure generation of the Son of God in the bosom of the Blessed Virgin. They were the dispositions thereto. It was necessary that the people of whom the Man-God was to be born should be purified in so many ways, and sanctified by so great a number of holy ceremonies.

§ III.

The epithalamium of the sacred marriage of Mary with the Holy Spirit, and the incarnation of the Word, which was to be the fruit thereof, is the Canticle of Canticles, wherein the spouse, even according to the literal sense, is, first, the sacred Humanity of our Lord; secondly, the Blessed Virgin; thirdly, holy Church; fourthly, each holy soul in particular, as well those that have preserved their virginity as those that having lost it, and having washed themselves in the sacred bath of penance, have afterwards reached the highest degree of chastity.

§ IV.

We ought to celebrate continually the nuptials of the divine union of our souls with Jesus Christ. Confession disposes us thereto by the grace of purity which it imparts to us, the Mass is the wedding-feast, and Holy Communion its consummation.

§ V.

The guards of the heavenly spouse march under three banners, in three several troops.

The first is that of the Martyrs, who represent by their death that of Jesus Christ, God never failing to grant them charity in virtue of the death they suffer for Him. Whence it comes that the Church, as is observed by St. Thomas, Suarez, and nearly all theologians, with the exception of a few moderns, has never in their canonisation inquired whether they were in a state of grace or not before their martyrdom, being content to establish that they died for the faith, or in defence of some other virtue. Death sets them free, not only from the guilt, but also from all penalty due to their sins, and for them there is no purgatory. In heaven they have a special crown, which is called the *aureole*, the mark of their love for Jesus Christ.

The second is that of the Doctors, who in their office represent that of Incarnate Wisdom: for the Son of God, who is the Wisdom of the Father, having made Himself man, it is to Him that it belongs to teach mankind; and this He did whilst He was on earth, and this He continues still to do by the ministry of the doctors, filling them with the lights of divine wisdom and science, that they may make Him known to the world. They are, then, especially consecrated to the mystery of the Incarnation. All their study and all their labours ought to tend to making Jesus Christ known and loved. To this end He set them in His Church, and in heaven He gives them an aureole which marks the share they have had in His office of teacher, and the resemblance they bear to Him in this regard.

Chastity is closely allied to wisdom. They appeared one day both together to St. Gregory of Nazianzum, and chastity seemed to take him by the hand in token of espousing him. Accordingly, as St. Thomas has remarked, he is the only one of the holy Fathers who has not broached material heresy, that is to say, who has not entertained some erroneous opinion since condemned as heretical.

The doctors most remarkable for their chastity have also been the most enlightened; witness St. John the Evangelist, St. Thomas Aquinas, St. Bonaventure, the blessed Albert the Great, Cardinal Bellarmine.

The third troop is that of the Virgins, who by their state honour that of the Humanity of Jesus Christ, sanctified by the unction of the Divinity which is united to it in the Person of the Word. The aureole by which they are distinguished in heaven marks their union with the divine spouse, and the intimate familiarity they enjoy with Him. These are they that "follow the Lamb whithersoever He goeth."

CHAPTER V.

ON IMITATING OUR LORD IN HIS OBEDIENCE.

"Jesus Christ became obedient even unto death for us."

THE excellence of obedience consists in this, that by it we are certain of accomplishing the will of God. And this our Lord exemplified in the most perfect manner possible, as head and restorer of the human race. We may make three considerations upon this, in order to excite ourselves to the imitation of His obedience.

1. Let us consider in what esteem we ought to hold the will of God, which we are certain of accomplishing when we obey. The will of God is not like our will. The human will is of itself indifferent to good or evil. Virtue is not essential to it. It leans more to the side of vice; it is blind, and has need of lights and of the guidance of the understanding, in order to know objects and to regulate its conduct. It is feeble, inconstant, full of imperfections. The will of God, on the contrary, being essentially and necessarily right, just, and holy, is so infinitely and illimitably. It is itself rectitude, equity, holiness; and consequently, as eloquence, if it spoke in its own person, could not but speak eloquently, so the will of God can will nothing except justly and holily. Now we are assured by faith that it is the will of God which is manifested by obedience.

Jesus Christ knew this infinitely better than we do. He knew perfectly that the will of His Father, even in the slightest things, is infinitely precious. He esteemed it infinitely; and this it is that made Him prize obedience more than life.

2. Let us consider what ought to be the degree of that affection with which we should attach ourselves to the will of God, and of the fidelity with which we should follow it. It is beyond the power of our mind fully to conceive. First, it has perfections and attractions which render it worthy of all love, and of being preferred before every thing that is not God. Pain, ignominy, every thing most terrifying in nature, become sweet and pleasant when we recognise in them the will of God. Secondly, we are under greater obligation, if we may so express it, to the will of God than to any other of His attributes, than to His immensity, His wisdom, or His power. It is the will of God that gave us being; it is by it that we exist, that we have the ability with which

we are endowed, that we possess what we possess, that we hope what we hope. Thirdly, the will of God is the rule of all our duties; it is the very source of them; and no one whatever has any claim upon us but such as is founded on the will of God, and derives thence all its force.

Jesus Christ knew all this perfectly, and therefore it was that from the first moment of His life He made this great sacrifice of submission to the will of His Father. What did He not do to give us an example of obedience to the Divine will? Such charms had it in His eyes, even as beheld in the torment of the Cross, that it made Him desire it with ardour and suffer it with joy.

3. Let us consider in our Lord His character of head and restorer of mankind. This character it was that obliged Him to redeem them by His obedience, as Adam, their first father, had ruined them by His disobedience. Thus it may be said that obedience has saved us, and that it is the cause of all the good we enjoy and the happiness we hope for; as disobedience was the cause of all our evils and the misery into which we have fallen.

This virtue, then, belongs especially to apostolic men who are employed in promoting the salvation of souls. And it is for this reason that St. Ignatius urges it so much upon us, and desires that it should be the peculiar characteristic of his Company, and the mark distinguishing it from other religious orders.

CHAPTER VI.

ON IMITATING OUR LORD IN HIS HUMILITY.

" Learn of Me, because I am meek and humble of heart."

JESUS CHRIST alone can teach us to be humble. To become so, we must make His humility our particular study, by entering into His mind and imitating His example.

First point. The measure of our Lord's humility is the self-annihilation to which the Word submitted in making Himself man. We may remark five principal qualities in this self-annihilation.

1. It is infinite; for there is an infinite distance between God, who is the universal and necessary Being, and the creature, which, however perfect it may be, is still in itself but pure nothingness.

2. It is as great and as profound as it could be, supposing, which is true, that God cannot unite Himself hypostatically to an irrational creature; for of those which are gifted with reason and free-will man is the lowest. Moreover, in assuming a body He took all that is lowest in nature, and subjected Himself to a thousand humiliations attached to the condition of men.

3. It is substantial, and not merely accidental like our self-annihilations. When we humble ourselves or are humbled, we lose only certain advantages, the deprivation of which, however, does not degrade us from our being. Often even our humiliations are only imaginary; but that of the Word reduces Him to a degree of being lower than His own, abasing Him even to the becoming truly man.

4. It is complete and total: this it is St. Paul indicates when he says that "in Jesus Christ dwelleth all the fulness of the Godhead corporally." For we may

say that the Godhead annihilates itself according to the measure in which it communicates itself to humanity.

5. It is eternal, and will never cease, the Word remaining eternally man.

Marvellous annihilation ! incomprehensible mystery ! annihilation which is the cause of all the greatness and all the glory of angels and men !

Second point. Jesus Christ, in His sacred Humanity, beholding the annihilation of the Word, has, after this example, annihilated Himself in all possible ways, and above all in the holy Eucharist, which bears wonderful relations to the Incarnation. The grounds of His humility are, first, the continual sight of the annihilation of the Word ; secondly, the clear knowledge of what He is as man—that the human nature He has taken, and which its union with the Person of the Word renders impeccable and infinitely holy, is in itself subject to sin, miseries of all kinds, and damnation ; thirdly, the infinite rectitude of His will, which, in the knowledge that nothing is due to the creature but lowliness, abjection, poverty, labours, and pains, makes Him desire nothing else ; and this it is He chose for His portion on the earth.

Third point. We are very far from having these humble sentiments of ourselves. We think only of exalting and aggrandising ourselves. Our own excellence is the centre in which all our thoughts, all our desires, all the movements of our heart terminate ; and nevertheless in the sight of God, who is Truth itself, the high notions we entertain of our own merit are nothing but error and falsehood ; the desire we have to be esteemed, praised, and honoured, is nothing but injustice ; and that vain-glory, that height we aspire after, is, in fact, the depth of degradation ; that distinction and worldly greatness after which we seek is nothing but misery and poverty : as, on the contrary, true greatness consists in humbling ourselves, loving abjection, and desiring only contempt. The holy angels rose to glory by their humility ; the rebel angels fell down to hell by their pride.

CHAPTER VII.

ON IMITATING OUR LORD IN HIS INTERIOR LIFE.

ONE of the first characteristics in our model which we ought to copy in ourselves is His hidden life, His life of retirement and recollection, and, above all, His interior life.

It consisted in the application of His heart to God, His aims, His knowledge, His love, His zeal, and His desires, which were infinite in their scope ; so that we may say that all He did and suffered externally is nothing in comparison with what took place in His interior.

In order to stimulate ourselves to imitate Him in this regard, we ought to lay it down as certain that all our perfection depends on the interior life. We acquire perfection by the communication which God makes to us of His graces, and by our faithful co-operation with these graces. Now this communication is made especially to souls which enjoy an intimate familiarity with God, and consequently it is by means of the interior life that we make greater progress in perfection.

First, because therein we exercise the sublimest virtues and the most excellent gifts of the Holy Spirit— faith, hope, charity, which are the theological virtues ; religion and penance, which are the noblest of the moral virtues ; wisdom, understanding, and science, which are the most perfect gifts of the Holy Spirit.

Secondly, because therein not only do we converse

with God, but God works with us and makes Himself known unto us; so that having a more perfect knowledge of His perfections and virtues, and being, as it were, wholly imbued therewith, we proceed to practise them with regard to our neighbour. One day God revealed to St. Catherine of Sienna, while engaged in prayer, some effects of His divine mercy towards a sinful soul, which left the Saint in a rapture of joy, and with a marvellous increase of zeal for the salvation of souls.

Thirdly, because He sometimes bestows upon us in one single prayer, by the effusion of His Spirit, more graces and succours than we should acquire during several years in exterior actions even of zeal and charity. Nothing furthers more our spiritual advancement than the time and application we devote to the exercises of the interior life. It is as if a gentleman in the royal favour, instead of labouring to improve his estate, should reside at court with the king: he would push his fortune far more in a single month by the liberality of the prince, than he would have done in twenty years by remaining in the country.

The Saints attained perfection by the way of the interior life, conversing familiarly with God. St. Ignatius in his Constitutions would have us regard this familiar converse with God as the chief instrument of our own salvation and that of our neighbour, for which our vocation obliges us to labour.

CHAPTER VIII.

HOW GREATLY THE MYSTERY OF THE INCARNATION SERVES TO ADVANCE US IN THE WAY OF PERFECTION.

THE incarnation of the Son of God conduces to our perfection, first, by removing the hindrances thereto;

secondly, by providing us with more powerful and more abundant means to arrive thereat.

The hindrances to perfection are the various attachments we have to creatures. For our perfection consists in our union with God, which also constitutes our beatitude. Now what leads us to attach ourselves to creatures, instead of tending to God, in order to unite ourselves to Him, is, that we do not sufficiently understand either the dignity of our nature or the infinite good we might acquire by uniting ourselves to God; but the incarnation frees us from this error, teaching us both the value God sets upon us and the price we cost Him, as also the happiness to be attained by union with Him, and the ease with which we might arrive at the enjoyment of that happiness.

The means we possess to this end are the virtues. Now in the incarnation we find new attractions to excite us to the love and practice of the moral virtues; for ever since a God made man has practised them, they are endued with an excellence and a beauty quite different from what they had before. They are, as it were, deified in the Person of Jesus Christ; besides which, He has taught us many which were unknown, or very little known, before—as humility, poverty, the love of enemies. A Man-God is the model of virtues, the most noble, the most perfect, the most attractive that can be proposed to the imitation of men.

With regard to the theological, virtues, which, by uniting us to God, begin, as it were, our beatitude even in this life, the incarnation marvellously facilitates the practice of them. In the first place, faith; seeing that God, who aforetime spoke only by the prophets, has come in His own Person to teach the truths we are to believe. Secondly, hope; since God, having given to us His Son, and that too after such a manner, can no longer refuse us any thing. Thirdly, charity; since God, having prevented us by that excess of love which He exhibits towards us in the incarnation, even to making Himself like unto us and becoming our brother, demands our love by every kind of title, and we on our part are under every conceivable obligation to love Him.

CHAPTER IX.

A MODE OF EFFECTUALLY HONOURING THE INCARNATE WORD, THE BLESSED VIRGIN, AND ST. JOSEPH.

§ I.

THE most effectual devotion we can practise in honour of the Incarnate Word, the Blessed Virgin, and St. Joseph, is:

1. To take as our model of self-contempt the Word in His annihilation, wherein He abased Himself to our miseries by the incomprehensible mystery of the Incarnation.

2. To take as our model of purity the Blessed Virgin, who was so pure in mind and body that she merited that the Son of God, being pleased to become man, should take her for His Mother.

3. To place ourselves under the guidance of St. Joseph, who having been entrusted by God the Father with the direction and control of the exterior actions of His Son, as also of the Blessed Virgin, fulfilled herein an office infinitely more exalted than if he had had the government of all the angels, and the direction of the interior of all the Saints.

We ought, then, to address ourselves to him in our functions and employments, and earnestly entreat his guidance, not only in the interior, but also in the exterior life; for it is certain that this great Saint has a peculiar power to aid souls in the interior ways, and that we receive much assistance from him in the matter of exterior direction.

§ II.

Every soul which desires to advance in the interior ways must endeavour to excel in devotion to our Lord and the Holy Spirit, uniting therewith devotion to the Blessed Virgin and St. Joseph, with the hope of attaining humility by the merit of the self-annihilation of the Incarnate Word; purity, by the favour of the Blessed Virgin, the purest of all pure creatures; and the guidance of the Holy Spirit, by the intercession of St. Joseph: for this holy patriarch having discharged, under the Holy Spirit, the office of governing the Son of God and His holy Mother, by the merit of this charge has acquired, as it were, a kind of right to direct interiorly faithful souls. And, in fact, we have sensible proof that they who take him as their director make wonderful progress under his guidance.

SEVENTH PRINCIPLE.

THE ORDER AND DEGREES OF THE SPIRITUAL LIFE.

Of all the instructions that Father Louis Lallemant gave on the order and degrees of the spiritual life, we have only what concerns mental prayer. He speaks of prayer in general, and of three sorts of prayer in particular, which belong to the three degrees of the spiritual life, and he enlarges most on that of the perfect.

CHAPTER I.

OF PRAYER IN GENERAL.

ARTICLE I.

The great advantage of being a man of prayer.

A man of prayer is attached to nothing; for he values neither talents, nor offices, nor honours, nor the friendship of influential persons, nor any other temporal advantages. He has no esteem or love except for the treasure he bears within himself, and which no external force can take from him. In comparison with this treasure he despises all else; and so that this only good be preserved to him, he is careless of losing every thing beside. It is as if some connoisseur in precious stones had by him a false one, which however, in common estimation, passed for being real; he would willingly give it to any one who wanted it, because he knows it to be worth nothing, notwithstanding the high value set upon it by those who are unskilled in the matter, and who judge of such things only by their appearance.

When a man has wholly given himself to God by a life of prayer, he is no longer pained either by calumnies or by any thing that may befal him, however grievous. He is like men protected with armour of proof; whether the missile be snow-ball, or stone, or bullet, it matters not, it may strike them, but it cannot penetrate their armour; it does them no harm. In like manner, a man of prayer, when his reputation is assailed, examines his conscience, and if he finds himself guilty, confesses his fault and makes satisfaction to the party aggrieved. If he is innocent, he blesses God for the opportunity of suffering for Jesus Christ.

ARTICLE II.
Advice on mental prayer in general.

1. The spirit of devotion and prayer will never visit us until we have blotted out the ideas of our past life, the images and the memory of innumerable things which foster our self-love and vanity.

2. In prayer our only object ought to be, to perfect the will, and not merely to become more enlightened.

3. It is only our sins and our evil habits that prevent the will, in prayer, from flying instantly to its Sovereign Good and being enkindled with love. This obstacle removed, the will would soon be all on fire without any long exercise of the understanding.

4. Whatever has most impressed the mind out of prayer will not fail to return to us in prayer more readily than in our other actions. The reason of which is, that in the time of prayer the mind being in a state of quiescence, it is more disposed to receive disturbing impressions of this kind than during the excitement of other actions which occupy it more.

5. Before prayer it is necessary to regulate and dispose the mental powers: the imagination, by repre-

senting to it some place on which it may fix itself; the memory, by arranging the several points; the understanding and the will, by providing beforehand some special end of meditation, as the deep realisation of some truth, exciting the affections towards some virtue, combating some vice.

6. One good method of prayer, according to the holy Bishop of Geneva, is to place ourselves silently in the presence of God, and there without the active use of the understanding remain in the presence of God, as listening to Him, although we do not deserve that He should speak to us. He will bestow this favour upon us when we shall have, in a manner, satisfied His justice for having neglected so many times to obey His inspirations.

7. Some in their prayer leave the sacred Humanity, and fly to the contemplation of the Divinity. Such proceeding is generally rash and ill-advised; and if we examine such persons strictly, we shall find them full of imperfections, attachment to their own judgment, pride, and self-love, because they have not sufficiently applied themselves to acquiring self-knowledge and purity of heart before soaring so high. The safest path for them is to return to meditation on the mysteries of Jesus Christ, and the virtues, particularly mortification and humility.

8. Prayer presupposes a tranquil and recollected soul, which is neither agitated by violent passions, nor mastered by any irregular affection, nor burdened by too many occupations, nor embarrassed by cares; nor does God ordinarily communicate Himself until we have been faithful in the exercise of prayer for some time, according to the method prescribed to beginners.

9. Every one ought to adhere faithfully to the kind of prayer suited to his degree and state in the spiritual life. There are three sorts of prayer. Meditation, or

discursive prayer, is suited to beginners who are in the purgative life; affective prayer to those who have made progress and are in the illuminative life; contemplation and prayer of union to the perfect who are in the unitive life.

CHAPTER II.

OF MEDITATION.

1. For meditation, which is also called discursive prayer, we must prepare the points on which we would meditate the evening before, and observe exactly the rules St. Ignatius prescribes.

2. In the actual exercise of prayer we meditate on the subject we have chosen; we draw conclusions from it; we make reflections on the past, examine our present dispositions, and form resolutions for the future. We stir up the affections, encourage ourselves to persevere, and ask the assistance of Heaven. At times God makes known some truth to us, memory suggests others, the hour passes in recollection with but few distractions, which do not last long. This sort of prayer belongs to the virtue of religion; and when it is accompanied with purity of heart, it is the shortest and the surest way to arrive at the other gift of prayer.

3. In meditation, beginners ought to use the easiest discursive method, which is that of reasoning from the more to the less, or from the less to the more. For instance, if the highest angel fell, if a creature so perfect, free from concupiscence and the corruption of original sin, possessed of more grace than I shall ever have, unassailed by any temptation, nevertheless perished miserably, how fearful ought I to be of falling, whatever the degree of perfection I may have attained! If God pardoned not a creature so noble, who might have been the

source of so much glory to Him, am I to expect that if I fall into His hands in a state of mortal sin He will pardon me?

CHAPTER III.

OF AFFECTIVE PRAYER.

In the second kind of prayer, which is called affective, we give ourselves more to affections of the will than to considerations of the understanding. We consider a mystery, a passage of Scripture; for instance, the words, *Verbum caro factum est.* On these we make acts of faith, hope, and charity, admiration, thanksgiving, &c. We take one of God's perfections, as His wisdom, His goodness, His holiness. We consider how it was communicated to Jesus Christ and the Blessed Virgin, to Angels, to some Saint; we praise God for it; we ask for a participation of it, and dwell as much as we can on the affection with which we are most touched.

CHAPTER IV.

OF CONTEMPLATION.

ARTICLE I.

There are two sorts of contemplation.

1. We must distinguish between two kinds of contemplation, the ordinary and the extraordinary.

2. Ordinary contemplation is a supernatural habit, by which God raises the powers of the soul to sublime knowledge and illuminations, lofty sentiments and spiritual tastes, when He no longer finds in the soul such sins, passions, affections, cares, as prevent the communications He would make to it.

3. They who possess this habit pray easily, and have,

as it were, at their disposal the particular grace of the Holy Spirit necessary for the exercise of the theological virtues ; so that they make acts of it whenever they will, after raising their heart to God to obtain His succour, which is always ready.

4. There is another higher kind of contemplation, which consists in raptures, ecstacies, visions, and other extraordinary effects. The former leads to this ; and we make more progress in it in a short time than we do in meditation during many years, that is to say, we acquire more virtue, and that more speedily. By meditation, the soul walks afoot with labour ; by contemplation, it flies without trouble. Thus St. Theresa said, that when God had admitted her to this sort of prayer, all her difficulties ceased at once, and she experienced a powerful attraction towards acts of all virtues, attended with a marvellous relish and sweetness.

They who possess this last gift of prayer commonly pray without knowing they are praying, or being aware of it ; and it is then that prayer is perfect.

In this sort of prayer we place ourselves in God's presence. We remain thus without making distinct or repeated acts, occupied either in the simple contemplation of God with awe and love, or in some pious sentiment which God inspires, and which lasts sometimes an hour, two hours, a day, two days, according to the disposition of the soul and the state of perfection and purity to which it has attained : in souls perfectly pure, the presence of God becomes almost unceasing.

It is usually said that in this kind of prayer no acts are made. This is not strictly true, for some are always made, but in a manner more exalted, more simple, and as it were imperceptible. A complete suspension of all act is simple idleness of a very dangerous kind.

Directors are apt to commit two faults in respect to

contemplation. Some, but little spiritual, or too timid, close the door of it altogether against the souls under their charge, although God may be calling them into it. Others, on the contrary, admit every body indiscriminately, and talk of nothing but prayer of simple regard, extraordinary graces, interior voices, visions, revelations, and ecstacies.

ARTICLE II.

Of the gift of the presence of God. The first step in contemplation.

§ I.

When, after a long cultivation of purity of heart, God would enter into a soul and manifest Himself to it openly by the gift of His holy presence, which is the first in order of His supernatural gifts, the soul finds itself so delighted with this new state, that it feels as if it had never known or loved God before. It is astounded at the blindness and stupidity of men; it condemns the indolence and languor in which we generally pass our lives; it deplores the losses it believes itself to have incurred by its slothfulness; it accounts the life it has hitherto led as not deserving the name of life, and that it is only just beginning to live.

§ II.

In vain do we labour to have this sense of the presence of God unless He Himself bestows it upon us. It is a pure gift of His mercy. But when we have received it, by that presence and in that presence we see God and the will of God in our actions, as we behold at one and the same time the light and the body which it enables us to see. This grace is the fruit of great purity of heart, and leads the soul to close union with God. He bestows it upon us, when, on our part, we do what we can and ought to do.

Were we fully possessed with God, we should be able to practise incessant prayer. It occasionally happens that some passion, or resentment, or vexation of mind, so possesses us, that we are altogether engrossed by it for two or three days together, and think of scarcely any thing else. Not an hour in the day passes without our experiencing this ill feeling; and though we fancy we resist it, yet if God were to shew us the real disposition of our heart, we should see that we had no desire to be free from it, and yielded it some sort of secret consent.

In like manner, if we had a tender devotion to our Lord, to the Holy Sacrament of the altar, we should think of Him a thousand times a day. If our heart were wholly occupied with God, we should cherish an unceasing remembrance of Him, and should experience no difficulty in realising His presence. Every thing would serve to raise us to Him, and the least occasions would excite our fervour.

Let us be assured that our Lord and the Blessed Virgin behold us from the height of heaven, even with their bodily eyes, the perfection of their powers of vision compensating for the greatness of the distance. Thus we ought to perform all our actions as in their presence; and this is the means of attaining the most exalted sense of the presence of God, wherein the prophets Elias and Eliseus walked, and which made them say: "As the Lord liveth, before whom I stand;"—a presence, the sense of which is more lively and more piercing than what we have by faith.

ARTICLE III.

The advantages of contemplation.

§ I.

Contemplation is true wisdom. This it is the books of Wisdom, Ecclesiastes, and Ecclesiasticus recommend so much. They who dissuade others from it are guilty of a great error. There is no danger in it when we bring to it the requisite dispositions. True it is that there is danger of illusion in raptures and ecstacies, especially while grace is still weak, and the soul as yet unaccustomed to such things; but in contemplation there is no danger.

§ II.

We see in the first Epistle of St. Paul to the Corinthians that the most marvellous gifts of God were commonly granted to the first Christians, the gift of tongues, of healing the sick, of working miracles, of prophecy, and of discernment of spirits; and the holy Apostle exhorts the faithful to desire these spiritual gifts, and particularly that of prophecy, which consists not only in predicting things to come, but also in understanding the Scriptures, in expounding them, and instructing the people.

Now-a-days, if any one aspires after some gift of prayer a little above the common order, he is plainly told that such things are extraordinary gifts which God gives only when He will and to whom He will, and that we must not desire them or ask for them: thus the door of these gifts is for ever shut against him. This is a great abuse. True it is that we must not of ourselves intrude into these kinds of prayer; but at the same time we ought not to refuse them when God offers them, nor actually do any thing which may have the effect of preventing His admitting us to them when He pleases.

§ III.

Meditation wearies and fatigues the mind, and its acts are of short duration; but those of contemplation, even such as is of a common order, last whole hours without labour and without weariness; and in the purest souls contemplation may easily continue several days together, in the very midst of the world and the engagements of business. In the state of glory, the first act made by a holy soul on beholding the beatific vision will last to all eternity without satiety or fatigue, ever the same and ever new. Now contemplation is a participation in the state of glory. It resembles it in its facility and duration. It injures neither health nor strength.

§ IV.

Contemplation opens a new world to the soul, with the beauty of which it is enraptured. St. Theresa, when passing out of a state of prayer, used to say that she came from a world incomparably more vast and beautiful than a thousand worlds such as this.

St. Bernard, returning from converse with God, went back with regret to the society of men, and dreaded attachment to creatures as hell itself. That holy priest, Father John Avila, on leaving the altar, could scarcely endure intercourse with the world.

In contemplation a pure soul discovers without labour, or any exertion of its powers, truths which throw it into ecstacy, and which, withdrawing it from all the operations of the senses, cause it to experience within itself a foretaste of paradise.

§ V.

Contemplation leads souls to heroic acts of charity, zeal, penance, and other virtues, as, for example, martyrdom. The Saints, who had received this gift from God, desired their sufferings to be increased tenfold; and to form these desires they had not to undergo those struggles and repugnances which we commonly experience in our good resolutions. They found therein nothing but consolation.

§ VI.

By contemplation we obtain a perfect knowledge of things human and temporal, supernatural and heavenly. The former we perceive to be so vile and contemptible as to be convinced that to set any value upon them is the greatest illusion possible, and that to attach our heart to them is the worst disorder we can fall into. We judge infallibly of the value of both one and the other, and distinguish between them as easily and with as much certainty as a man who understands coins, having several pieces before him, is able to pronounce, only by looking at them, or touching them, "This is good gold, and that is not."

§ VII.

When God has admitted a soul to contemplation, it discovers in itself faults and imperfections it did not see before: for instance, a habit of letting the eyes dwell on the countenance of a person of pleasing appearance, seeking willingly the company and conversation of this person, and loving him, because he is attractive. Such looks, such conversations, such individual likings, are in God's sight a kind of impurity, and the principle of them is vicious.

ARTICLE IV.

Contemplation, so far from being opposed thereto, is necessary to the Apostolic life.

§ I.

Contemplation, far from hindering zeal for souls, on the contrary, augments it by three considerations, of which it gives the mind a vivid appreciation.

First, that souls are capable of possessing God; and that viewed in this light, there is not one which is not incomparably more precious than the heavens and the earth with all their glory and riches.

Secondly, that souls belong to the Son of God; that He has given His life to redeem them; that He has washed them in His Blood; and that being His inheritance and His kingdom, there is no labour which should not be undertaken, no sufferings which should not be endured, for their salvation and perfection.

Thirdly, what is the state of a soul in mortal sin! how wretched it is, and nigh unto hell!

These considerations it was that made St. Paul desire to be anathema for his brethren, and has caused many Saints to wish that they might suffer, if God had permitted it, the pains of hell without sin, so that they might prevent the loss of a single soul.

Such were the sentiments of a St. Catherine of Sienna, a St. Catherine of Bologna, an Alphonsus Rodriguez.

§ II.

Without contemplation we shall never make much progress in virtue, and shall never be fitted to make others advance therein. We shall never entirely rid ourselves of our weaknesses and imperfections. We shall remain always bound down to earth, and shall never rise much above mere natural feelings. We shall never be able to render to God a perfect service. But with it we shall effect more, both for ourselves and for others, in a month, than without it we should accomplish in ten years. It produces acts of great perfection, and such as are altogether pure from the alloy of nature; most sublime acts of the love of God, which we perform but very rarely without this gift; and, in fine, it perfects faith and all virtues, elevating them to the highest degree to which they are capable of rising.

§ III.

If we have not received this excellent gift, it is dangerous to throw ourselves too much into active occupations of charity towards our neighbour. We ought to engage in them only experimentally, unless imposed upon us by obedience, otherwise we ought to occupy ourselves but little in external employments,—the mind in such case having enough to do in acquiring self-knowledge, in purifying continually the natural acts and sentiments of the heart, and in regulating the interior, so that we may walk always in the presence of God.

ARTICLE V.

What contemplation is.

§ I.

Contemplation is a perception of God or of divine things, simple, free, penetrating, certain, proceeding from love, and tending to love.

1. This perception is simple. In contemplation we do not exercise the reason, as in meditation.

2. It is free; because to produce it the soul must be liberated from the least sins, irregular affections, eagerness, and unprofitable and disquieting cares. Without this, the understanding is like a bird tied by the feet, which cannot fly unless it be set at liberty.

3. It is clear and penetrating, not as in the state of glory, but as compared with the knowledge we have by faith, which is always obscure. In meditation we see things only confusedly, as it were from afar off, and in a dryer manner. Contemplation enables us to see them more distinctly, and as it were close at hand. It enables us to touch them, feel them, taste them, and have an inward experience of them. To meditate on hell, for instance, is to see a painted lion; to contemplate hell, is to see a living lion.

4. It is certain; because its objects are the supernatural truths which the divine light discloses to it; and

when this disclosure is made immediately to the understanding, it is not liable to error. When it is made either through the senses or through the imagination, some illusion may at times mix with it.

5. It proceeds from love, and tends to love. It is the employment of the purest and the most perfect charity. Love is its principle, its exercise, and its term.

§ II.

Suarez holds that an act of contemplation is an act of faith or of theological reasoning; but it seems to be an act of those supernatural habits which are called gifts of the Holy Spirit, and which perfect faith and the other infused virtues.

It is a received maxim among theologians, that God reveals no new articles of faith, but only makes known more clearly and more distinctly those He has already revealed; and besides, by contemplation we may have truths manifested to us which only suppose the presence of faith, and do not directly proceed from any theological reasoning, although this may sometimes be their origin.

§ III.

The gifts of the Holy Spirit which serve to contemplation are particularly those of understanding, wisdom, and science, in regard to the intellect; and those of piety and fear, in regard to the will.

By the gift of science we have knowledge of creatures, and despise them, beholding their frailness, their fleetingness, their nothingness. By the gift of wisdom we know the greatness of God and of heavenly things; and hence we are led to detach ourselves from all affection to creatures, in·order to unite ourselves solely to God. The effect is pretty much as when one has just been seeing the Louvre or some extraordinary picture. The mind, filled with these beautiful objects, deigns not so much as to cast a look at some peasant's hut or some school-boy's daub. Thus a soul to which God manifests Himself in prayer ceases to find any thing great on earth. St. Anthony possessed so rare a gift of contemplation, that he passed whole nights in this holy exercise without perceiving that he had spent a moment in it; and on receiving letters from the Emperor Constantine, did not deign even to send him one word in reply.

§ IV.

They who say or imply that the object of contemplation is, properly speaking, God alone, are mistaken. Every thing relating to God may be so. By the gift of contemplation, St. Theresa saw hell in so palpable a manner, that ever after she had no difficulty in performing acts of mortification, or any other acts however arduous. Another time she beheld, in an ideal representation, the sacred Humanity of our Lord, which delivered her for all the rest of her life from all affection for the things of earth, so that she could no longer love any thing but the divine beauty she had seen. By which we perceive what power the visits of God have in them, seeing they produce effects so wonderful; and often there needs only a single supernatural vision to work an entire change in the heart.

ARTICLE VI.

Of the properties and effects of contemplation.

The properties and effects of contemplation are: elevation, suspension, admiration, raptures, and ecstacies.

1. Contemplation elevates the mind above its ordinary mode of action, and draws it supernaturally to sublime operations, whether with regard to God simply or any object relating to God. This elevation is produced either by the gift of wisdom or by that of

science : by the first, if contemplation is occupied with the perfections of God ; by the second, if with some other subject relating to Him. The gift of understanding also contributes thereto, inasmuch as by its means the mind is enabled intimately to penetrate whatever appertains to wisdom or science.

2. The mind thus elevated remains, as it were, suspended in the knowledge of the truth with which it is enraptured. This may be explained by comparing it to the flight of birds, which do not always continue mounting, but after raising themselves aloft, keep themselves sometimes suspended in the air without vibration of their wings or any other apparent movement. In this state of suspension sometimes it is the understanding, sometimes the will that is most exercised, according as God communicates to the soul more light or more affection.

When it is said, that the will is more exercised than the understanding, it is meant that its action is strongest and most sensible, and not that it acts alone, without the understanding acting at all, as some with little probability maintain. The will, then, in this condition is so penetrated, so inflamed with its object, that the action of the understanding is imperceptible. It is as if the will absorbed all the forces of the soul, so preoccupied and possessed is it by the Spirit of God.

3. Suspension is followed by admiration ; which may spring from two sources, viz. either the ignorance of the mind, or the greatness of the object.

4. Sometimes admiration is so strong that the mind no longer acts externally ; and this is the cause of raptures and ecstacies. Rapture, properly so called, is a sudden transport of the powers of the soul, elevated in an instant by the Spirit of God. Ecstacy is the state and the repose in which the soul continues when thus

elevated above itself. Some would have ecstacy to be that kind of transport which takes place gradually and gently, and is called by others "the flight of the mind."

Raptures are marks of imperfection, and of a certain remaining earthliness, when they happen to a soul simply because it is as yet unaccustomed to the objects which throw it into rapture; but when they proceed from the greatness and the extraordinary excellence of the light communicated by God, they are not marks of imperfection.

In first raptures the impression made by supernatural objects upon the soul and body is so powerful that we are unable to support it without being carried out of our senses; but in course of time the soul becomes accustomed to it, and gradually grows stronger, so that the impression produced by the divine communications it receives ceases to be attended with violent effects, except when God, who is infinite in bounty, imparts some new and very extraordinary light; for on such occasions the soul will still fall into rapture, although it has become accustomed to those objects which heretofore produced that effect upon it.

In fine, when the soul, being perfectly strengthened and habituated to the most wonderful communications of grace, is no longer liable to be ravished out of itself, it experiences the effects of rapture without being actually in a state of rapture. The impressions of grace are then purely spiritual, and act no longer on the body, as was the case when it was not perfectly subject to the spirit, and as pure as it is now become.

For it is a maxim of philosophers, that "every thing received into a subject is received therein according to the disposition of the subject." Thus, when the soul is still somewhat sensual, and the body not entirely purified, the operations of God, meeting with this obstacle, are more feeble, less sweet, and less perfect.

St. Theresa said, that after receiving graces of this sort, it is martyrdom to live among creatures; the soul, on returning to itself, feels more keenly than ever its exile and its miseries.

These wonderful effects of grace cannot be explained even by those who experience them, and much less by those who have no experience of them. Generally they fill the soul with so much sweetness and such solid contentment, that St. Francis Xavier used to say, that for the least of such consolations he would willingly have undertaken a second voyage to Japan, fearless of the toils he had endured in the first.

This is quite a different thing from those sweetnesses and tears of sensible devotion which God sometimes gives to beginners.

Whence we may see how great is the misery of spending our life in trifles and sensual satisfactions, which deprive us of the favours of our Lord; and that there is incomparably more pleasure in serving God in self-abnegation than in remaining always attached to self and to creatures, and never arriving at union with God. This is to participate in the pain of loss which constitutes the eternal woe of hell.

God sometimes favours souls with such wonderful communications and such transporting sentiments concerning some of the objects of faith, that ever after the mere remembrance, the mere thought, the very name of them, is enough to throw them into ecstacies; as was the case with the blessed Giles of Assisium when he heard the word "Paradise" pronounced.

Raptures and ecstacies happen commonly rather to women and persons who are less actively employed than to others, because their life more disposes them thereto, and health, which is extremely affected by graces of this kind, is not so necessary in their case for the promotion of the glory of God. On the other hand, the devotion of Apostolic men who have to labour for the salvation of souls is less sensible in its effects, more spiritual, and more solid. Generally speaking, God does not grant them the grace of ecstacies, unless it be that He desire thereby to give authority to their ministry, as is the case sometimes; witness St. Vincent Ferrer and St. Francis Xavier: and He communicates to them rather by the way of the understanding, which is capable of receiving lights of the highest order, than by that of the imagination, in which the divine lights are of a more sensible character, and their effects more externally manifested.

When a person falls into a state of suspended consciousness, in which the mind does not act, and receives no operation on God's part, it is not an ecstacy, but a plain illusion of the devil, or a dangerous lethargy.

The connexion between the soul and its senses is never interrupted, save in sleep, without much injury to health; for such disjunction is like the death of the senses: it is a commencement of that complete separation of the mind from the body which happens at death.

There is danger in desiring raptures and ecstacies, in wishing to have visions and revelations during such a state, and in hankering after other ways than those by which God is pleased to lead us: but there is no danger in asking for the gifts of the Holy Spirit and His guidance, solid virtues, and a high order of prayer.

ARTICLE VII.

Different divisions of the degrees of contemplation.

§ I.

The degrees of contemplation, according to some

are, first, recollection of all the powers of the mind; secondly, semi-rapture; thirdly, complete rapture; fourthly, ecstacy. But this division expresses not so much the essence of contemplation as its accidents; for sometimes a soul without rapture will be favoured with a sublimer light, a clearer knowledge, a more excellent operation from God, than another who is favoured with the most extraordinary raptures and ecstacies. The Blessed Virgin was more elevated in contemplation than all the Angels and Saints united; and yet she had no raptures. Our Lord enjoyed the beatific vision without ecstacy. The blessed in heaven will have a perfectly free use of all their senses.

Others distinguish the degrees of contemplation by different acts of the will, or by different states of fervent charity. Richard of St. Victor reckons four: 1. the wounds of love, *charitas vulnerans;* 2. the captivity of love, *charitas ligans;* 3. the languors of love, *charitas languens;* 4. the faintings of love, *charitas deficiens.* In the first, love pierces the heart and makes itself master of all the affections; in the second, it takes the mind captive and possesses itself of all the thoughts; in the third, it prevents the action of the external senses and the internal powers; in the fourth, it throws the soul into swoons and into a sort of death-like state by the boundless longings of its zeal, which it is unable to endure, as it perceives that all it does and all it can do is nothing, and that all it cannot do is infinite. Some mystical theologians add to this what they call the sepulchre of the soul, in which it is reduced, as it were, to dust and annihilated, afterwards to rise again and become a new creature in Jesus Christ, a creature wholly transformed into God.

The progress of these degrees is as follows:

1. When a person has applied himself for some time

to the keeping of his own heart, the love of our Lord, and other such exercises, remaining the while faithful to God, so it is that he receives from heaven lights of a more abundant grace, which cause the soul to know its own state and its miseries; that what it has hitherto done for God is as nothing; that it owes every thing to Him, and that He merits that all hearts should burn with His love, and all beings be consumed in His service.

At this sight the soul is filled with confusion; then, rousing itself, it abandons itself to love; and love, seeing it given up into its power, pierces it to the heart with its flaming arrows. It feels itself wounded, and the wound with which it is stricken causes it both pain and pleasure.

2. The heart being thus engaged, the mind can no longer think of any thing but the object beloved. Love takes the thoughts captive, recalling them from their wanderings among creatures to attach them to God; so that they can no more be drawn away from Him, save by compulsion. This, however, does not prevent a person still employing himself in indifferent matters. The merchant can attend to his commerce, the judge and the advocate to their suits of law, married persons to the management of their family.

3. The soul now wounded and captive, continually receiving new impressions of divine love, does nothing but languish, and becomes incapable of any action which is not either of God or for God. If it sees or hears any thing which has no reference to God, it is as if it saw or heard it not. In the two preceding degrees love makes itself master of the affections and the thoughts; in this it takes possession of the actions, permitting only such as are divine, that is to say, such as have God for their principle and end; and even in this state

a person can act but very little, and is capable only of certain exercises conformable to his attraction.

4. The soul being in such wise wholly possessed by God, whatever it may do for His service, whatever it may suffer for His glory, it is never satisfied; it is ever desiring to do and suffer still more; thus putting no bounds to its desires, it loses itself in their immensity, and perceiving that there is an infinity of other things that might be done for God, but which it cannot do, it feels itself ready to faint away. Thus our Lord, although He did and suffered so much for the glory of God His Father, counted it all as little or nothing compared with what was due unto Him; and the martyrs, full of esteem and admiration for the Divine Majesty, could not satisfy their desires of glorifying a God so great and so worthy of love. This was also the disposition of those holy heroes who shewed themselves insatiable of labours and sufferings.

§ II.

Some change the order of these degrees, making the second that state of languor which follows a deep and extensive wound; and the third that of captivity, which takes place, they say, when the soul, no longer sensibly experiencing the operations of God, is, as it were, abandoned to itself and its enemies, amid disquietude and suffering, feeling itself on the point of offending God, but that it finds itself bound, as it were, and restrained by a secret power.

In that mystical death which, according to some theologians, takes place in the soul previous to deification, the person in this state suffers sensible pains even in his body, because the process is that of severing him from the corruption of his nature, his evil affections and bad habits, which, through their intimate connexion with himself, cannot be torn away without the acutest pain. He must bear them courageously, and rejoice in the loss inflicted, seeing that he is but parting with his miseries to attain the sovereign good of this life.

Again, there is a state which, in mystical theology, is called that of burning love, in which the soul suffers a sort of fever, attended with fits and paroxysms, which even communicate themselves to the body and set it all on fire, causing revulsions, transports, and other marvellous effects—as was the case with St. Catherine of Genoa, the blessed Stanislas, and numerous other Saints.

§ III.

Some make four degrees of contemplation in this wise:

The first, they say, is when the soul, having attained great purity of heart, receives a new accession of the knowledge and love of our Lord by infused lights and extraordinary operations of grace.

The second, which some call the prayer of divine presence, is when the soul is ordinarily occupied with a simple attention to God; when it beholds itself before God with a profound awe for His adorable majesty and a holy horror of itself.

The third is a clearer and more penetrating knowledge of God, which enables the soul to see Him in a manner more and more perfect; for God does nothing but give and take away, as if He were saying: "This is not it yet, it is something more."

In this state the soul may say with the Spouse: "I sat down under his shadow;" such knowledge being, as it were, the shadow of God. There are souls which remain thus many years; and what they see of God creates such an ardent desire of beholding Him as He is, that it seems as if they would quit the body to fly towards God. In this state the symptoms exhibited are like those of death; the limbs remain cold, stiff, motionless, destitute of feeling, like those of a corpse; and to such excess might this love proceed as to cause actual death. St. Theresa, one Easter-day, fell into this state, and the effect was such as nearly to deprive her of life. And, indeed, there would be danger of death, unless an effort were made to dissipate the strength of this impression and distract the mind to some external object.

The fourth degree is called by mystical theologians the embrace of God, the chaste kiss of the Spouse. It is now that the soul is actually united to God as His spouse. Some would have it, that when arrived at this degree it already loves God as perfectly as in the state of glory; but this is not so. So long as He is seen only through the medium of faith and as in a glass, however vividly, He is never loved as much as He shall be hereafter in glory, where the blessed soul, being raised to the highest degree of contemplation, sees God face to face, and as He is in Himself.

ARTICLE VIII.

Another division of the degrees of contemplation.

Some reduce what concerns the essence of contemplation to four degrees.

The first is the knowledge and the love of our Lord, together with those supernatural effects which devotion to Him operates in pure souls.

Many err in the way of the spiritual life, thinking to arrive at union with God and the sublimest order of prayer without attaching themselves to our Lord; yet He is "the way," and it is through Him that we are to go to God. We must become filled with the knowledge of His perfections and His mysteries, His doctrine, His Spirit, and His love, joining thereto the careful study of His purity of heart; in proportion as we advance in this path, we approach the Divinity.

The progress made within the extent of this degree consists, first, in a certain recollection of all the interior powers, attended in the beginning, not by any vivid lights, but by a sweet peace which keeps the soul ever tranquil. Secondly, in a secret feeling of the nearness and the presence of God, which causes the powers of the soul to be still more collected and drawn together in order to their union with God; in the same manner as several needles which have touched the magnet turn all in the same direction and join their points together to meet at their centre. Thirdly, a presence of God more express and more formal than any hitherto experienced; not equal, however, to that enjoyed in the highest degrees, and which lasts a greater or a less time according to the disposition and co-operation of the soul.

The second, which mystical theologians call the state of divine darkness, is when God strips the soul of all the experiences it had before, all its lights and affections, and all its spiritual sweetnesses; and thus stripping it, He thereby disposes it for more perfect lights and a purer and more ardent love, making it rise continually by the way of deprivation, ever giving, in order afterwards to take away and bestow upon it something better still.

When God places a soul in this state of mystical darkness, and strips it thus of its first lights, He enlarges its understanding and its will, rendering them capable of performing acts of eminent perfection.

To arrive at this degree, there is need of a generous virtue, a faithful correspondence with grace, a complete detachment from self, and an unreserved surrender of ourselves to God: and as we are exceedingly pusillanimous, there are but very few who have courage enough to reach this point, and fewer still who advance further, because men cannot make up their mind to strip themselves perfectly of creatures.

St. Denis exhorts St. Timotheus to separate himself completely from all created things, to strip himself of all affection for them, of the very thought and remembrance of them, of all imaginations and ideas regarding them, and to rise above the senses and the ordinary modes of knowledge and of action; to the end that, having arrived at this perfect void and nudity of spirit, he might enter within the brightness of divine darkness and the luminous obscurity of the Divinity, to which no souls have access but such as are free and detached from every thing that is not God. This mystical darkness is a participation in that which surrounds the throne of God in glory, and which was figured by the smoke and clouds wherein God appeared to Moses when He spoke with him on the Mount.

The third is when God raises the soul to an extraordinary mode of action with regard to supernatural objects, communicating to it, through the medium of the imagination, lights and revelations which produce so powerful an impression upon it as to carry it out of itself. This it is that causes raptures and ecstacies, when the lights which the soul receives are so strong and so transporting as wholly to absorb it and abstract it from the senses and all exterior actions, to bring it into close application to the object manifested to it, which sometimes is of such a nature that all the powers of the soul combined are still too weak to endure or comprehend it. These raptures and ecstacies last as long as the operation of God continues, or as long as one operation is succeeded by others, or a single one by its strength and novelty arrests and captivates the soul.

In this state God is loved with a pure love, and acts of virtue are performed with great simplicity, acts which not being mixed with self-love or any of the impurities of nature, render more glory to God in a quarter of an hour than we ordinarily render to Him in many years.

The fourth is when the soul acts no longer through the imagination, the medium through which raptures and ecstacies are caused, but is wonderfully enlightened by God by means of mental species or intellectual illuminations, independent of the imagination and of phantoms.

Then it is the pure spirit alone that acts, or, to speak more correctly, that receives the operation of God, and this divine operation does not prevent the exterior action of the senses.

This degree is described in the words of David in the second book of Kings, where he says that God spoke to him "as the light of the morning, when the sun riseth, shining in the morning without clouds, and as the grass springeth out of the earth by rain." The sun shining in the morning without clouds denotes the operation of God in the soul, without admixture of sensible images and phantoms of the imagination.

Some say that souls that are raised to this degree are confirmed in grace. This at least is certain, that in it they exercise acts of virtue so pure and so perfect, that the honour rendered to God thereby, and the consequent increase of merit to the soul, are greater than we can conceive.

In this state God bestows, sometimes for a time, sometimes permanently, lights so penetrating, that without seeing with the bodily eyes those with whom they are in communication, persons behold them with the eyes of the mind, and know what they would say before they open their mouth. They know what to answer on every occasion and in all matters that come before them. They receive supernatural lights to guide themselves always and in all things by the Spirit of God.

This degree of divine union was the ordinary state of the Apostles, even in the midst of the world and their most important occupations. So also was it of St. Ignatius from the very first year of his conversion, ever after an intellectual vision which he had while gazing at a stream along the banks of which he was walking while at Manresa. After this he was so enlightened in all the truths of faith, that he used to say that even were they not written in the Gospel, he would be ready to shed the last drop of his blood in their defence; and that if the Holy Scriptures were lost, nothing would be lost for him.

ARTICLE IX.

Opinion on the above divisions of the degrees of contemplation.

§ I.

Of all the above divisions of the degrees of contemplation, the truest is that which is formed from viewing the subject on the side of the understanding, and the different modes of knowing God and divine things: the first mode being by the lights received through the senses; the second, by such as come through the imagination and phantoms; the third, by those which God Himself communicates immediately to the understanding, without the ministry or the co-operation of the lower faculties.

These are, as it were, three sources of contemplation. The first corresponds with the first degree, in which the object of the soul's study is the love and knowledge of our Lord. The second corresponds with the second degree, which is called divine darkness, in which progress is made towards the last by the way of deprivation; and with the third degree, in which souls are in a state of rapture and ecstacy. The third answers to the fourth degree, in which souls advance in the purest region of the mind and in the highest perfection which it is possible to attain on earth.

§ II.

Even in the lowest degrees of contemplation God communicates Himself with so much sweetness, that a thousand years' enjoyment of all the pleasures of the world are nothing compared with the delight the soul experiences in God. The perfections and the joys it finds in Him are so transporting to it, that it is, as it were, impossible for it to love any thing but God, or to seek any satisfaction out of Him.

The highest degrees are not attained until all sins have been remitted, as regards not only the guilt, but the penalty also; and if sins are still committed in the sublimest states (seeing there is no state so perfect as to exempt from sin), they are but slight faults, faults of surprise and infirmity, which are bitterly lamented, and forgiven immediately.

As it is not possible to attain these highest degrees except through extraordinary purity of heart, so neither is it possible to abide therein without the utmost fidelity to grace. And as God is lavish of His liberality to a soul in such a state, so is the soul, on its part, bound to the strictest correspondence with God; otherwise He withdraws His graces, and the soul fails to persevere in the degree to which it had been raised.

From the time that a soul receives these extraordinary gifts from God, and especially when it has attained to the highest degree of contemplation, it is marvellous how detached it is from creatures; it ceases to be eager after any thing whatever; nothing affects it save the love of God.

In these highest degrees of prayer, a person acts but very little from the formal motive of particular virtues. Since he is united to God by love, he does every thing from the principle of love and under the direction of love, without troubling himself, generally speaking, with motives of other virtues, which might distract the soul from its union with God.

When God bestows such grace upon a soul as to raise it to the highest degree of contemplation, He no longer refuses it any thing; it commonly obtains every thing it asks for. If it is requested to ask some favour of God, no sooner does it prepare to offer its petition, than it feels the Spirit of God carrying it away to the contemplation of admirable mysteries, in the midst of which it loses itself, thinking no more of the subject of its prayer, nor recollecting what it wished to ask; and yet God grants its request, and its desires are fulfilled without its bestowing any attention upon them. A soul that has attained to this point of perfection, may singly, by its prayers and merits before God, uphold a whole religious order or a whole kingdom.

§ III.

The union of the soul with God differs in every one of these four degrees of contemplation, each having that which is peculiar to itself.

The first and the most excellent, to which all the exercises of the active and the contemplative life tend, is an habitual union, by which the principal powers of the soul remain continually united to God at all times, in all places, even amid the disturbance of exterior actions and the most urgent affairs, without causing a person to be more abstracted or less capable of acting externally.

The second kind of union with God is not as perfect, nor as general, nor as lasting; it is when the will is united to God, but not all the other powers, in such a way, however, that the imagination occasions no more trouble than in the first.

The third is when the will is united to God, but not in such a way but that it is sometimes distracted and harassed, or is in danger of being so, by the aberrations and roving propensities of the other faculties. This it is that happens to us so often at Mass: our will is really united to God, and yet the lightness of our imagination, sounds, and external objects striking on our senses, are an occasion of disturbance to us.

They who are subject to this weakness, not being as yet firmly settled in a state of interior recollection, run in pursuit of their imagination and their discursive thoughts with a view of checking them; but they do but fatigue themselves in vain, and the trouble they take serves only to make them lose the small degree of union they had with God, and to fill their soul with disquiet and excitement, which is a worse disorder than the first. St. Theresa warns us of this, having herself experienced it.

In connexion with this subject we may remark, that after Communion to exert ourselves to converse with our Lord by eliciting acts, is not the best mode of thanksgiving; and many give themselves a great deal of trouble in this way without much fruit. Then is the time for enjoying, not for seeking; for if it is true that acts of virtue have no other end than to unite us to God, when once we have Him within us, and when once we possess Him, as we really do possess Him in the Holy Sacrament, what more do we seek? This should not prevent us from representing our miseries and our necessities to Him, but without much inward discourse. At such a time, the better way is to remain recollected in His presence, and let Him act in us according to His good pleasure, listen to Him, receive what He gives us, keeping the mind always in a reverential attitude, and observing the other duties of interior recollection, neither allowing it its usual excursions, nor letting it fall into the inaction and the false repose of quietism.

We ought to seek to put ourselves in the same disposition which St. Theresa speaks of being in: that great Saint seeking God alone in all things, and finding her repose only in God, did not even concern herself about virtues where it was question of God, His presence, and the enjoyment of Him. She left off making acts of the virtues, that she might enjoy God when He vouchsafed to communicate Himself to her; and in this there was no illusion: for what can we have without God? and if we have Him, what virtues can we want? It is to possess them all in an eminent degree and in a more excellent way than when we possess them formally, as theologians say, since they all tend only to unite us to God.

§ IV.

It sometimes happens to pure souls, that when they present themselves before our Lord in visiting the Blessed Sacrament, they experience immediately a transport of their spirit into the Heart of Jesus, where perhaps they remain for hours and whole days together.

§ V.

There are those who enjoy a certain union with God who may be compared to children at their mother's breast; at times they cling more closely to it and press it more tightly. So there are souls which at times are more recollected in God and drink more deeply of Him, according as the movement of grace draws them, and exterior occupations dispose them thereto.

§ VI.

In the various gifts and visits with which God favours souls, there is no fixed or definite order, so as that one might say, for example: After such an operation such another will follow; or from such a degree of prayer you pass on to such another. St. Theresa notices this, and says that the order she observes in enumerating the favours she received from God regards only herself, and denotes merely what she had herself experienced.

ADDITIONS.

CERTAIN THOUGHTS OF FATHER LALLEMANT;

COLLECTED BY

FATHER JOHN JOSEPH SEURIN, OF THE COMPANY OF JESUS, DURING HIS SECOND NOVICIATE IN THE YEAR 1630.

CHAPTER I.

OF PERFECTION IN GENERAL.

ARTICLE I.

Motives that excite us to perfection.

WE must go on to perfection. The motives which excite us thereto are: 1. The great advantages it brings with it; peace of soul, perfect liberty of mind, the delights of the love of God, the abundance of the riches of grace. 2. The assurance of our salvation, which is not to be had save in the way of perfection; whereas in the practice of it salvation is morally certain.

There is great wisdom in making haste to acquire perfection, because then we are at rest for our whole life, and enjoy a solid satisfaction, that interior joy which the world knows not, nor can take away from those who possess it.

ARTICLE II.

Wherein perfection consists, and what dispositions we ought to bring thereto.

Perfection consists in the operations produced by

interior grace, which proceeds from God alone; and as God is ever ready to operate in the soul according to His designs, all that he has to do who would become perfect, is to remove the obstacles that stand in the way of the Divine operation.

We remove them by cleansing the interior of the soul and those sentiments by which we seek God, that we may do so purely, to the exclusion of all the interests of the creature, convinced that nothing is worthy of consideration but God alone, nothing of importance but the accomplishment of His will, from whence His glory comes, and that all else is nothingness.

In order to be in a state to form acts of such perfection, it is necessary to clear away all the impurities of the soul, render the will pliant to the movements of the Spirit of God, and cut off all desires of our own ease and natural gratification.

There are three principal kinds of impurity: the love of earthly things; the desire of being in favour with men; and the pleasures of the body, whether illicit or excessive.

In order to acquire holiness, three things are requisite. 1. To have a high idea of it and a great desire for it. 2. To use great diligence in the pursuit of it, which diligence, again, must have three characteristics; it must be not only fervent and persevering, but exclusive. 3. To be courageous in resisting the opposition we shall meet with in the prosecution of our design.

The foundation of the spiritual life consists in conceiving a great idea of God and of divine things, and a very low idea of all created things, and then regulating our life according to these two ideas.

Three sorts of dispositions are necessary in one who aspires after perfection. 1. Great watchfulness and close application in all things, keeping the eyes ever open for every opportunity of personal advancement. 2. Great courage in surmounting all difficulties and conquering himself whenever there is need. 3. Great perseverance in the study of perfection, so as never to relax his endeavours, never to grow weary, never to cease from watching and toiling to the end.

ARTICLE III.
Of the practice of perfection.

The whole practice of the spiritual life consists in two things : first, in watching continually over ourselves, on the one hand, in order to do good, and on the other, in order to avoid evil ; secondly, in having the courage and strength both to do all the good and avoid all the evil we have a knowledge of.

Watching over ourselves includes three things. 1. The thinking almost continually of God, in order to prevent unprofitable thoughts. 2. The avoiding every kind of sin, and every thing that can stain the soul. 3. The mortifying ourselves interiorly by resisting all our inclinations.

The order of the spiritual life demands that we should commence with the purification of our interior, correcting whatever is disordered therein. This is so necessary, that if we devote ourselves to the practice of virtue without having first done this, we shall mix therewith a thousand effects of self-love ; we shall be always seeking ourselves in the holiest practices ; and the good we may receive from God we shall appropriate in a spirit of ownership, and shall thus remain always novices.

There are four things of high excellence which it is necessary to practise in the spiritual life. 1. To purify our soul by continual examination and detestation of its vices. 2. To take no satisfaction save in God alone. 3. To live in the practice of great fidelity, not doing the least thing which may displease God. 4. To exercise ourselves continually in the presence of God and the love of our Lord, meditating without ceasing on His perfections and His mysteries.

Every one who enters on the spiritual life must take pains to become filled with a threefold spirit, that of compunction, mortification, and prayer.

Compunction includes four or five excellent things: a serious and grave spirit, continual sorrow and inward moanings, profound humility, and devout solitude of heart.

Compunction has for its object three things in particular. 1. The vanity or miserable condition of man in this life, and the folly of the generality of Christians. 2. Our own sins and those of our neighbour. 3. The bloody passion of our Lord. These are the three motives which constrain devout souls, like gentle turtle-doves, to fly the vain joys of the world and the frivolities of life, that they may pass their days in continual plaints.

CHAPTER II.

OF PURITY OF HEART.

THAT the soul may be free to converse with God, it has need of being delivered from three sorts of hindrances: 1. from sins; 2. from passions; 3. from importunate distractions. These three sorts of hindrances are of very different degrees.

There are three degrees in true purity of heart. The first is, to do nothing in which there is appearance of sin. The second is, to attach the affections to nothing, either good or bad, which may interfere with perfect liberty of heart; but to study complete detachment from all created things. The third, never to perform an unprofitable act, or entertain any vain or petty thought, but always to be occupied in what promotes the glory of God. This is an excellent rule of life, which may be followed even in a state of dryness and interior suffering; affording, as it does, ample scope for the exercise of virtue, and an excellent test of our fidelity in the service of God.

The slightest faults and the least imperfections, when voluntary, inflict four evils on the soul: 1. they darken and blind it more and more; 2. they sully it; 3. they disturb and oppress it; 4. they diminish its strength and enfeeble it. The practice of virtue produces four contrary effects.

The resolution to leave some fault, whatever it may be, uncorrected, although such resolution be tacit and not express, although it be glossed over by excuses and reasons plausible in appearance, prevents in the soul any powerful operations on the part of God, and hinders the effects of the Holy Eucharist.

One of the causes which most retards the progress we might make in perfection, which keeps the soul in its native littleness, and of which we are least aware, is the allowing ourselves to be occupied with a thousand useless things. We ought to avoid all waste of time, and never do or think of any thing which is not to the glory of God. For want of this we make very little progress, and attach our heart to a thousand objects which disturb and distract it in prayer. One of the greatest efforts of fervour is directed to watching over self, and avoiding every thing unprofitable.

Until we combat as strenuously against the first disorderly movement of the heart as against sin itself, we shall never thoroughly correct our vices. And the reason that there is so little amendment in us is, that we fancy ourselves in the possession of virtue, notwithstanding the contrary movements of which we are sensible, not reflecting that such movements proceed from principles of sin which we take no pains to destroy. Thus we remain idle, under the pretext that first movements are not in our own power, instead of labouring with all our might to tear up the root of them. It is impossible to say how much harm we do ourselves by this error and self-indulgence.

There are three sorts of dangerous poisons which flow insensibly into the heart: 1. that of the pleasure of vain-glory; 2. that of sensuality and immodest love; 3. that of anger and bitterness of spirit.

CHAPTER III.
IN WHAT THE FAITHFUL SERVICE OF GOD CONSISTS.

To serve God faithfully is to serve Him: 1st, with exactness in all things, even the smallest; 2dly, in simple faith without the aid of consolations, or any large supply of interior lights; 3dly, without assurance that our services are agreeable to Him, and without seeking for considerations calculated to give this assurance; 4thly, without a hope of recompense, or thought of our own interests, or solicitude whether we are furthering our own ends in promoting those of God; 5thly, contented with the little God gives us, though it be the lowest place in Paradise; just as a beggar asking alms at a gate, after having long waited, receives with joy a morsel of dry bread bestowed upon him.

CHAPTER IV.
IMPORTANT ADVICE FOR THE ADVANCEMENT OF SOULS.

HERE are some secrets which it is important to know in the spiritual life: the first is, to remain constant, tranquil, and as it were balanced between God and nature, whenever there is question of passing from one motive of action to another (that is, from a less perfect to a more perfect one); the second is, to enter into the things of God rather by a submissive love than by the force of reasoning; the third is, to give ourselves to interior recollection; the fourth is, not to soar higher until our interior is purified, striving after a mode of operation for which we have not yet received the required disposition; the fifth is, not to read mystical books without great precaution.

In the illuminative way, we must perfect more and more the ideas we have conceived of our Lord, in order that the will may operate thereupon more effectually.

In the spiritual life there are long nights to spend and wide deserts to traverse, which afford good exercise for patience and fidelity.

He who cannot endure something within himself, or who desires something external to himself, does not possess perfect resignation.

Among the interior virtues, there are three which we ought especially to endeavour to acquire—a true humility, a perfect disengagement from all things and from ourselves, and a perfect obedience or resignation to God.

CHAPTER V.

OF HUMILITY.

THERE is no solid virtue without humility. One who is truly humble must comport himself like a little child, or a public slave, or a convicted impostor; that is to say, he must behave with simplicity like a child, depend on all the world like a slave, take shame to himself like an impostor whose tricks have been discovered.

Humility and patience are, so to say, the shoulders of charity, inasmuch as they carry its burdens.

The root of humility is the knowledge of God; for it is impossible to know and feel our own vileness, except by reference to something great with which we may compare it. It is in vain that we think of the little that is in us; we shall never be any the more humble, unless we compare it with the infinite perfections of God. It is thus that savages who inhabit forests are insensible to the wretchedness of their condition, until they come to know the manner of life of civilised people, who dwell in towns in the midst of every sort of accommodation; and so a poor villager will never have any true idea of his poverty, until he has seen the mansions of the rich and the palaces of princes.

We may endure contempt from different motives: 1. from a sense of the vanity of human esteem, for in truth the honour and esteem of men is nothing but vanity; 2. from a motive of humility, because we deserve every kind of disgrace; 3. from a motive of fidelity, which constrains us to render to God what belongs to Him, and to Him alone belong honour and glory; 4. from a motive of love and gratitude, inasmuch as our Lord clothed Himself with ignominies, and consecrated contempt and abjection in His Adorable Person.

CHAPTER VI.

OF HOLY SIMPLICITY.

TRUE simplicity consists in having, like God, but one thought, and that thought must be to please God in all things. The vices opposed to simplicity throw us into a state of *multiplicity*.

These vices operate particularly in three ways. 1. In what regards our passions; to gratify them we multiply our thoughts and desires, acting not with the simple view of honouring God, but from various other motives. Hence spring our distrusts, our suspicions, dissimulations, concealments, subtle inventions, precautions, refinements, distinctions, &c. 2. In what regards others, about whom we have our judgments, interpretations, conjectures, inquiries, questionings, &c. 3. In what concerns reflections upon ourselves, for our own satisfaction: reflections on the past, on the present, on the future; on our good works, to take a pleasure in them; on our bad ones, to excuse them or waste useless regrets upon them, to form vain resolutions respecting the future. All this is opposed to true simplicity; but we close the gate to all such faults, when the mind is occupied only with the simple thought of pleasing God.

CHAPTER VII.

OF THE SPIRIT OF DEVOTION.

THE spirit of devotion is the mainspring of the spiritual life, and consists in keeping the heart always united to God or our Lord Jesus Christ. And when this is done effectually and without difficulty, every thing else follows easily, as amendment of life, progress in virtue, forgetfulness of the things of the world, &c. So that to raise a soul to perfection in a short time two things are necessary.

The first is, to make it labour at knowing and correcting itself; the second, to fill it with ideas which excite it to devotion, and cause it to feel an interior relish for God.

When the soul has attained to this relish for God, it must endeavour to cherish it and render it enduring. To this end, it must despise the care of the body; it must discard all reflections on the life of others; it must give up a thousand little diversions which waste its time and retard its progress. Then also virtues will introduce themselves sweetly and easily into the mind.

Let us therefore constantly endeavour to draw near unto God; to unite ourselves to Him by our thoughts and affections, and allow nothing to divert us from Him, unless it be such actions as appertain to His service, for which we must quit every thing, even prayer and converse with God.

As soon as we find a void in our occupations, let us turn to the profitable employment of conversing with God in our own interior, or to Jesus Christ, in order to quicken devotion in us. The result will be, that our mind, being always occupied in some holy way, will give no admission to vices or a store of useless accomplishments; and will become noble and venerable in its own eyes and in those of others, breathing a perpetual odour of sanctity.

Of the three principal objects of our devotion, Jesus Christ, the Blessed Virgin, and St. Joseph, we may say that what forms the glory and special lustre of Jesus Christ in His mortal life is His humility and meekness; that of the Blessed Virgin, her purity; that of St. Joseph, the wisdom of his conduct.

Three things are injurious to the spirit of devotion in some religious communities: 1. excess of unprofitable recreations; 2. a spirit of raillery; 3. particular friendships, and too great an intimacy between individuals.

CHAPTER VIII.

OF DIFFERENT KINDS OF RELIGIOUS, AND OF THE THINGS THAT ARE MOST PREJUDICIAL TO CERTAIN HOLY COMMUNITIES.

THERE may be said to be four kinds of religious: some perfect; others bad, proud, full of vanity, sensual, opposed to all regularity; others, again, tepid, slothful, careless; and lastly, such as are virtuous and on the way to perfection, although they may perhaps never attain to it.

The holiest orders in religion may contain these four kinds of members, as well as those orders that have fallen into laxity; with this difference, however, that in an order that has fallen from its first fervour, the majority are tepid persons, and the remainder consists of some that are positively bad, a few who are labouring after perfection, and a very few who are perfect. But in an order in which discipline is still strictly observed, the bulk of the community is composed of those who are tending to perfection, and the remainder comprises some who are perfect, a few who are tepid, and a very few who are bad.

One very important remark may here be made: it is, that a religious order inclines to degeneracy when the number of the tepid begins to equal that of the fervent,—I mean those who labour from day to day to make fresh progress in prayer, recollection, mortification, purity of conscience, humility. For those who do not use this diligence, even though they keep themselves from mortal sin, must pass for tepid persons; they corrupt many others, inflict extreme injury on the whole body, and are themselves in danger, either of not persevering in their vocation, or of falling into interior pride or great disorders.

The duty of superiors in religious houses is to labour, as well by their own good example, as by exhortation, private conversation, and prayer, that their subjects may persevere in the ranks of the fervent who are aiming at perfection; otherwise they will themselves bear the penalty of it, and that a terrible penalty.

There are four things that are injurious to the spiritual life, and which form the basis of the evil maxims that insinuate themselves into holy communities: 1. esteem for natural talents, and such qualities as are purely human; 2. anxiety to make friends from human considerations; 3. a conduct directed by policy, and one that follows mere human prudence—a crafty spirit, and such as is opposed to evangelical simplicity; 4. superfluous recreations, which become indispensable to the soul; or such conversations and books as afford a merely natural satisfaction to the mind.

The three concupiscences of the world find easy entrance into the best-regulated orders: 1. ambition, through a desire of being promoted to offices and employments of distinction; 2. avarice, through a desire of acquiring and accumulating knowledge; 3. the lust of the flesh, through sensuality and a desire for bodily ease and comforts.

CHAPTER IX.

OF THE SPIRIT OF THE COMPANY OF JESUS.

The spirit of our Company is a participation in that of Jesus Christ, and consists particularly in this, that the Company is connected with Him as a body specially appropriated to Him. This is why it is called the Company of Jesus.

St. Ignatius, who would have obedience to be the mark by which his children should be distinguished from other religious, enjoins them to "pay no regard to the personal qualities of their superior, but to see in him our Lord Jesus Christ, whose place the superior holds, and for the love of whom they are to obey him." This is the spirit of the Company, and an excellent mode of exercising ourselves in the presence of God.

For the same reason he wished to have the Company bound by an express vow to the Sovereign Pontiff, as the one who of all the world best represents Jesus Christ, being His Vicar on earth.

Our spirit ought to imitate that of Jesus, in that as Jesus was possessed of two natures, one divine and the other human, so our spirit, in relation to these, consists of two natures, the divine and the human, the interior and the exterior. According to the exterior, Jesus Christ appeared a mere man like others; and interiorly He was hypostatically united to God. So ought we to be externally like other men in our ordinary life, but interiorly to be united to God by attention and love. We are bound to occupy ourselves with offices of zeal and charity towards our neighbour; and for this end we ought to make great exertions and practise virtue largely: such is the exterior of our spirit. The interior is to be possessed by God, and to have our soul filled with a holy disposition, which influences all we do externally, and animates it.

An interior spirit is formed by two things: 1. great self-abnegation and a great contempt of the world; 2. a great knowledge of spiritual things, a relish for God, much prayer, dependence on the Holy Spirit, freedom of heart, and an ardent zeal.

To form the exterior spirit, what we need is great obedience, great fortitude in labours, and a great prudence in conversation.

The resemblance of our spirit to that of Jesus Christ

consists in the combination of things which in appearance are contrary one to the other; as knowledge and humility, youth and chastity, diversity of nation and perfect charity, &c.: just as our Lord unites in His person the divinity and the humanity, immortality and a mortal life, sovereign dominion and the condition of a servant, &c. At the same time that He was governing the whole universe, He was conversing familiarly with sinners. So also ought we to be disposed to perform one while the sublimest actions, at another the lowliest. This is the spirit of the Company.

The culminating point of the highest perfection in this world is zeal for souls. To form this zeal, a certain temperament is needed which is difficult to be met with, and which is the result of a mixture of opposite elements. For example, our life must combine a strong affection for supernatural things with the study of the sciences and other natural pursuits; and it is easy to lean too much on one side. We may have too great a fondness for the sciences, and neglect prayer and spiritual things; or if we desire to be spiritual men, we may not sufficiently cultivate natural talents, as doctrine, eloquence, prudence, from which we derive the implements of success in our ministrations.

The Spirit of God bestowed on St. Ignatius a special light for combining these things in our Institute. Others who had not this light have been so attached to solitude, penance, contemplation, that they seem to have carried the contempt of human talents to an excess.

Hence we may learn the excellence of the spirit of the Company, which honours and imitates the mode in which the divinity was united with all that was human in Jesus Christ, the faculties of His Soul, the members of His Body, His Blood, and made all divine. Thus is the Spirit of God joined in us with all that is good naturally, as natural and acquired talents, and makes all divine that can contribute to the glory of God.

This combination is difficult; and this is the reason why those amongst us who do not apprehend the perfection of our spirit attach themselves to natural and human advantages, being devoid of such as are supernatural and divine. That which may do us most harm, unless we are on our guard, is an ambition for distinguished employments, vanity, a desire to be conspicuous, or carefulness about bodily comforts, unprofitable conversations, and amusements. We necessarily fall into these faults when we do not give ourselves up wholly to the interior life, because the needy hungry soul seeks something on which it may fasten and satisfy itself.

There is no vice so opposed to our Institution as vain-glory, because we are bound to promote the greater glory of God in all things.

By the terms of our Institute we have no peculiar ceremonial or especial offices, like other religious, because our mode of life is in this respect ordinary, and according to the practice of the Church at large. We are not on that account exempted from the particular devotions of other orders, but rather we are fitted to embrace them all, not being confined to any exclusively.

St. Ignatius desired that we should have scarcely any thing distinctive, because the end of our Institute is the greater glory of God; and as this is preferable to all other ends, and under certain circumstances requires things incompatible with particular ends, it is necessary that we should not have any special one assigned us. But this does not prevent our embracing all on occasions when the greater glory of God demands it. The spirit of the Company renders us independent in such a manner, that we are able to enter into the spirit of other orders, and share their devotions, without in this doing any thing contrary to the spirit of the Company, which, by reason of its universality, sympathises with all. It is the spirit of Jesus, who is the General of the Church. The spirit of the Company is universal in so noble a manner, that there is no state or order within the Church, distinguished by any spirit of virtue, which ours does not embrace; it comprehends all, so far as they are not exclusive of each other.

We ought to have a high idea of our vocation, a great esteem and a profound respect for our office, seeing that we are established, by the authority of the Church, of the Holy See, and of a General Council, to render to God the most noble service of which we are capable. We have succeeded to the ministry of the Apostles, not in what concerns dignity and authority, which in the sight of God is the least considerable part of their office, but in what is truly great, viz. labour for the salvation of souls, and the propagation of the kingdom of God.

Our portion is that of the Apostles. "*Nos autem orationi et ministerio verbi instantes erimus.* But we will give ourselves continually to prayer, and to the ministry of the word." The functions of the Apostles are committed to us, the glory of God is entrusted to our hands; what can be more exalted? This it is to which our profession engages us. Accordingly, we ought to treat each other with great reverence, although externally we lead but a mean and ordinary life. This very fact serves only to increase our glory; for thus it was that Jesus Christ and the Apostles lived; and every thing that is most eminent in the kingdom of God is based on lowliness. Jesus Christ founded His glory, the salvation of the world, and all His designs, on His poor and abject life, His ignominies, and His death.

Our aim ought to be so high, that in all things we

may seek, as St. Ignatius says, *quod est optimum*, what we judge best and most perfect; so that the spirit of the Company obliges us to aim, not only at what is good, but at what is best. It imposes on us the strict obligation of performing all our functions in the most perfect manner; for otherwise we are not necessary to the Church, since there are others who do the same things that we do.

We ought to judge of the dignity and perfection of the spirit of the Company not so much by what is ordinarily accomplished, as by the design of our founder St. Ignatius. This design is so high, that the holy patriarch, to render his children capable of executing it, looks for peculiar qualities in them. He obliges them to undergo extraordinary trials. He does not admit them into the body of the Company till after several years' probation. Doubtless, without this, our functions might have been creditably and profitably performed; for we see that persons of ordinary virtue succeed tolerably well in the same employments. Whence we ought to conclude, that St. Ignatius wished to lead us to a sublime and arduous height of perfection; that is to say, he would have us join together things difficult of combination, continual prayer, great self-abnegation, a perfect disengagement from all things, great contempt of the world, the fulness of the Holy Spirit, with conversation, study, missions, travelling, and exterior ministrations. Now it is plain that to accomplish this combination and admixture successfully, all that our holy founder enjoins upon us is indispensable. And if we discharge our several duties in a mere commonplace way, we render profitless most of the provisions of our Institute; for instance, the distinction of degrees, and those various and lengthened probations. It is evident, then, that in order to correspond with the essential object of our Institution, we must be distinguished for eminent virtue, and possess the apostolical spirit in an excellent degree; otherwise we cannot attain to the perfection of our constitutions; we give occasion to deserved reproach; and it may be justly said, that the design of our Institute is not fulfilled, and that the establishment of the Company was needless.

CHAPTER X.

OF THE KINGDOM OF GOD IN SOULS.

ARTICLE I.

In what the kingdom of God consists, and its advantages.

GOD's kingdom is threefold: that of nature, that of grace, and that of glory. The first is connected with the second, and the second with the third.

The kingdom of grace is within us, and its end is a holy beatitude. For the beatitude of man results from his union with God, which is holiness.

This kingdom, as regards its exercise, consists in two things: 1. in the government of the King; 2. in the dependence of subjects: or, to use the language of Scripture, in the ways of God towards souls, and in the ways of souls towards God.

The ways of God towards souls are, justice and mercy, and a mixture of both one and the other. God has different kinds of wills. There are those of positive command and of simple permission. There are such as are evident and such as are hidden. He consoles and afflicts. He caresses and chastises. He inspires terror and excites confidence. He proceeds openly and as it were stealthily. He makes assaults and wins by sweetness, &c.

The ways of souls towards God are, dependence, humility, resignation, abandonment of all care, mortification of self-love, purity of heart. The more we possess these holy dispositions, the more is the kingdom of God established in the soul.

The excellences of this kingdom are: the wisdom of the King, His power, His goodness; the nobility and dignity of His subjects; the peace, the security, the liberty, the goods, the pleasures they enjoy: wherein the kingdom of God has advantages infinitely above the kingdoms of the earth.

What a difference between the kingdom of grace and that of sin! Their chiefs, their wars, their arms, their laws are different. They are both interior. Both one and the other are found within us; the one is founded on Adam, the other on Jesus Christ. They are based on the destruction the one of the other. St. Paul sets this forth in an admirable manner. It is left to us to choose of which of these two kingdoms we would be the subjects. Salvation consists in withdrawing from that of sin and entering that of grace; and perfection in destroying within us the law of sin and the flesh, and in living according to the law of the spirit.

ARTICLE II.

Of the governance of the kingdom of God.

The first operation of God in the governance of His kingdom, according to St. Denis, is the purifying of souls. And for this end He puts into the hearts of His subjects the knowledge of themselves, and gives them a light which discovers to them all their most secret perversities; and that for three reasons: 1. to shew that He is the King of the heart, seeing that He penetrates and lays open its most intricate folds, bringing to light faults which they would never have themselves perceived; 2. to maintain the order He has prescribed to Himself of sanctifying men by their own co-operation, which consists in renouncing all their past infidelities—a thing they cannot do unless they have a full knowledge of them; 3. to render His kingdom firm and enduring by means of true interior humility, which cannot be better formed within us than by an experimental knowledge of our miseries, and the horror with which we regard them. Now this serves to establish the kingdom of God; and without it we naturally pride ourselves on the graces which God bestows upon us.

This operation of God, which is the beginning of His ways, discloses to the soul: 1. the vast amount of its malice; its refusals of divine grace; the movements of its will, not only such as lead it directly to evil, but also such as are indirect, interpretative, and virtual, which disorderly affections commonly conceal, or which are excused on false pleas: 2. the depth and gravity of that malice, which it is most important for it thoroughly to know, that it may be solidly grounded in the spirit of humility, and correct itself effectually of its faults.

All this is accomplished by means of a supernatural light, terminating finally in the light of glory. It gradually increases, until it becomes a light of contemplation, which has more power to manifest to us our sins and weaknesses than all the reflections and self-examinations we can make. The knowledge of our miseries which this light gives us serves to encourage us, and prevents our being confounded at the sight of our sins at the hour of death.

God, who is light, begins to reign in a soul by chasing away the darkness of sin. He delivers it: 1. from actual sin; 2. from the habit of sin; 3. from the obligation of undergoing the penalty of sin; 4. from the corruption of nature; and at last He proceeds even to purge it more and more from the imperfection of a created being. But this is never wholly effected in this life.

The reason why God commences in this way is, that He would have His kingdom to be eternal. Now this process is necessary to render it enduring.

The second operation of God in the governance of His kingdom is, to teach souls the science of the Saints, which is the only true science. Other sciences, taken in themselves and without reference to the glory of God, lead to pride, folly, and error.

The truth of science and wisdom, says Aristotle, must be ascertained by reference to the last end. Science which is not referrible thereto is not simply and absolutely science; it is so only in a certain limited sense, and is compatible with a state of error. The really learned man is one who knows truths which lead to happiness, and not one who knows only mere human things.

God is very different from the doctors of this world. 1. The latter do not inform the understanding. The lights they impart leave the heart cold. God is able to move the will. His light carries heat into it. 2. They impart instruction only by means of discourse and a series of propositions. God communicates truth in an instant, and by a simple view. 3. They cannot teach their doctrine to any one who is deficient in intelligence. God gives understanding to those who have it not; and there is no mind so dull but it is capable of acquiring the science of the Saints when God is pleased to teach it.

ARTICLE III.

Of the happiness of the kingdom of God.

The subjects of the kingdom of God are truly kings.

"*Fecisti nos Deo nostro regnum, et regnabimus.* Thou hast made us a kingdom to our God, and we shall reign."

Three things attend on royalty : dignity or splendour, riches, and pleasures ; to possess much of these three things is to reign in the world. Now souls in which God has established the kingdom of His grace possess these three advantages in an eminent degree.

1. Their state is one of surpassing dignity, inasmuch as they obey God immediately, and depend interiorly on Him alone. They have full liberty, a perfect dominion over the world, the flesh, and the devil. They walk with head erect ; they fear nothing ; they have a courage proof against every thing that can happen in this life. Josephus calls the government of the Israelites before they had kings a *Theocracy,* that is to say, a divine government. And thus also we may name the government of souls " the kingdom of grace."

2. The riches of this kingdom are incomprehensible. "*Investigabiles divitias Christi,* the unsearchable riches of Christ," says St. Paul, who admirably describes them in several passages of his epistles. They are of two kinds : an abundance of wisdom, science, and interior lights ; and a plenitude of exalted sentiments of God and divine things. In this kingdom souls are so filled with the fulness of God, as St. Paul says, that they desire no other goods. This is to be truly rich.

3. The pleasures, the delights, the sweetnesses, the consolations, the peace, which are tasted in the kingdom of God, surpass every thing the heart can desire and every thing the mind can conceive.

These treasures of God's interior kingdom have two qualities which marvellously enhance their value. The first is, that they are eternal, or based on eternity ; for the splendour of the kingdom of grace is the shadow of the light of glory. The riches of grace are the earnest of glory. The delights of the Saints in the present life are a foretaste of Paradise. This is why St. Paul calls grace "life eternal." The second is, that these great goods are compatible with the opposite evils; a peculiarity which is not found in temporal goods. The glory, the riches, the pleasures of the kingdom of God, subsist together with shame, poverty, and suffering; and this alliance is a source of merit to the Saints.

These are the goods we may possess even in this life: royalty, boundless treasures, torrents of delights. This is what we lose for trifles that lead us to hell; for every attachment to the things of earth puts our soul in danger of perdition.

ARTICLE IV.

Of the practice of the interior kingdom of God, or the means of establishing it within us.

To establish the kingdom of God within us we must do three things.

1. We must banish from our heart every other dominion than that of God, and render ourselves interiorly free from those affections which subject us to creatures. Men commonly wish to join together the kingdom of grace and that of sin. They seek for accommodations by which to reconcile the laws of the one with those of the other: and self-love suggests a thousand contrivances. Hence it is that the ordinary state of men is full of disorders and greatly distracted. "No man," says Jesus Christ, "can serve two masters." God must reign alone in the heart; He will endure no partner. Therefore to constitute Him the sole undisputed possessor, it is necessary to drive out of it the tyrants who contest with Him the sovereignty, that is to say, those objects which through an ill-regulated

affection bear sway therein to His prejudice. The means of ascertaining them is to observe what is the point to which our thoughts ordinarily tend, and what is the mainspring in us of the four passions to which we are most subject: joy, sorrow, desire, and fear. When we have discovered it, we must apply ourselves vigorously to dislodge it and to destroy it by contrary inclinations.

2. After having overthrown the dominion of creatures, we must attach ourselves to God's guidance by a strict dependence, which requires that we should abandon ourselves to Him without reserve and without anxiety about the future; that we should resign our affairs and our interests into the hands of God, especially in whatever concerns obedience, doing nothing of our own impulse, but letting ourselves be guided like little children; that we should offer ourselves generously to whatever may be the future will of God concerning us, and submit ourselves fully to His present dispensations, accepting every thing at His hand, without complaining, and without allowing ourselves to desire any thing else.

3. In all this we must proceed in an interior way, and lead a life not merely good, but truly interior, regulating all the movements of our heart by the instinct of God. Such a principle of life comprises three acts. First, to consult in all things the interior oracle and the divine Spirit, lest the human spirit should forestall its operation. Secondly, to perform faithfully what it prescribes; otherwise it withdraws and hides itself. Thirdly, to do every thing as in God's sight, by paying homage to His sovereign being and uniting ourselves to His Spirit. Unless we accustom ourselves to proceed thus, we act only on law and unmortified principles, even in the holiest actions, and ever with a

view to ourselves: we seek self and find self in every thing.

Let us conclude, then, that we must devote ourselves to the interior life. "Learn," says the Book of the Imitation of Jesus Christ, "to despise exterior things; enter into yourselves, and you will see the kingdom of God come into you." Let us be wholly God's. Live, O God! As for me, I belong to God, let the world follow whom it will. Alas, my God, am I not Thine? Art Thou not my king? And yet men desire none of Thee, and say in their rebellion, "*Nolumus hunc regnare super nos.* We will not have this man to reign over us." But for me, O Lord, I will say aloud, I will cry without ceasing, "*Adveniat regnum tuum. Veni, Domine Jesu, aufer scandala de regno tuo.* Amen. Thy kingdom come. Come, Lord Jesus, take away all scandals from Thy kingdom."

THE END.

CPSIA information can be obtained
at www.ICGtesting.com
Printed in the USA
LVHW030136190719
624596LV00023B/784/P